GREATNESS

THE 16 CHARACTERISTICS OF TRUE CHAMPIONS

Second Edition

Don Yaeger

GREAT BOOKS

GREATNESS
The 16 Characteristics of True Champions

Published by
Great Books
413 North Meridian Street
Tallahassee, FL 32301
Web: www.donyaeger.com

Visit our Web site at www.donyaeger.com.

Printed in the United States of America

Second Edition: February 2016

10 9 8 7 6 5 4 3 2 1

ISBN 978-0-692-54591-1 (hardcover)

GREATNESS

Be great!

To Dale Brown:

For more than twenty years you've been everything
from my best friend to my Best Man,
helping to shape my thoughts, my career,
and, most important, my life.
I am honored by your investment in me!

DY

ACKNOWLEDGMENTS

This book is the culmination of nearly twenty-five years of interviews during my career in journalism. As a result, I owe a tremendous debt of gratitude to every editor who ever assigned me a story, giving me an opportunity to live out a dream. While still in high school, my father offered me a simple challenge: Make sure to learn something from each champion I interviewed about what allowed them to separate themselves from their peers. So for that, I owe my father as well.

To the staff who worked exhaustively to help me organize and grow my observations on Greatness from a collection of ideas to the fully-developed pillars you see here, I offer my sincerest thanks: to Jenny Fernandez, who helped me manage my first foray into speaking about Greatness; to Anjie Cheatham, who then stepped in and has done wonderful work opening doors for speaking; to Lee Williams, who has done such a great job every week getting my *Moments of Greatness* newsletter distributed – you are such a tremendous worker; to Elton Gumbel, who knows better than almost anyone how best to tell a story; to Linley Wartenberg, who provided some great examples and shared her vast knowledge of hockey; to Kelly Wiggains and Edric Sanchez who provided updates to storytelling and edits to this revised edition; and finally, to the dozen or so interns who faithfully added to and maintained my collection of Great quotes – I know it wasn't the most exciting part of your workday, but it made a difference, and I thank you all for it.

But the real Great one in the project has to be Tiffany Brooks, who brings such writing skill to everything we do. You are truly one of the most amazing champions I've met because you bring your A game every day!

It is fair to say that Harry Helm at Hachette Book Group was the perfect editor for the initial version of this book. It was his suggestion that it be written after he read a few newsletters, and his passion and direction guided it through to the finish. Harry, your contagious enthusiasm, intense preparation, visualization of victory, and professional integrity are just a few of the things that make you truly Great. Ian Kleinert at Objective Entertainment, who has represented me as a literary agent for several years, helped turn Harry's enthusiasm into a contract in short order.

This book would, of course, not have been possible without the insight, wisdom and perspective of so many incredible athletes and coaches. There are far too many to even begin to name here, but their stories grace these pages and their lessons have changed my life profoundly. Thank you, from the bottom of my heart, for opening your lives and sharing your stories with me and with everyone who is pursuing Greatness. You not only showed what true Greatness is, but how to achieve it…and that is the Greatest lesson of all.

Finally, my wonderful wife Jeanette, who has put up with the unbelievable amount of travel and hectic schedule that comes with being married to a journalist, is, as always, a champ. And to my children, Will and Maddie, thank you for sharing your daddy for interviews, speeches, and while writing this book. And someday, when you're all grown up, I hope these stories will provide a road map to a championship life.

Also written by Don Yaeger

Books that have appeared on *The New York Times* Best Seller list:

Under the Tarnished Dome: How Notre Dame Betrayed its Ideals for Football Glory (1993) – By Don Yaeger and Douglas S. Looney – **Publisher:** Touchstone

Never Die Easy: The Autobiography of Walter Payton (2001) – By Walter Payton and Don Yaeger – **Publisher:** Random House

Ya Gotta Believe: My Roller-Coaster Life As a Screwball Pitcher and Part-Time Father, and My Hope Filled Fight Against Brain Cancer (2004) – By Tug McGraw and Don Yaeger – **Publisher:** NAL Hardcover

It's Not About the Truth: The Untold Story of the Duke Lacrosse Scandal and the Lives it Shattered (2008) – By Don Yaeger with Mike Pressler – **Publisher:** Threshold Editions

I Beat the Odds: From Homelessness, to the Blind Side, and Beyond – By Michael Oher with Don Yaeger (2012) – **Publisher:** Gotham

Play Like You Mean It: Passion, Laughs, and Leadership in the World's Most Beautiful Game (2012) – By Rex Ryan with Don Yaeger – **Publisher:** Doubleday Books

Nothing to Lose, Everything to Gain: How I Went From Gang Member to Multimillionaire Entrepreneur (2013) – By Ryan Blair with Don Yaeger – **Publisher:** Portfolio

George Washington's Secret Six: The Spy Ring That Saved the American Revolution (2014) – By Brian Kilmeade and Don Yaeger – **Publisher:** Sentinel

Thomas Jefferson and the Tripoli Pirates: The Forgotten War That Changed American History (2015) – By Brian Kilmeade and Don Yaeger – **Publisher:** Sentinel

All other books

Greatness: The 16 Characteristics of True Champions; First Edition (2011) – By Don Yaeger – **Publisher:** Center Street

Beating Goliath: My Story of Football and Faith (2014) – By Art Briles and Don Yaeger **Publisher:** St. Martin's Griffin

Wish Granted: 25 Stories of Strength and Resilience from America's Favorite Athletes (2013) – By Make-A-Wish® with Don Yaeger – **Publisher:** HarperOne

Any Given Monday: Sports Injuries and How to Prevent Them for Athletes, Parents, and Coaches – Based on My Life in Sports Medicine (2014) – By Dr. James R. Andrews with Don Yaeger – **Publisher:** Scribner

Devoted: The Story of a Father's Love for His Son – (2012) – By Dick Hoyt with Don Yaeger – **Publisher:** Da Capo Press

Starting and Closing: Perseverance, Faith, and One More Year (2013) – By John Smoltz with Don Yaeger – **Publisher:** William Morrow Paperbacks

Gold Medal Strategies: Business Lessons From America's Miracle Team (2011) – By Jim Craig and Don Yaeger – **Publisher:** Wiley

Never Give Up on Your Dream: My Journey (2009) – By Warren Moon with Don Yaeger – **Publisher:** Da Capo Press

A Game Plan for Life: The Power of Mentoring (2011) – By John Wooden with Don Yaeger – **Publisher:** Bloomsbury USA

Tarnished Heisman: Did Reggie Bush Turn His Final College Season into a Six-Figure Job? (2008) – By Don Yaeger and Jim Henry – **Publisher:** Pocket Books

Running for My Life: My Journey in the Game of Football and Beyond (2009) – By Warrick Dunn and Don Yaeger – **Publisher:** It Books

Turning of the Tide: How One Game Changed the South (2008) – By Don Yaeger with Sam Cunningham and John Papadakis – **Publisher:** Center Street

Pros and Cons: The Criminals Who Play in the NFL (1998) – By Jeff Benedict and Don Yaeger – **Publisher:** Grand Central Publishing

A Shark Never Sleeps: Wheeling and Dealing with the NFL's Most Ruthless Agent (1998) – By Drew Rosenhaus with Don Yaeger and Jason Rosenhaus – **Publisher:** Atria Books

Tiger in a Lion's Den: Adventures in LSU Basketball (1994) – By Dale Brown with Don Yaeger – **Publisher:** Hyperion

Shark Attack: Jerry Tarkanian and His Battle With the NCAA and UNLV (1993) – By Don Yaeger with Jerry Tarkanian – **Publisher:** Harpercollins

Undue Process: the NCAA's Injustice to All (1991) – By Don Yaeger – **Publisher:** Sagamore Publishing

This Game's the Best! So Why Don't They Quit Screwing With It? (1999) – By George Karl and Don Yaeger – **Publisher:** St. Martin's Press

Contents

GREATNESS

If we are to be a really great people,
we must strive in good faith to play a great part in the world.
We cannot avoid meeting great issues.
All that we can determine for ourselves
is whether we shall meet them well or ill.

— THEODORE ROOSEVELT
(U.S. president, military leader, and author, 1858–1919)

There are countless ways of attaining greatness,
but any road to reaching one's maximum potential
must be built on a bedrock of respect for the individual,
a commitment to excellence,
and a rejection of mediocrity.

— BUCK RODGERS
(American baseball player, b.1938)

= INTRODUCTION =

Defining GREATNESS

"Defining greatness is perhaps even harder than achieving it."

— JOHN WOODEN

GREATNESS. I'm fascinated by it, riveted by what allows some people to achieve at a high level for an extended period of time. What allows some to make the move from good to Great when most simply are stuck in conversation?

Of all the discussions I had with Coach Wooden while writing a book that was released on his ninety-ninth birthday, my favorites always came back to the topic of Greatness. Who would he, the greatest coach of all time, call "great"? Why? How did he define the term? We spent hours mulling the subject. As we ultimately agreed, finding a definition for Greatness is a much bigger challenge than it might seem, and it seems that there are as many definitions as there are people seeking Greatness itself.

It's something over which countless bar-stool debates have raged: Who is the greatest hitter ever? Who is the greatest quarterback of all time? Which team is the greatest representation of their sport—or any sport?

After spending more than 25 years as a sports journalist, I have found myself engaged in countless "greatness" discussions with some of the most exceptional winners of our generation and the recurring impression I've had during all of them has been that we seem to be begging the question: *What is Greatness?* It seems to me that this concept must be defined first before anything else can actually be resolved.

And, truth be told, the debate over the definition of *Greatness* isn't that different from the debates over who earns the title "the greatest." The challenge, of course, is that Greatness can't be quantified the way other things in sports can. For example, there is no debate as to whether or not Kareem Abdul-Jabbar was the highest scorer ever in the NBA, because the number 38,287 doesn't lie; and no one can object to the fact that the 1972 Miami Dolphins hold the only perfect season in NFL history. Those are facts that aren't subject to interpretation. But does the achievement of those numbers make them the Greatest?

It seemed to me that what set the truly Great athletes apart were small, almost imperceptible things that made them dramatically different from their peers. There were incremental improvements in who they were and how they acted. These were the tiny changes, the ever-so-slight differences that gave them an edge in competition and in life.

Athletics, after all, are rife with examples of how small the difference is between good and great. Just in the past few years there have been some remarkable examples. During the 2010 NCAA men's basketball championship game, Butler University's best player, Gordon Heyward, let loose with a half-court shot at the buzzer that would have allowed his Bulldogs to beat Duke. The shot rimmed out, and Duke claimed the title. A re-creation of Heyward's shot suggested that had it hit the backboard less than one inch from where it did, Butler would have been crowned champion in one of the great Cinderella stories of all time.

In the 2008 Beijing Olympics, Usain Bolt of Jamaica broke American Michael Johnson's world-record time from 1996 for the 200-meter by .02 second. He defended his title four years later at the London Olympics, becoming the first man in history to defend the 100m and 200m titles. Also in 2008, America's Michael Phelps took an extra half-stroke in the 100-meter butterfly to propel his fingertip to the wall just .01 second before Croatia's Milorad Čavić, and helped to seal his unprecedented eight gold medals. Similarly, in the ladies' downhill event at the 2010 Vancouver Olympics, Andrea Fischbacher of Austria finished just 1.49 seconds behind American skier Lindsey Vonn—yet it was enough to make the difference between going home with the gold and going home with no medal at all.

The smallest bit of extra training or effort or stamina or preparation changed everything. The small things come together to make a huge difference. But what, exactly, are those incremental changes that can impact performance so dramatically? That is much harder to nail down than concrete numbers and finishing times—because Greatness is about so much more than just professional rankings, and so much more subtle than world records or championships.

The undeniable fact that we can debate Greatness indicates that it is something more than statistics and figures. It's a concept, an idea, a state of being—and it seems to defy a single definition in concrete terms.

Despite its abstract nature, it is still necessary to have some kind of a tangible definition of Greatness. Even if we can't boil it down to a concise sentence or two, I believe there is a workable meaning that we can use when we engage in those inevitable arguments.

Even more important than having it in our debate-settling arsenal, though, is having a working definition of Greatness for our own lives—which brings us back to the original question: *What is Greatness?*

Everyone, it seems, has an opinion. From someone as inspiring and uplifting as Helen Keller to someone as ambitious and maniacal as Napoleon Bonaparte, there are as many different views on Greatness as there are issues to debate.

In seeking my own meaning of the term, I have found it necessary to consider a number of different aspects of Greatness—

both what it is, and what it is not—and it is these attributes that can help to steer us towards a better idea of What Makes the Great Ones Great.

GREATNESS is . . .

GREATNESS is available to all of us.

"Excellence is a better teacher than mediocrity. The lessons of the ordinary are everywhere. Truly profound and original insights are to be found only in studying the exemplary."

— WARREN BENNIS
(author, international corporate leadership expert, 1925–2014)

To begin, anyone seeking Greatness must understand that it is something truly unusual. Its uniqueness is part of what makes it so special—it is not something that is easily achieved because it is not something ordinary. It is available to each of us, but it is uncommon.

John Wooden once remarked to me, "If you didn't have to work to get something, it probably wasn't worth getting." If Greatness were easy, it wouldn't be Greatness—it would be the norm. Greatness reaches beyond the status quo. Greatness can be achieved only through sweat and struggle because it is not something that happens automatically. Instead, we must actively seek it through an investment of time, effort, sacrifice, discipline, and dedication to our individual pursuit. Your Greatness will be different from mine, and mine is different from Coach Wooden's. Greatness takes a unique form for every person.

It may be uncommon, but that's not because it is impossible to achieve. Greatness is available to each one of us *if we are willing to do common things uncommonly well!* However, as we will see in the next point, what makes it so rare is that most people aren't willing to do what it takes to get there.

GREATNESS does what others will not.

"You have to be willing to do things the masses would never do; that's how you separate yourself from the masses."

— STEVE BISCIOTTI
(NFL owner)

"There are no traffic jams along the extra mile."

— ROGER STAUBACH
(NFL Hall of Fame quarterback)

"I'm not saying Earl is in a class by himself, but whatever class he's in, it don't take long to call the roll."

— BUM PHILLIPS (coach, Houston Oilers)
on his running back Earl Campbell

If you were to ask a room full of people how many would be willing to make sacrifices in order to be Great, 95 percent would raise their hand, but 99 percent of those would never actually do what is necessary. The Great ones are unique because they live differently from those around them.

Many people will never begin the effort to change because it appears too daunting, uncomfortable, or inconvenient. Beyond just hard work, though, is the fact that Greatness recognizes opportunity, even if it presents challenges, and refuses to be intimidated by obstacles. Greatness seizes the moment.

It requires more than just muscle. Greatness demands a new way of thinking and a different perspective. It never allows itself to stagnate or grow complacent. It refuses to be put aside until a more convenient time. Greatness never rests from its quest for realization because it always sees ways to improve, room for growth, and lives to touch. It embraces the challenge rather than fleeing from it.

GREATNESS lifts—and recognizes—those around it.

"To become truly great, one has to stand with people, not above them."

— CHARLES DE MONTESQUIEU
(French politician and philosopher, 1689–1755)

"Responsibility is the price of greatness."

— WINSTON CHURCHILL
(British prime minister)

It is essential to remember that Greatness takes others along, raising them up, inspiring and challenging them to Greater things, too. Greatness recognizes its responsibility to reach beyond itself to encourage and empower others.

Greatness does not happen in a vacuum. Even if it practiced in private, its results are broad-reaching and impact the world in a positive manner. People who are in the presence of someone actively seeking Greatness cannot help but be inspired by their spirit, attitude, and commitment.

GREATNESS is well-rounded.

"Success at one single thing is not the same as greatness."

— CHRIS EVERT
(American tennis player)

An individual who truly espouses Greatness pursues it in every avenue of life. It goes beyond success and becomes a philosophy instead of just a marker. Greatness is concerned with overall improvement rather than attention on just one single skill.

Someone who swings a tennis racquet well, who jumps fastest from the starting blocks, or who wins 14 golf majors , but is a failure in other aspects of his life, has not achieved Greatness. Instead, Greatness strives to develop every area of one's life in order to create a whole person rather than just an individual, talented in a single pursuit.

GREATNESS has vision.

"Man's greatness lies in his power of thought."

— BLAISE PASCAL
(French mathematician, philosopher, and physicist, 1623–1662)

Greatness has a firm grasp on the reality of each situation—an understanding of goals and of the Big Picture. Greatness keeps things in perspective, appreciating what is truly important as well as what is trivial.

Greatness also has a long-range view of things, understanding that sacrifice in the present can mean major dividends in the future. Every workout, every obstacle—whether physical or mental—is not about the uncomfortable moment but about preparing for the ultimate goal. By viewing each situation with an eye toward opportunity and preparation, Greatness looks beyond the immediate and into the promise of the future.

GREATNESS is humble.

"I long to accomplish a great and noble task, but it is my chief duty to accomplish humble tasks as though they were great and noble."

— HELEN KELLER
(American author, 1880–1968)

"A great man is always willing to be little."

— RALPH WALDO EMERSON
(American poet, lecturer, and essayist, 1803–1882)

Greatness is not only about raising up. It also works for the goal and not for praise, because the goal is more important than ego. True Greatness gains recognition because it has been observed by others, not advertised by the individual.

Simply believing yourself to be Great is not the same as achieving Greatness. Greatness readily accepts blame, and acknowledges responsibility and ownership of a situation. It requires action and dedication, not simply patting yourself on the back.

Likewise, the Great ones acknowledge the influence of others who have helped to shape their pursuit. Teachers, coaches, mentors, families, peers—all these contribute to how a person develops in their quest for Greatness. No one achieves it alone, and the Great ones recognize this.

GREATNESS overcomes.

"The spirit, the will to win, and the will to excel, are the things that endure. These qualities are so much more important than the events that occur."

— VINCE LOMBARDI
(legendary NFL head coach and general manager)

Often Greatness comes from moving beyond difficult circumstances in one's past or clearing unexpected hurdles. Other times, it is the result of challenges that were faced with determination. Whatever the case, Greatness does not make excuses—it makes progress. It recognizes that there will always be obstacles in one form or another, and it uses those challenges as a means of growing stronger and wiser.

Anyone who achieves success without a fight is probably not Great. Greatness is more than inborn ability—it is the struggle to develop and hone the skills necessary for mental and physical victory. It is not easily defeated. Giving up, throwing in the towel, surrendering without a fight, are not signs of Greatness. Greatness is not a guarantee of achieving goals, but it is a guarantee of pursuing them with heart and effort.

GREATNESS is the product of choices.

"Greatness lies, not in being strong,
but in the right using of strength."

— HENRY WARD BEECHER
(American abolitionist and minister, 1813–1887)

Choices, not circumstances, are what determine Greatness. It is achieved through a series of decisions that consistently tend toward the better option. Greatness lies not in what we're given, but in what we do with what we're given.

As the expression goes, "Our choices are what define us." And we are surrounded by a multitude of choices every day, from how we spend our spare time, to the friends we choose, to what food we put in our bodies. We control our own decisions, the only area in life we can control. The Great Ones make those decisions wisely.

GREATNESS is a way of life.

"We are what we repeatedly do.
Excellence then, is not an act, but a habit."

— ARISTOTLE
(Greek philosopher)

"Greatness consists in trying to be great. There is no other way."

— ALBERT CAMUS
(French philosopher and author, 1913–1960)

Working toward Greatness is a process—it isn't a one-time action. It is a developing, changing, and adapting journey, and it is cumulative. All aspects of it are necessary to achieve the overall goal, and as we hone one area of our lives to be targeted toward Greatness, we find that the other areas also become sharper and more focused.

Greatness is the persistent pursuit of professional and personal excellence. It doesn't take a day off. It is what we wake up to each morning; it is how we think and how we work; it is how we act and how we interact. Greatness is all-consuming because it is about how we live our lives, not simply what we do for a living. Greatness is more than a catchphrase or a gimmick—it is who we strive to be and, therefore, who we are.

GREATNESS is not. . .

Every bit as important as defining what Greatness is, is determining what it is not.

GREATNESS is not genetic.

It is not something that is the result of the gene pool; it is something that everyone must actively pursue in order to achieve. We all possess the potential for Greatness, but Greatness itself is not an inborn trait. Greatness should never be confused with talent—Greatness is what one does with his or her natural abilities, but they are not the same thing.

If you were to say to any Great athlete, "You were born great. Your mother and father set you up for your success," every single person would balk at the suggestion. LeBron James, Peyton Manning, or Derek Jeter—anyone could point to someone of the same size, same strength, or same talent who had the same potential but not the same drive.

No one is born Great. No one is inherently Great without making a significant effort toward reaching the goal. Greatness is defined by the very struggle it requires, because the desire to be Great is the first step in achieving Greatness. It can be reached no other way.

GREATNESS is not about the record book.

It is not measured by records, rings, championships, wealth, or fame. In 2008, Dick and Rick Hoyt were inducted into the International Iron Man Hall of Fame, even though they never won a single race. In chapter eight, we will explore what is about them that makes them worthy of such an honor.

The simple truth is that Greatness is not about winning but is something achieved only through a wholeness of self. It is directly linked to the integrity of an individual's character and the way in which they approach their sport, profession, or life.

If your vision of personal Greatness is defined only by a statistic or a number, it is not likely to last, because there will always be someone coming along behind you who will be poised to surpass it. Greatness must be rooted in something more substantial than records.

GREATNESS does not take shortcuts.

Greatness cannot be achieved by seeking a backdoor to success. Marion Jones, who "won" five medals in the 2000 Summer Olympics, has an empty shelf where her medals used to be to prove that winning achieved through cheating counts for very little. Barry Bonds may hold the all-time home-run record as well as the record for most homeruns in a season, but the BALCO drug scandal will forever taint his career. In my book, he's not the record holder. He doesn't deserve to be mentioned with Hank Aaron, and he certainly doesn't qualify for the term *Great.* Greatness does not seek a quick and easy solution, and it is not convenient.

Instead, Greatness understands that improvement comes only through repeated and deliberate work toward a goal. Just simply breaking a record does not make someone Great; adherence to the discipline, dedication, and rules required to get to that point is what shapes a person's Greatness.

GREATNESS isn't perfect.

Great players have bad games. Great people have bad days. Flaws don't eliminate you from the pursuit of Greatness; they make you human. Everyone discussed in this book is a flawed individual, but the truly Great work through their flaws. Great ones do make mistakes.

Anyone who desires to be Great must understand that failure, disappointment, and letdowns are a part of life. The Great ones learn from those experiences and become stronger as a result. No person is whole without understanding losing as well as winning.

Perfection is impossible, but the pursuit of it allows the truly Great to thrive.

GREATNESS is not a fad.

Greatness is not defined by one moment. There are plenty of one-hit wonder bands out there, but very few true artists whose music defies generational or categorical boundaries.

In many arguments over who or what is the Greatest at something, the standards and criteria change depending upon the ideas of the moment or the tastes of the participants. Greatness is much bigger than a shifting idea based on a situational agenda. It is something whose meaning extends far beyond the immediate. It is not defined simply by current values or trends, but is proven to have staying power. It is not something that is here today and gone tomorrow. Greatness never goes out of style.

Greatness transcends the moment to be lasting and timeless.

GREATNESS is not the same as fame.

Some Great individuals never see their names in the front-page news, but through quiet actions like parenting, mentoring, teaching, and giving, they touch the lives of countless others and make their impact on the world in a manner far more lasting than fame.

Many people desire to be famous, but most are not willing to do the work required to become Great—and the difference is vast. Fame is attention gained through a person's public image. Greatness is a philosophy gained through the genuine manner in which a person lives his or her life.

A common theme of all of these ideas is not necessarily Greatness itself, but the *pursuit* of Greatness. It is in the chase of this ideal that character develops, and in that development that the habits, thoughts, and behaviors of Greatness begin to emerge. This is a "doing" list, a series of actions. The pursuit of Greatness does not happen through passivity, through wishing, or through half efforts and shortcuts. Greatness is both the goal and by-product of its own pursuit.

This book discusses what I like to call the Sixteen Characteristics of Greatness—qualities that are present in truly Great winners but that can be translated into anyone's life. Each chapter will focus on one aspect of Greatness, offering anecdotes, discussions, tips, inspirational quotes, and recommended reading.

Over my more than twenty-five years as a sports writer, I have had the opportunity to not only witness skills and moves, but also to personally ask countless world-class athletes about the behaviors they have embraced, honed, and utilized to propel themselves forward.

When I started out, I was fascinated by what seemed to be some kind of secret formula, separating the merely talented, noteworthy, remarkable, headline-grabbing, or flashy from the ones who just seemed to have something more. It didn't matter if they were rookies or veterans; there was just something that seemed to elevate certain athletes to a different level. It was in something they brought to their game and something they brought to their lives.

In hundreds of interviews, I found myself coming around to a few key questions over and over again: What separated you from the competition? What took you from good to Great? I was determined to find the answer to one pervading question: What makes the Great ones Great?

At first, these questions were for my own benefit—ideas and tips about their individual Greatness that I would ask them for in the course of the interview; but eventually, I realized the advice I was receiving was significant in the big picture, too. Almost none of the athletes told me their success was due to their physical gifts; almost to a one, they pointed to something else. And the longer I examined these practices, the more certain patterns started to emerge, and they all seemed to fall into one of four categories: thought, preparation, work, and life.

If Great athletes past and present seem to consistently exhibit certain traits, then perhaps there is something in these ideas that can be applied to any one of us. The next sixteen chapters will break down each category of Greatness into its individual elements, and we will examine how these characteristics can have a place in your own life.

The first step in pursuing Greatness is to consider the way you think. What are your passions? What are your beliefs? And how do you react to the situations around you? Proper mental preparation and a healthy mind-set are traits that the Great ones share. There is always emphasis on how an athlete keeps his or her body in peak physical shape, but the same is true for an athlete's mind, attitude, and spirit. Chapters one through four will guide you through these traits of mental Greatness.

1. **It's Personal.** The Great ones hate to lose more than they love to win. Here, we will examine the intensity with which athletes approach their sport and the personal interest they have in every loss and every move they make—with no excuses.
2. **Rubbing Elbows.** They understand the value of association. This chapter takes a look at our "pacers"— the people around us who push us to be better. It is our responsibility to surround ourselves with the very best people, those who can push us, challenge us and encourage us.

3. **Believe.** They have faith in a higher power. Many famous athletes today seem to worship at the altar of self. But there are others who understand that life is so much more than personal gain and glory, that talents and opportunities are blessings, and that moral grounding and strong faith are essential elements in creating a well-rounded, healthy person.
4. **Contagious Enthusiasm.** They are positive thinkers. They are enthusiastic, and that enthusiasm rubs off on those around them. They aren't just optimists; they are encouragers who motivate their teammates to victory.

The second step in attaining Greatness is to examine the way you prepare. Are you directing your energy and resources to the right places? Are you working toward the winner's circle or just the finishing line? Preparation is more than just practice—it is precise, measured effort that is goal-oriented and motivated for success. The Great ones are always ready to rise to the occasion, and they never lose sight of what they are working toward. The next four chapters will challenge you to approach preparation in a new and more effective way.

5. **Hope for the Best, But . . .** The Great ones prepare for all possibilities before they step onto the field. They anticipate needs and keep themselves relevant so that when their opportunity comes, they can calmly step in and do what needs to be done—because they've already prepared for it.
6. **What Off-Season?** They are always working toward the next game. They understand that the goal is what's ahead, and that there's *always* something ahead. These athletes refuse to back off from their training because they know there is always someone waiting on the bench who will be happy to fill their shoes. Because of this, they push themselves to grow, stretch, hone, and continually develop.

7. **Visualize Victory.** They see victory before the game begins. They refuse to entertain the possibility of defeat but, rather, see themselves as winners with the ability to succeed again and again. Rather than allowing themselves to get distracted by unimportant things, they direct their energy and resources toward the positive goals they have set.

8. **Inner Fire.** They use adversity as fuel. Some people use difficulties as an excuse to fail, but the Great ones use it as a springboard to propel them forward. It's a lot easier to achieve success when things are comfortable, but what about when they turn upside down? Rather than allowing themselves to be held back, the truly Great use adversity to take them some place they wouldn't otherwise go.

No victory can be gained without effort, and the third step toward Greatness is to look at how you approach your work. How do you handle the prospect of failure? How adaptable are you to changing circumstances? How do you relate to the rest of your team? An athlete's profession is their sport, and the principles that the Great ones use to dictate their approach to competition are applicable to any job field. Chapters nine through 12 encourage a closer look at how you take on your professional pursuits.

9. **Ice in Their Veins.** The Great ones are risk takers and don't fear making a mistake. They have to contend with fears and nerves like anyone else, but they refuse to be controlled by them. Rather, they force themselves to charge on.

10. **When All Else Fails.** They know how—and when—to adjust their game plan. Instead of stubbornly refusing to change when the conditions change, the Great ones will tweak their technique or modify their methods to adapt to their circumstance.

11. **The Ultimate Teammate.** They will assume whatever role is necessary for the team to win. Placing the needs of their teammates above their own desires or preferences, they are willing to take on different responsibilities in order positively affect the desired outcome of their team's aspirations.

12. **Not Just About the Benjamins.** They don't play just for the money. The Great ones recognize that there is more to the game than which team will write them the biggest check. They make decisions based on what will be best for the people around them, for supporting the organization, and for achieving the ultimate goal.

The final step in reaching Greatness is to live your life in a way that reflects Greatness. How do you interact with those around you? What do you do with your success? Where do you look for fulfillment? What do you consider your Greatest accomplishment? Achieving Greatness means having a ready answer to these questions thanks to a life dedicated to something bigger than yourself.

For athletes, that means being able to appropriately handle the pressures placed upon them by fame and recognizing the importance of staying grounded. For the rest of us, it means developing our personal side apart from our work, cultivating a life lived for something Greater than the bottom line, and setting goals for things more important than our professional pursuits. The final four chapters of this book examine the way in which a life—not just a career—can be truly Great.

13. **Do Unto Others.** They know character is defined by how they treat those who cannot help them, so they dedicate a portion of their time and resources to enriching their communities and giving back to those in need.

14. **When No One Is Watching.** They are comfortable in front of the mirror and they live their lives with integrity. They incorporate their values in every aspect of their lives, from the playing field to the home—not because the eyes of the world are upon them, but because it is the right thing to do.
15. **When Everyone Is Watching.** They embrace the idea of being a role model. Whether they chose it or not, athletes are some of the most visible mentors in our society. While some use this notoriety for material gain or as an excuse for reckless behavior, the Great ones recognize the responsibility they have to their fans and to the next generation.
16. **Records Are Made to Be Broken.** They know their legacy isn't what they did on the field. They are well-rounded. While their career is obviously a huge part of who they are, they have also recognized that there are some things, like family, faith, and community, that are more important and last longer than a few seasons on top. The Great ones work to cultivate these relationships and associations in order to develop their full selves.

The thing that makes the Great ones Great cannot be boiled down to one simple idea, catchy mantra, or trick of the trade. It is the realization and daily pursuit of each of these characteristics that helps an individual—athlete, career person, parent, friend—truly achieve Greatness. It is within reach for all of us. Let yourself become one of the Great ones.

PILLAR ONE

How They Think

CHAPTER

1

It's Personal

The truly great hate to lose more than they love to win.

The only person with any expectations of the 38-year-old entered in the US Open tennis tournament was himself. No one else thought the man who'd been ranked at No. 947 in the world the year before had a chance to win. He'd earned a wild-card bid to the tournament, which meant the world to him.

The aged underdog faced a top-10 player in the first round, 25-year-old Patrick McEnroe, the younger brother of John McEnroe. The elder player lost the first two sets and the first three games of the third set. He was down love–40, serving, and literally just moments away from being swept out of the tournament.

With everything in his favor, a calm McEnroe waited for the serve. He was relaxed and lackadaisical, and then he did something that would change the course of that evening: he yawned.

Across the net, the 38-year-old could not believe his eyes. Insulted, he swore under his breath, "I am not going to let that kid beat me."

He came back to win the third set 6–4; then went on to win the fourth set 6–2. After four hours and 20 minutes of play, he won the fifth set—and the match.

"In the old days I used to win a lot because of my reputation," the underdog said. "I'm not 24 or 25 years old now. But there's been a pattern that developed over my career that you have to kill me to beat me."

When Jimmy Connors—yes, the former world No. 1 Jimmy Connors—walked off the court at 1:36 that morning, he understood that his performance that night was driven by a feeling he had often expressed in a 20-year professional career: "I hate to lose more than I love to win."

For the truly Great, victory is not just something they get a chance to enjoy; it is something they come to expect. Winning lasts only momentarily...losing lingers. The Great ones take losing personally, and that is what drives them to higher levels of competition.

Connors went on to win the next round of the US Open against a player five years younger than he was, and the next against an opponent 12 years younger. On September 2, 1991, in the fourth round of the tournament, Connors found himself down again two sets to love. But just as before, he won the next three sets to beat 24-year-old Aaron Krickstein and went on to become the oldest player ever to compete in the US Open semifinals. The four-hour-and-forty-one-minute match took place on Connors's 39th birthday.

Jimmy Connors understood that losing is a painful obstacle waiting to be overcome by those who rise to the challenge. Despite the odds and against opponents often an entire decade younger than himself, he elevated his game to new levels by refusing to lose.

More from the Truly Great

Hating to lose was certainly a defining trait of legendary college football coach Bear Bryant. A few years ago, I had the opportunity to work on a book about Coach Bryant and the University of Alabama football program, interviewing people all over the country who had known him—old coaching buddies, friends, family members, and scores of former athletes who played football under this remarkable man. I asked them all what made him so successful, and time and again, the answer was the same, simple truth: "He hated to lose more than he liked to win."

His drive toward excellence was contagious; it spread to his fellow coaches and on to his players. Bryant's desire to lead his teams to victory was so great that under his leadership, the Crimson Tide earned six National Championships and thirteen conference championships. When Bryant retired in 1982, he was the winningest head coach in college football history.

"Losing doesn't make me want to quit," Bryant once said. "It makes me want to fight that much harder."

It really stood out to me that those who knew him best all attributed Bryant's success not to an elaborate formula of coaching secrets but to the very simple fact that he hated to lose, and he cared enough to invest himself into the pursuit of Greatness.

The work it takes to win may hurt, but losing hurts even more.

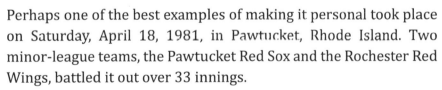

Perhaps one of the best examples of making it personal took place on Saturday, April 18, 1981, in Pawtucket, Rhode Island. Two minor-league teams, the Pawtucket Red Sox and the Rochester Red Wings, battled it out over 33 innings.

Technically, the game should have ended at 1:00 a.m. on Sunday, but the umpires were unaware of the League's ruling on when to call a game in such extraordinary circumstances—so they kept on until 4:07 a.m., 32 innings in, with a score of 2–2. Finally, the League president, over the phone, called the game to a halt and ruled that it would be resumed when the teams were next scheduled to play at Pawtucket in June. On June 23, in what was technically the 33rd inning of the game, Pawtucket managed to pull ahead 3–2 and clinch the win in a marathon game that lasted eight hours twenty-five minutes.

Each team wanted the game to be over, but neither wanted to be the one to call it quits. Both teams cared enough to keep plugging away, tied inning after tied inning, until one was the clear victor. For all the players, managers, coaches—and even the 19 diehard fans who stayed until 4:07 a.m. on April 19—the game wasn't just a game. It was a testament to the passion and drive that each team shared to never throw in the towel.

It's even more significant when you realize that in that matchup, officially the longest professional baseball game ever played, Wade Boggs was playing for Pawtucket and Cal Ripken Jr. was playing for Rochester. Both men, future Hall of Fame major leaguers, were part of that intense determination not to be the team that walked away from the game with a loss.

"We were now in uncharted territory. We wondered what was going to happen next," Ripken recounted in his book *Get in the Game.* "We were having fun again. And make no mistake about it, as time wore on, we really wanted to win that game."

And, true to his character of relentless energy and hard work, Cal Ripken Jr. played every single one of those 33 innings. *And* he was the first player to show up for the team's next game, which was played the very same afternoon following the marathon.

"I never even considered not showing up. I wanted to play that afternoon game," Ripken recalled. "A lot of my teammates felt exactly the same way."

Patrick Roy was the ultracompetitive netminder during his National Hockey League days, and the guy hated to lose. During the first round of the 1994 playoffs, Roy developed appendicitis. From his hospital bed, he watched his Montreal Canadiens lose the third game of the series, and he just couldn't accept it. He talked the doctors into postponing surgery, giving him antibiotics and letting him compete with his team. Roy went out and stopped 39 shots in a 5–2 win, then made 60 saves in the fifth game of the series. It wasn't until the Boston Bruins eliminated Roy's Habs that he finally allowed the doctors to remove his appendix.

During his NHL career, Roy won four Stanley Cups—two each with Montreal and Colorado—and pushed not only himself but also his team to excel. Losing wasn't an option. "I have the love to win. I hate to lose," Roy said more than once. "Maybe it's more the hate to lose than the love to win."

In the 1996 Stanley Cup Final, Roy's Colorado Avalanche played the Florida Panthers, a team that threw rubber rats on the ice when their team scored a goal. During the second game of the best-of-seven series, the Panthers scored two quick goals, which resulted in two waves of rats. Roy skated over to his bench while the ice was being cleared and told his teammates, "No more rats." He didn't allow another goal in the series, and the Avalanche swept their way to their first championship.

"I admire how he hates to lose," former Montreal coach Jacques Demers, now a member of the Canadian Senate, said. "He cares only...about the team winning. That's the ultimate pro."

Duke basketball, no question, is synonymous with Greatness. In talking to Mike Krzyzewski, head coach since 1980, I asked him when he knew he carried his team to the level of Greatness, fully expecting the answer to be a pivotal game or event during one of the five seasons he coached the Blue Devils through March Madness to the national title. "Coach K" surprised me when he told me Greatness began at the end of his third season at Duke.

At the end of that season (in which they had a losing record) they had to face nationally No. 2 ranked Virginia in the tournament. The Cavaliers pummeled Duke, 109–66, embarrassing the Blue Devils badly on television. After the game, Krzyzewski stood, staring at the scoreboard, then finally left the arena to meet some booster friends for a late meal. As he arrived at the restaurant, he noticed someone laughingly pulling the knives off the table, just in case the coach took the loss too hard.

After sitting down, one of the boosters raised a glass of water in a toast. "Here's to a night let's soon forget," he said. But that was not what Krzyzewski wanted.

Shaking his head, he looked at the boosters and said no, that was the wrong toast. Coach K then lifted his own glass corrected it: "To a night we'll *never* forget."

That 2:00 a.m. toast illustrated the Greatness of Coach Krzyzewski. He had taken an underdog Duke team into the Atlantic Coast Conference tournament and gotten humiliated by one of the best teams in the nation—but he didn't make excuses for the loss. He used it to build a better team.

At the team's first practice the following year, Coach K walked out onto the court and turned on the scoreboard, illuminating the 109–66 reminder and stinging loss. He accepted no excuses and used the losing game as a teaching moment. He wanted the Blue Devils to remember the sting of the loss and how badly it had hurt to walk off the court. And that year, the team won thirteen more games. Two years later, Duke played for the National Championship with Coach K on the bench.

He used a humiliating loss on television as a springboard for improvement. "It was that loss, and turning the energy from that loss and remembering the pain that came from losing like that allowed us to become a more successful program," Krzyzewski explained.

Serena Williams was a perfectionist long before she was a serious competitor on the tennis court.

"When I was five years old and in kindergarten, we had a project due and I was up late working on it, so late that my mom had to force me to go to bed," she told me in an interview. "But I kept getting back up because I wanted to redo the project until it was 100 percent perfect. Eventually, I fell asleep and didn't get it done because I wanted it to be perfect more than I wanted to just get it done."

Her work has always been a point of personal pride, a trait that is reflected in her impressive career. By 2015, she had been the top-ranked player, according to the Women's Tennis Association, on six separate occasions, and had won twenty-one Grand Slams: one win at the French Open; three at the US Open; four at the Australian Open; and four at Wimbledon.

While she used to lose her temper and lash out when she lost a match, she learned to channel that personal disappointment and frustration into a much more constructive outlet. "I don't like it, and what I do is go home and practice harder. I work harder. I train harder. When I step on that practice court in the days after a loss, I have an anger in me. It is subconscious. I don't mean to be that way. But now I use that anger to make me better. It propels me to work harder."

And for the Truly Great in Business

Hating to lose is a philosophy that fuels many top business leaders as well. The National Retail Federation studies trends in sales, and found that 48 percent of all salespeople will make one call and quit if the answer is no. That's almost half who quit after one setback.

When the rest of the people called back, another quarter gave up after getting a second no. Fifteen percent more got three no's and abandoned the potential sale. Just 12 percent continued to call until they got the results they wanted.

The NRF's study didn't stop there. It analyzed the sales figures, which showed that the 12 percent who didn't accept losing accounted for 80 percent of total sales. A full 88 percent of sales staff gave in to defeat, but the persistent staff—the ones who made it personal—not only closed the deal, but are the Great ones who are overall responsible for their company's success.

Stanley Bing, in his best seller, *Sun Tzu Was a Sissy,* writes, "In battle, attitude is all. And true warriors are united in the fact that they hate to lose even more than they love to win." In many work environments, second place is termed the "first loser"—a term many leaders acknowledge but struggle to accept. Other leaders see second place as a "tie for last."

Second place is not even on their radar screens. Robert Goizueta, former CEO of Coca-Cola, summarized it this way: "I hate to lose... I'd rather not play." Jack Welch, former CEO of General Electric and best-selling author, responded, "No, I'd rather play. But I like to fight like hell before I lose."

Many executives admit that the "love to win—hate to lose" mentality is based on expectations and intensity of pleasure versus pain. The "can't win 'em all" attitude, common in many sporting events, simply does not resonate with CEOs who expect nothing less than 100 percent victory.

The thought of coming in second place—or worse—has lead many business leaders to share former Cincinnati Reds and Detroit Tigers manager Sparky Anderson's opinion that "losing hurts more than winning feels good." Hating to lose in business settings takes on additional significance for company leaders. If Phil Mickelson misses a putt and finishes second at the Master's, or if Serena Williams gets bounced in the middle rounds of Wimbledon, there is another opportunity to win right around the corner for most athletes with the next tournament, next match, or next game.

But business is not as forgiving, as coming in second place can send shock waves, perhaps even leading to a company's ruin. According to Sam Simon, chairman and CEO of Atlas Oil, "I hate to lose. That in itself is a great motivator. I also love what I do and have 192 people working for me who I don't want to let down."

Business leaders hate to lose just as badly as athletes do. For many, the potential for losing business and changing the livelihoods of thousands of valued employees is the Greatest motivator—and the one that requires the most work.

After booming to become the nation's third-largest pizza chain, John Schnatter, the "Papa" in Papa John's Pizza, nearly had to close one thousand stores. But Schnatter, who hated the thought of losing franchises, studied the chain's losing ways. He realized they'd gotten away from the fundamentals of the business. "The one thing that Papa John's had that was solid was that people thought we had a better pizza," he told a reporter. "So we focused on that."

He hated losing so much he was willing to go back and pore over every mistake the company ever made to never lose again.

The GREATNESS Challenge

You may never be Jimmy Connors, one of the most competitive athletes in the history of tennis; you may never be Bear Bryant, one of the winningest coaches in the history of college football; you may never be in situations like Wade Boggs, Cal Ripken Jr., or Serena Williams—but you will certainly have the opportunity to bring the pursuit of excellence to your office, your family, and your life.

You will lose, but how you react to that loss and what you learn from it will demonstrate your level of greatness. Will you accept it, or will you hate it?

How do you handle the prospect of loss? Do you hang up after the first rejection and not try again? Does it mire you in a self-fulfilling prophecy of defeat? Take some time to honestly assess the ways you deal with losing. Sam Walton, former CEO of Wal-Mart and once the richest man in the world, was fond of saying, "I expect to win. I go into tough challenges always planning to come out victorious. It never occurred to me that I might lose, it was almost as if I had a right to win. Thinking like that often seems to turn into a self-fulfilling prophecy." Champions expect to win; why shouldn't you?

Think about the last time you finished second—or worse—in something that was meaningful to you. What was your reaction? Did you explain it away somehow, or did you commit yourself to work harder?

When you lose—and you will—don't make excuses. Figure out a better way to approach the same situation when you encounter it again, and prepare for it. Sportswriter Bob Nightengale once asked pitching great Greg Maddux about the most memorable batting situation he'd faced. Maddux, known for his excellence in preparing for each situation, didn't cite a famous slugger or pennant-chasing circumstance. Maddux, an eight-time All Star with four Cy Young awards, eighteen Gold Glove awards, and a World

Series championship, said his most memorable situation had been striking out Dave Martinez to end a regular-season game.

Perplexed, Nightengale asked why. Maddux said, "I remember that one because he got a hit off me in the same situation (full count, bases loaded, two out in the ninth inning) seven years earlier. I told myself if I ever got in the same situation again, I'll pitch him differently. It took me seven years, but I got him." The odds were against Maddux meeting Martinez in that exact same situation again, let alone pitch to the same count again, but Maddux had been beaten before and lost. His hatred of failure in the previous matchup drove him to success when he encountered it again.

No matter how small the loss is, learn something from it. Six-time NBA champion Michael Jordan hates to lose at anything—even a charity basketball event. Even if no one knows about the loss except Jordan and the person who bested him, Jordan mulls it over for days, trying to figure how he could have prevented it. "I hate to lose at anything I do," he said. "It doesn't matter what the stakes, or who the audience is." Most people might blow it off as something inconsequential, but Jordan cares enough about the small battles to make them personal. When you come in second, don't justify it. Challenge yourself to work harder.

Do you care enough to make it personal? Does the desire to win with honor steer you to continually strive towards victory? Hating to lose is not bad sportsmanship—it means that you have a drive to succeed and hate to fall short of your best.

The pursuit of Greatness is an inherently personal one; do you care enough to make it your own?

CHAPTER

2

Rubbing Elbows

The great ones understand the value of association.

John Wooden is the Greatest coach of all time. It is tough in the world of sports to make any statement that declarative, but in this case I can. Besides being a man of impeccable character and a mentor to thousands, he was an incredibly gifted and insightful leader. Over the last twelve years that he was the head coach at UCLA, he guided the Bruins men's basketball team to an unbelievable ten national championships. That is among the few records in men's sports I feel comfortable will never be broken.

So when Coach Wooden offered advice on what made the Great ones Great, the lesson was sure to be a valuable one. When I asked that question a few years ago, Coach explained to me that among the most important things he looked for when trying to get a sense of a person's capacity for success was who that person included in their inner circle. "Their associations told me everything I needed to know about them," Coach said. "I could tell what their future held by how important it was to surround themselves with the right people."

To illustrate his point, Coach said he wanted to share the story of "one of the best players I've ever coached." I immediately assumed I was about to hear about a legendary Bruin like Kareem Abdul-Jabbar or Bill Walton. Instead, Coach smiled and said: "Do you know about Swen Nater?" I did not.

Nater was born in Holland and raised in an orphanage there before immigrating to the United States at the age of nine to grow up in Southern California. It might have appeared he was destined for basketball because of his great height—he would eventually grow to seven feet tall—but he was too gangly and awkward to even make his high school's team.

His body matured and he got a second shot at playing basketball competitively, this time at a small community college not far from his home. Over the next two years, Swen Nater went from a boy who couldn't make the high school team to one of the best junior-college basketball players in the country. He quickly drew the interest of a number of four-year colleges that hoped to add Nater as the star player on their roster for his final two years of eligibility.

As Nater was weighing offers from those schools, his coach at Cypress Creek Community College suggested he not make any decision until they could talk to John Wooden. Swen laughed at the unlikely prospect of playing for the Bruins, who had just won their fifth consecutive national championship. But he listened as his coach phoned Wooden and made one of the Great sales calls of all time.

"It appears you have one scholarship left for next year," the Cypress Creek coach said to Wooden. "And I have your player sitting right here."

Wooden asked why he was so confident and the other coach replied in a rather gutsy way, "Coach Wooden, here's your problem: as I look at your roster, you have one of the best players in the country starting at center for you next year, Bill Walton. But what you don't have is anyone big enough to compete against Bill Walton…in practice! You need *my* big guy to make *your* big guy work harder every day to get better."

Coach Wooden got the point immediately: Walton would improve more rapidly if he had better competition every day. What he needed to push him to his full potential was someone who could match him and drive him forward. Walton, Nater, the Bruins—they would all be made better if these two men chose to associate themselves with one another, if they chose to make each other a key part of the other's inner circle.

The value of association—it made sense to John Wooden, and after the pitch from Cypress Community College, he offered Nater his last remaining scholarship to play at UCLA.

The scholarship came with an understanding, however. Nater was told he'd probably seldom make it off the bench during games; however, he would have the opportunity to practice each and every day with the best players and best coaches in the nation.

Nater didn't wait a second before he signed that scholarship, and as John Wooden promised, he rarely played in games and certainly never started. But he mattered.

When Bill Walton, as a senior, was poised to be the first choice overall in the NBA draft, all of the scouts and reporters seemed to want to know one thing: who did the best guy think was the best guy *he'd* ever had to play against?

He didn't look across town to Pepperdine or across the country to Kansas. Bill Walton looked down the bench and said "that guy down there"—Swen Nater—was the best competition he'd faced.

Nater, who played with heart and drive and passion and soul, had grown every day as a player at UCLA because he had understood the importance of training against the best and surrounding himself with greatness. This no-name athlete with almost no playing time became the first-ever first-round NBA draft pick who never started a senior college game.

John Wooden agreed with Walton: the best ones are those people who can recognize the strengths of others, as well as their own weaknesses. They surround themselves with excellence and accept the challenge to propel themselves forward to greater things.

Wooden treasured this story because he understood that the value of association is the first step to achieving greatness. Despite not starting a single college game, Swen Nater went on to play 12 years in the NBA and is now vice president of Costco. And the admiration is reciprocal: Nater says that to this day, associating himself with John Wooden and Bill Walton was the best decision he ever made.

More from the Truly Great

The value of association can take several forms. Think, for a moment, about how different kinds of challenges and associations helped other athletes realize their Greatness.

Wilma Rudolph's inspiring story of Greatness illustrates the impact that association can have on pushing individuals beyond themselves. Struck with polio at age four, the doctors told her parents that Wilma would never walk without assistance again. Her mother tirelessly helped her daughter regain the use of her legs by researching home remedies and massaging the muscles to keep them from total atrophy. She repeatedly promised her daughter that together they would beat the disease and shed the braces.

Her mother's efforts were monumental, but the thing that really inspired young Wilma to keep going was watching her older sister play basketball. After watching her sister from the sidelines for several years, twelve-year-old Wilma decided that walking wasn't just enough—she was going to reach beyond that. She was going to be an athlete.

Just four years later, at sixteen, Wilma Rudolph won a spot on the US Olympic track-and-field team and brought home a bronze medal for the 4×100-meter relay at the Melbourne Olympics in 1956. Four years later, at the 1960 Olympics in Rome, she won three more track-and-field medals, breaking an Olympic record for the 100-meter dash and setting a new world record with her teammates for the 4×100 relay—and all because she had felt a push to reach for something more.

Simply the presence of the right people—some who encourage

and some who challenge through example—can be the force that makes people work for goals far beyond what they ever thought possible.

The Romanian gymnast Nadia Comăneci had no equals on her native team. Easily sweeping numerous national awards before she hit her teenage years, it was in preparation for the 1976 Summer Olympics in Montreal that she faced her stiffest competition in the form of Soviet gymnast Nellie Kim.

Coming in second place to Kim in vault, floor, and uneven bars in pre-Olympic qualifying, Comăneci used the challenge to attack her training and performance at the Games with a new level of ferocity. It paid off. At just fourteen years of age, Comăneci earned a perfect 10 for her routine on the uneven bars, making her the first person to ever achieve that honor in modern Olympic history. She remains the youngest woman ever to do so, and she earned it in a category where she had lost to her stiffest competition in the preliminaries.

Nadia Comăneci was clearly an athlete who understood the importance of having a challenger. It was the ongoing rivalry between Comăneci and Kim that would spur both of them on to earn numerous perfect 10s and countless honors for the next five years. But the distinction of being the very first perfect 10—and the association of her name with such an outstanding accomplishment—remains with Comăneci.

Have you ever noticed how Great athletes often seem to emerge in groups? It's not a coincidence. The presence of other Great athletes challenges each one to become even better.

Think about the so-called Four Horsemen of the Apocalypse who dominated the Notre Dame backfield in the 1920s. Quarterback Harry Stuhldreher, halfbacks Jim Crowley and Don Miller, and fullback Elmer Layden were a force the likes of which college football had never seen before. Of course their combined talent made playing time that much tougher, but the presence of other fierce competitors forced each one to stay on top of his game.

Consider, too, the famous friendship and rivalry between Mickey Mantle and Roger Maris. Each man benefited from the talent of the other in challenging his own hitting. They were able to use that competition to not only improve their own game but also to propel their shared team, the New York Yankees, to consecutive World Series victories in 1961 and 1962. Not coincidentally, these are the same years that saw the height of both men's pursuit of Babe Ruth's home-run record.

Venus and Serena Williams have used their sisterly rivalry to push each other to greatness. Their performance at Wimbledon in 2008 illustrates this point perfectly. Together they made a formidable pair on the court, winning the women's doubles competition. But they also both channeled their talent and competitive spirit to outplay the other, as they battled through the rankings to face one another in the finals, in which Venus won her fifth Wimbledon women's singles title. The presence of the other sister as both a friend and rival has encouraged each to grow as an athlete until both are among the world's best.

Prior to the Williams sisters rise to Greatness, rivals Martina Navratilova and Chris Evert dominated women's tennis throughout the 1970s and 1980s. They faced each other eighty times in professional play, sixty-one of those matches played in tournament finals. Bud Collins, famed sportscaster and journalist for professional tennis, called theirs "The rivalry of the century."

Evert and Navratilova each hold 18 Grand Slam victories in the singles division, currently fourth on the all-time highest list of career Grand Slam players in the open era. From November of 1975 through August of 1987, either Martina Navratilova or Chris Evert ranked No. 1 in all but twenty-three weeks, and most of the time, the other ranked No. 2. Of the eighty matches where they faced each other, Navratilova won 42 and Evert won 37.

At the screening of *Unmatched,* a 2010 ESPN documentary featuring the famous rivalry, Evert said, "The beauty of our rivalry was not only we met so many times, but the contrast. We were night and day, so different in every way and brought our own set of fans to the mix. It was drama."

Navratilova's emotional and passionate play became famous on the court. She displayed her anger, frustration, tears, and excitement for all to see. Her drive to compete and to win was always evident through her passion. With the off court perception as America's Sweetheart, Evert's strategic game for cool calculation and a calm temperament earned her the name Ice Maiden during play.

Even more impressive than the stats on the court, in retirement, and throughout different points in their lives, Navratilova and Evert credit each other for their successful careers. Longtime friends, each sees the other as the principal motivation for their success. Their rivalry drew popular attention to women's tennis, and it elevated the sport for two decades. In *Unmatched,* both women praise the rivalry as the reason for staying in competition for as long as they did and for accomplishing their career successes. They built a lasting friendship through their competitiveness.

On their quest for Greatness, Evert and Navratilova propelled each other to sports history. Navratilova encapsulated their rivalry and camaraderie by saying, "There never will be another Chris and Martina show. There never was another like it, and there never will be another."

In 1955, Igor Larionov jump-started his NHL career in Detroit, where Coach Scotty Bowman acted on the idea to team up the Russian legend with his fellow countrymen Sergei Fedorov and Slava Kozlov on offense, and Slava Fetisov and Vladimir Konstantinov on defense. "Four Russian guys alongside you, of course to make your job easier," Larionov said.

Normally, offensive players have two linemates and two defensemen skate in pairs, but although it was commonplace for the players' Red Army team back in their homeland, Bowman was the first NHL coach to use a five-man unit. The success of the "Russian Five" illustrates how common background, values, and training can help the greater goal.

"Finally, I had a chance to play the style I was taught to play in Russia, with a team that could win the Stanley Cup, a team that played puck possession, with skating and creativity. Those were unbelievable years," Larionov remarked before his induction into the Hockey Hall of Fame. "I was proud to be a part of that team."

All kids who lace up their skates dream of eclipsing Wayne Gretzky's unbelievable 215 points in one season. They may not ever get close to it, but it's the challenge looming out there that makes them try. Athletes who set their sights on records to beat understand the value of association.

Not too long ago, I spent some time catching up with the Manning family: Archie and Olivia, and their sons Cooper, Peyton, and Eli. The result of this fascinating visit was another pretty impressive lesson in the power of association.

Archie had no intention of starting a football dynasty. A highly successful quarterback at Ole Miss, he went on to play in the NFL for thirteen years, including ten seasons with the New Orleans Saints. As a result, his three sons grew up around football and developed an innate love for the gridiron, even though their dad never pushed them in that direction. The competitive bug must have been in their blood, though, because no matter what activity the family shared, it always became a fight to the finish.

Even shooting hoops in the driveway was an epic battle. "As their father, you don't want to let them just win, but you do want them to feel like they can compete," Archie laughed. "When the games got close, we'd have trouble finishing a game to 20 because by the time you get to 18, no one's going to get a shot off. They'd hack at you to keep you from scoring. A competitive nature is something they all had."

That nature served all three boys well.

Cooper, the oldest Manning son, earned all-state honors as a wide receiver in high school. His senior year he played on the same team as his younger brother, Peyton. The two were a force to be reckoned with on the field; Peyton always looked first to his brother, and Cooper almost always managed to get open to catch the pass. Their years of competing against each other had helped them hone their instincts for how to read each other, as well.

Cooper was offered a football scholarship at Ole Miss, but during his freshman year it was discovered that he suffered from a narrowing of the spine, an extremely serious medical condition that would end his athletic career. Instead of mourning his own unfortunate situation, however, Cooper channeled his competitive spirit into his brothers' efforts, cheering them on and pushing them to keep working.

Peyton went on to play quarterback for the University of Tennessee, where he became the school's all-time leading passer and set the Southeastern Conference's record for career wins, was named First Team All-American and received numerous other prestigious awards. He was selected as the No. 1 overall pick in the 1998 draft by the Indianapolis Colts, whom he led to two Super Bowls, besides setting numerous records and being voted NFL MVP an unprecedented five times. After missing the 2011 season with the Colts due to a neck injury, Peyton Manning moved on to play for the Denver Broncos, leading them to a Super Bowl appearance.

Eli, younger than Peyton by five years, also had an outstanding college career. As quarterback for Ole Miss, he set or tied forty-five separate records, earned numerous national awards, and was the No. 1 overall draft pick when he went pro; he currently leads the New York Giants. In Super Bowl XLII and Super Bowl XLVI, Eli led his team to beat the New England Patriots in both games, and he earned MVP honors for both performances.

Even as professionals, the Manning men check on the others' teams after every Sunday game and call each other that evening to discuss how they played that day. Cooper, now a partner at an energy investment firm, calls both his brothers during the week and joins them and their father at the Manning Passing Academy, a summer football camp for high school players held each year at Nicholls State College in Thibodaux, Louisiana.

The special bond that these men share comes from more than just being a family. By challenging one another and competing all their lives, they have helped to propel each other forward toward not only outstanding careers with their respective teams or companies but also toward Greatness in terms of their personal lives. Following the example set by their parents, the second generation of Mannings in the spotlight has a reputation for being intelligent, personable, down-to-earth, and charitable to the community. In a lot of ways, no one wanted to be the first Manning labeled as a troublemaker—their competitive spirit helped keep them on the straight and narrow, both on the field and off.

And for the Truly Great in Business

The value of association is a huge motivator in the business world, as well. Consider just a few examples of how major corporations benefited from understanding the powerful motivation competition can provide.

Sam Walton, founder of Wal-Mart, provides an example of how sometimes the best lessons are learned from those who have more experience and are in direct competition with you. Walton opened his first retail store across the street from a competing store managed by an excellent manager named John Dunham.

Walton had sales experience, but the five-and-dime store was the first operation he'd owned. He delved into studying retail magazines to educate himself on how to make it better, but he also took notes on his competitor's example, visiting the store to get ideas on displays as well as to check out Dunham's prices. "I didn't just learn from reading every retail publication I could get my hands on, I probably learned the most from studying what John Dunham was doing across the street," he said in his memoirs, *Sam Walton: Made in America.*

Similar self-imposed competition can be seen in the way Avis does business. Since 1962 the company's mantra has been "We try harder," and the rental car company tripled its volume in the first year after the slogan was adopted. It wasn't a gimmick, the company says, but a philosophy each of its employees embraces to this day. The company sets its sights on the leader—whoever it happens to be in the industry each year—and, even if they can't beat them in market share, Avis aims to work harder for their customers than does their biggest competitor. "The message was about the extra effort and service...but I think 'We try harder' has always been about service," Maria Miller, Avis's senior vice president of marketing told *Newsday* in 2000.

Ray Kroc sold a billion hamburgers between 1955 and 1963, and there's no question that his McDonald's restaurants are the undisputed champions of fast food. Still, the man who applied the assembly line concept to burger making looked to his challengers as competition in order to jump-start his own business. "If any of my competitors were drowning, I'd stick a hose in their mouth," he's credited as saying with a wink.

Kroc's methods were tough because his goal was to outwork whatever competition stood in front of him. He always used the momentum of outselling someone as an opportunity to improve on the service of his own product. McDonald's thirty-one thousand restaurants and worldwide brand recognition attest to his business savvy.

By keeping a close eye on market-share rivals, companies can often find ways to strengthen their weaknesses or hone their unique edge.

The GREATNESS Challenge

Runners call them "pacers"—those people who are just a little bit faster and, consequently, make you run a stride or two more quickly in pursuing them. And runners will swear by them. Having someone just ahead whose back is taunting you, or just behind whose footsteps are always drawing closer, can be the biggest motivator in moving a runner forward. As former NFL coach Jan McKeithen famously said, "If you cannot win, make the one ahead of you break the record."

Do you know anyone in your personal or professional life who is a kind of pacer for you? Is there someone who challenges you to reach for the next level either through example, rivalry, or encouragement? It's important to remember that those we associate with can offer us any or all three of these ways of pushing us forward. The question is: will you allow them to do so?

That's the secret: you have to recognize those individuals who have the potential to motivate you, and you have to be willing to let yourself be stretched. It's all up to you as to if and how you let your associations influence you.

It's tough sometimes when our pride wants to tell us that we're already the best, or when we feel we're already working at maximum capacity. Bill Walton was certainly the best, but he still had a chance to be better. Nadia Comăneci was one of the top three or four gymnasts in the world, but she still saw a place she could improve and she used her competition as motivation to do just that.

Who are the power players at your company? What is it about their presentations, reports, or meetings that is so effective? Keep in mind, though, that the people who are the best often aren't the ones who are out front.

Determine one or two areas in which you feel you would like to see some improvement and then find the one person in your office who emulates those characteristics. If you feel comfortable doing so, ask that person what it is that makes them so good. People are naturally sympathetic to someone who expresses a genuine interest in their lives and abilities, so you're sure to get some good tips.

Don't be content with being good—always be driven to be better. You probably can't be the office champ in every area of your professional life, but figure out what your best asset is and focus on developing that. Don't be afraid to challenge yourself; muscles can grow only if they are worked beyond their current capacity.

Surround yourself with people who will pace you. Look for the ones who set an example, like Wilma Rudolph's sister. Look for the ones whose competition will challenge you to do better as you both work for a common goal, like Mantle and Maris. And look for those who will motivate and encourage you to develop your potential, like the Williams sisters.

We are who we associate with. The five people you spend the most time with in life are going to decide just how successful you are. Are these five people you are closest to taking you to Greatness? The right ones can make all the difference.

On your own team, is there someone who brings out your competitive nature? Too often in the professional world, the notion of "competition" is a rival company or product; but competition can be a positive force, as well.

We all owe it to ourselves to find those people whose presence inspires us to do more with our talents and opportunities. By developing and maintaining meaningful relationships with people who continually push us to grow, we learn not only how to develop ourselves but how to celebrate the accomplishments of others. Much like how the Mannings both challenge and cheer one another, so too do Great individuals.

Who drives you to try harder, study more, prepare better, or reach higher? Whose friendship motivates you to work just a little bit more? If you can point to someone on your team who fills that role, reflect on the recent way his or her presence has helped you raise your own game a notch or two and consider how to use that in the future. If you don't have such a person in your life, find someone whom you can respect and engage with as you work together to improve your performance and stretch your professional muscles.

Invite a friendly rival to lunch or to share a cup of coffee, and talk frankly about what each of you has done to challenge the other. It might surprise you to learn how you have motivated someone else to grow, and your honesty might just lead to even greater growth as you discuss how your relationship can help to move your team ahead.

It is no coincidence that success often runs in families or among tight groups of friends. Greatness surrounds itself with Greatness. It is your responsibility to find—and keep—those people who challenge you to always do better, even as you return the favor to them. Amiable rivalry teaches us to work harder, applaud others, and always keep looking ahead.

We are all blessed to have the opportunity to interact, on occasion, with Great winners. It is our job to rub elbows with those who aspire to Greatness and want to get better; we should approach them and try to understand what makes them successful and what keeps them going. And if you just so happen to be one of those star players in your field, it is your job to accept the invitation to teach us, to help us learn, and to challenge us to improve our lives daily, just as Bill Walton taught Swen Nater. It's not how good you are coming in that matters, it's what you learn from those around you that help you to grow.

Remember the value of association, and make sure that you're making the most of what others around you can offer in terms of motivation and challenge.

Remember to always reach for Greatness.

CHAPTER

3

Believe

The truly Great have faith in a higher power.

Biting at the heels of a picture-perfect season with a 13–0 record in 2005, the NFL's Indianapolis Colts suffered their first defeat at the hands of the San Diego Chargers. Weeks later and still considered the best team in the league, the Colts suffered another blow as they were eliminated in the first round of the playoffs by the eventual champions, the Pittsburgh Steelers.

That was the Colts' biggest loss of the season, but wasn't the biggest loss for the Colts' head coach, Tony Dungy.

On December 22, 2005, Dungy's eighteen-year-old son, James, who suffered from depression, took his own life.

The death of James Dungy, who was close to the players and coaches who worked with his father, was a loss felt deeply by all who knew him. But it was, of course, an especially immense loss for Coach Dungy, who called upon his faith for the strength to carry on. Facing his grief, Dungy's belief was the only thing he had, but it was everything to him.

Like so many Great winners, Tony Dungy's faith was central to his success.

Dungy said it was his faith that allowed him to take something positive out of the tragedy his family faced and to help others in the process. In an emotional eulogy at his son's funeral service, Dungy encouraged other parents to hug their children. He implored parents to let their children know how special they are and to not take for granted their time with them.

A coach who always put faith and family before football, Dungy was known for kicking his assistants out of the office after hours so that they could spend time with their families. For years he had been a father to his own children and a father figure to his players, and he volunteered to provide fatherly advice for everyone from foster children to inmates.

In 2007, after four consecutive playoff appearances and four straight seasons with twelve or more wins, Dungy and the Colts overcame another season of adversity and criticism on their way to a 29–17 victory over the Chicago Bears in Super Bowl XLI.

It was a championship the team said they won for their leader, Tony Dungy—the man who kept his faith through tragedy and triumph, and who still held to his beliefs despite all he had been through. "If you don't believe in God you will find yourself spending hours trying to understand things that can't be understood," Dungy explained. "My faith actually frees me to focus attention on other areas of my life and career."

Dungy never cared about fame or fortune, but he knew he could use his position and his success to influence people in a positive way. Dungy always put his values before football, and he encouraged his players to do the same. He always led by the example of his character, and he proved that he could motivate his team to be the best without sacrificing his morals or the relationships he had built with his players.

Dungy quietly earned respect through his leadership, his work ethic, the passion through which he coached and—most importantly—his faith. It's what sets him apart from those who are merely confident or driven or talented. Dungy recognized that after the awards and accolades, the championships and cheering, there was something more, something both higher and deeper—and he built his life around that unshakable belief.

As Dungy showed throughout his career, the truly Great have faith in a higher power. A little faith can go a long way in your life as well—with it you may accomplish things you never before believed you could.

Do not let challenges or failures keep you from accomplishing your ultimate goals. Create a formula for success, adjust it as necessary, but stick with it. Believe that there is a reason for all that happens, and believe that you have a place in that plan.

Living your faith will not only give you strength, but it can lift up others. You may not impact as many lives as Tony Dungy, but having faith can help you make the best of difficult situations and inspire those around you in the process.

More from the Truly Great

Belief has had an essential part in the careers of many Great ones, such as Sandy Koufax. Koufax, a remarkable player by all accounts, spent his entire career with the Los Angeles Dodgers, where he was named the National League's MVP in 1963, and won the Cy Young Award—by unanimous vote—in 1963, 1965, and 1966. Those same three years, he not only won the pitcher's Triple Crown but also led all of baseball in wins, strikeouts, and earned run averages. He pitched the first professional no-hitter thrown by a left-hander since 1880, and he became the youngest player ever voted into the Hall of Fame.

Despite the amazing statistics he recorded during his career, one of the things for which he is most remembered is the day he chose *not* to take the mound. Game One of the 1965 World Series fell on Yom Kippur, the most important of the High Holy Days on the Jewish calendar, and Koufax's Dodgers were scheduled to play the Minnesota Twins.

Koufax was slated to pitch that day but informed his coaches that he would not be able to play. To him, it was far more important to honor his faith than to play a game of baseball and so, instead of taking the field, he fasted and prayed and went to shul. His team suffered a loss with the Dodgers No. 2 pitcher, Don Drysdale, but Koufax knew he had made the right choice.

He went on to pitch Games Two and Five before clinching the title in Game Seven with a performance that many enthusiasts consider one of the best-pitched games ever in a World Series. Not only did he win his second World Series MVP award that year, but he was also named the *Sports Illustrated* Sportsman of the Year for 1965.

Koufax was true to his faith beyond all else, and it was this devotion that earned him respect that can't be measured with awards. He became a hero to a generation of children who saw a man quietly but firmly make a difficult choice that honored his heritage and his beliefs—and still managed to lead his team to victory.

In short, Sandy Koufax proved that it really is possible to have it all when he stood up for his faith.

Dave Dravecky, another left-handed pitcher, had a promising career ahead of him. In 1983, just his second season in the majors, he represented the San Diego Padres in the All Star Game, and the following year he helped the Padres win their first pennant. In 1987 he went to the Giants and pitched a shutout against the St. Louis Cardinals in that season's pennant series. Everything seemed to indicate that the young player had start potential—until a tumor was discovered in his pitching arm.

Dravecky calmly accepted the news and relied on his belief that this was all part of a greater plan. During the 1988 season, Dravecky underwent surgery and rehabilitation for his cancer, and ten months later he returned to the majors to pitch eight innings and lead the Giants to a victory. It seemed too perfect a story to be real. Then, during his very next game only five days later, bones snapped in his arm, benching him for the rest of the season.

When the Giants won the National League pennant in October 1989, Dravecky was right there with his teammates. His amazing work ethic and inspiring attitude had been a rallying point for the team because despite the terrible luck that seemed to plague him, Dravecky had never lost his positive outlook and drive to win. Tragically, during the postgame celebration, his arm broke a second time, and in the X-rays doctors discovered another tumor. His cancer had returned, and this time it was aggressive.

Two more surgeries followed before the doctors determined that they would have to amputate the arm and shoulder in order to save Dravecky's life. Once again, Dravecky refused to give in to depression or anger.

Instead, he used his experiences to author inspirational books for both adults and children. He and his wife, Jan, also established a ministry for cancer patients, amputees, and their families. Called Outreach of Hope, his message is simple: Don't allow yourself to lose sight of what ultimately matters. Have hope in your faith to carry you through whatever trials you are facing, because belief is the only thing strong enough to get any of us through life.

Kareem Abdul-Jabbar converted to Islam as a student-athlete at UCLA, and he has found his faith to be a source of strength both in his basketball career and in his life after retiring from the pros.

"My decision to convert had to do with me having a moral anchor," he wrote in John Wooden's book, *A Game Plan for Life.* "I realized that was the faith I wanted to embrace."

Formerly known as Lewis Alcindor, Abdul-Jabbar has been a peaceful proponent for the Muslim faith. Diagnosed with leukemia in 2009, Abdul-Jabbar told me that he found the peace to accept his trial and the strength to fight it because his deeply held beliefs gave him a sense of perspective.

Now, with a clean bill of health and a renewed sense of purpose, he is working to share the lessons he learned by bringing hope and encouragement to other cancer patients and their families.

Kurt Warner is one of the most successful quarterbacks ever to have played in the NFL, being named the league's MVP in both 1999 and 2001, but his primary goal is to live as a person of faith.

His story is the stuff of fairy tales. Until his senior year at the University of Northern Iowa, he was ranked only third on the depth chart and was not drafted by a professional team out of college. After a tryout for the Green Bay Packers failed (he was competing against no less a formidable talent than Brett Favre, among others) he returned home to Iowa and worked in a grocery store, stocking shelves, before playing Arena Football for three seasons.

But he didn't give up on his goal of playing for the NFL, and his incredible on-field accuracy soon caught the attention of several coaches. More important, however, as Warner will tell you, he placed his primary focus not on his career but on God.

As Kurt and his wife, Brenda, challenged and encouraged one another about their religious beliefs, they began to grow in the understanding and practice of their faith. It was in this process that Warner matured both as a person and as a player, a transformation that finally helped get him noticed by the St. Louis Rams, who signed him in 1998. The following year, he led the team to a victory in Super Bowl XXXVI and was named the MVP of the game.

He went on to set franchise records with several of his subsequent teams, and he ranked among the NFL's top quarterbacks in a number of areas before his retirement in 2010. But for Warner, he's about much more than his statistics.

In each interview, Warner carries his Bible with him and tries to make a mention of his faith. Despite the honors and accolades piled on him, he remains a humble person who acknowledges everything as a blessing that he is proud to receive, not a celebration of himself.

He and his family work with a number of charities to enrich the lives of others by sharing the blessings in their own lives. Warner seeks to be a role model not only for his children but for his fans as well.

Former heavyweight champion George Foreman believes people who hold fast to their beliefs will always be in demand. Prior to his first retirement, he was all business in the ring and kept a cold personality outside it. During that retirement, he became a preacher and loosened up his public image, becoming a likable and funny character, and letting his personality show through.

As a result, Foreman began a sales and endorsement career, starting with Meineke Car Care Centers and continuing with the George Foreman Lean, Mean, Fat-Reducing Grilling Machine. In recent years, he has promoted health shakes, shoes for diabetics, and even a reality television show following his family called *Family Foreman.* Foreman staged a comeback in order to fund the youth of the George Foreman Community Center in Houston, and he remains conscious of the image he projects.

As a Christian, he won't compromise his religious principles. At one point, he was approached to create a line of restaurants, but when he discovered the business plan included sales of alcohol he turned it down. Many successful athletes own eating establishments, and no one would have thought twice about Foreman opening a restaurant and bar chain. But the deal would have included something that clashed with his personal religious values, so he said no.

"You've got to believe in something. And you've got a line that you can't cross," he said. "But at least have something you believe in and you cannot be talked out of by dollars and cents. And that's what I try to pass on."

The numbers that detail former Florida State football coach Bobby Bowden's career are mind-boggling: 389 wins, twelve ACC titles, two national championships, two Heisman Trophy winners, and fifteen straight seasons where his team finished ranked in the Top Five.

But for Bowden, football was just his job—it was never the most important part of his life. He was asked recently how he felt about his retirement, and his response was simple: "I'm not paying a lot of attention to it. I have never tried to make football my God. I think coaches that make it their God have a struggle. For me, I'm just starting a new life."

It is this steadfast faith in something higher that carried Bowden through the peaks and valleys of his career and his personal life. His faith is so important to him that he wanted each player who came to FSU to have some exposure to what it means. As a result, he spent thirty-four years asking permission from the parents of every new Seminole recruit to include that player in the two Sunday trips the team took each season. One was to a church whose membership was predominantly black, and the other was to a church that was predominantly white.

Bowden told me that in all the years he coached, only two parents asked that their sons not be part of those trips. "I understood why in each case," he said, "and I think they understood what I try to do with these trips. I just want to make sure our young men knew where they could go when things got tough...and they will get tough."

When he lost a grandson and former son-in-law in an automobile accident during Hurricane Frances in 2004, Bowden insisted it was no time to question God but instead to deepen his trust that there is an ultimate plan to all things.

Bowden told the Associated Press he sought to put his faith first: "I've tried. I don't want people to think that 'Bobby really thinks he's a good boy.' No, I don't think I'm good. I try to be good. But the thing about it is that God has taught me that if you try to be obedient and try to follow the rules and try to do what He asks you to, you still can be a success."

He urged his players towards sportsmanship, prayer, and charitable involvement—and he practiced these things himself. In fact, in 2004, the Fellowship of Christian Athletes established the Bobby Bowden Award to honor one college athlete who stands out as a prime example of someone living his or her faith and principles.

Bowden's coaching career may have ended, but his faith is—and has always been—in something much bigger and more lasting than college football.

And for the Truly Great in Business

What place does belief have in the highly competitive and sometimes even cutthroat world of business? As it turns out, belief is central to the corporate structure of many successful corporations and their leaders.

What would allow a college dropout, who was forcefully removed from the company he cofounded, and who later survived both a rare form of cancer and a subsequent kidney transplant, to become the leader of one of the most innovative and respected consumer electronics companies in the world?

In the case of Apple CEO Steve Jobs, it was his belief, as his spiritual journeys guided him through failure and illness and restored a "beginner's mind" view of technological development.

What would drive a humble boy born in a small New Mexico mining town to achieve great success in the hotel industry despite the obligations of running his family's store following his father's unexpected death, near bankruptcy during the Great Depression, and numerous early career failures?

In the case of Conrad Hilton, it was his faith, as he readily admits that his belief in a higher power was his foremost guide of professional decision making.

Brad Anderson, former CEO and current vice chairman of consumer electronics retailer Best Buy, instilled a faith-driven philosophy of failure and forgiveness that influenced employee decision making across all levels. Anderson understands that decisions often come with risk, and that the most innovative ideas also have the greatest potential for failure. Employees are told that being afraid to fail is failure in itself, and that forgiveness is just around the corner.

Also, Anderson's core company values reflect an emphasis on spiritual principles such as honesty, integrity, embracing challenges, allowing people to make a difference, and having fun. These ideals were put in place to help employees see work as not just a job, but also as a higher calling.

In one of the most well known testaments of personal faith, Chick-fil-A founder S. Truett Cathy adopted a "Closed on Sunday" policy, which has remained steadfastly in place for more than five decades. Despite the estimated $500,000,000 in lost annual income, the practice has allowed employees to focus on things other than the business, including spiritual pursuits. The rule, which is based on the fourth of the Ten Commandments ("Honor the Sabbath and keep it holy"), allowed Cathy to teach Sunday school classes to thirteen-year-old boys—a job that he embraced for over fifty years.

Larry Julian writes in his book *God Is My CEO,* "What impresses me most about Truett Cathy is that he has had the courage to follow his beliefs even though he's pressured by the world to do otherwise. Even though the business world said it didn't make sense to take Sundays off, Truett insisted on a day of rest."

Hobby Lobby founder and CEO Steve Green takes a similar view as Cathy. Not only are all Hobby Lobby stores closed on Sundays in order to give their employees an opportunity to spend time with their families and worship together, but Green also puts the Bible first in his company's statement of purpose: "Honoring the Lord in all we do by operating the company in a manner consistent with Biblical principles." Similarly, S. Truett Cathy said his company's corporate mission was to "glorify God."

In another impressive demonstration of faith, Domino's founder and CEO Tom Monaghan sold all of his holdings (including the Detroit Tigers baseball club), often at a sizable loss, to develop as many faith-based students, teachers, and religious leaders as possible. With $250 million of his own money and partnerships with local organizations, Florida-based Ave Maria University opened in 2008 with an initial enrolling class of almost six hundred students.

The GREATNESS Challenge

Belief can be the thing that gets us through difficult times. It can be the source of strength we didn't know we had. It can be the one fixed point in our life when everything else seems chaotic. It can be the center of our life when we stop to take stock of what we really hold true.

Allow yourself to realize your beliefs and not to feel hindered by them. Evaluate your life honestly and consider how you live your faith in terms of your decision making and your priorities. What do you believe in? How do you take a stand? Where do you turn in times of trial?

The Great ones understand that career accomplishments are not the ultimate measure of a person. Instead, they know that a life lived with belief is a life of purpose and direction.

The truly Great strive to keep their faith at the center of all they do. Faith in God—by whatever name you use—determines how we treat people, how we react to circumstances, and how we view the opportunities that we've been given.

What do you believe? What tenets dictate your decisions, your attitude, and your outlook on life? What standards do you hold for yourself, and how do you live them out? Take ten minutes today to write down answers to these questions. The more clearly you understand your beliefs, the more active a part they can play in your life.

Reconnect with your Higher Power. Carve out the time daily to re-center yourself. Prayer or meditation can help reduce stress, have positive health benefits, improve concentration, and give peace of mind. If you do not already have a regular quiet time, find a way to incorporate your beliefs into your everyday routine. Whether it is a prayer to start your day during your morning commute or a few minutes of mediation before bed, see if you can carve out a short block at the same time each day to reflect on your beliefs and re-center yourself.

Some people find times of trouble as a time of spiritual growth; others find difficult periods to be times when their faith slips away from them. Think about the most difficult periods in your life—did you find those were times when you felt closer to your beliefs because they were all you had to trust in, or further from them because you felt alone? If you can identify the pattern by which you seem to react, you may be better prepared for your next spiritual challenge.

Consider several ways that you can make a stand for your faith that will encourage others. Allow your beliefs to be a way of reaching out as well as strengthening your own convictions. Even if it's something as simple as turning off a violent television show or refusing to gossip about a coworker, the example you set as you live your beliefs can be an inspiration to the people around you.

Look at what Mahatma Gandhi accomplished in India simply by refusing to compromise his nonviolent beliefs. By staying true to the values of his Hindu faith, he helped to bring about lasting change and helped to alter the course of history for his nation. Faith has power.

Greatness believes we are accountable to a Higher Power, which the truly Great look to for guidance and from which they find strength. Talents and opportunities are blessings from this Higher Power, and faith is essential in being a well-rounded person. In short, the truly Great believe in something Greater.

CHAPTER

4

Contagious Enthusiasm

They are positive thinkers, they are enthusiastic, and that enthusiasm rubs off!

"Run! Run!" Team USA first base coach Margie Wright screamed at Laura Berg.

It was the 1996 Olympics in Atlanta, and Team USA had just jumped out to a 2–0 lead in the gold medal softball game against China. Well, they *would*—just as soon as Laura, who was jumping up and down deliriously at first base, remembered to run.

Shortstop Dot Richardson had just blasted a two-run homer over the right-field fence. Laura, the USA base runner on first, was so excited that she had forgotten to advance to the next base, and was instead waiting ecstatically to congratulate her teammate.

But you could hardly blame her. That was the kind of impact Dot

Richardson had on her teammates. She encouraged and inspired them. She mesmerized and energized their spirit of competition and teamwork. In fact, that's the kind of impact Richardson has on a lot of people.

"We must always have confidence in our teammates," Richardson said. "It is believing that we are winners that produces the ability to win." Everyone believed in her—and she returned the favor.

People like Richardson are few and far between. She doesn't just *enjoy* what she does; enjoy isn't a strong enough word, because Richardson is spilling over with excitement. Few athletes can say they love their sport as much as she genuinely loves softball, and it showed. With every ball she gloved, every throw she made, and every swing she took, her passion was joyfully obvious.

Richardson and her teammates won the gold medal in 1996, the first year softball was officially recognized as an Olympic sport. In the bottom of the third inning, Richardson hit what proved to be the game-winning home run—something she had always dreamed of doing as a kid.

As positive a thinker as they come, Richardson never failed at anything she ever tried. Two Olympic gold medals to go along with numerous national champion and All-American honors weren't the culmination of her career. Richardson used the precision, discipline, and focus that softball taught her to earn a medical degree. Because her enthusiasm for the sport was so strong, she wanted to help others keep playing, too—so she became a successful orthopedic surgeon.

Juggling softball and medicine at the highest levels was tremendously difficult, often forcing Richardson to fly from her residency program at USC to softball games on the opposite coast. But, always bursting with enthusiasm, she rarely complained. After all, she was getting to do the two things she loved most in life. How much better could it get?

After the crowds were gone and the celebration of winning the Olympic gold in Atlanta was drawing to a close, someone in the stands shouted, "Olympic gold, baby!" Those were the words she had used often in softball clinics to let athletes know they were doing things the right way.

The yell came from four girls who couldn't have been more than fourteen years old. Richardson raised the gold medal to them and shouted back, laughing: "Olympic gold, baby! Now, go get yours!" Even in her greatest moment yet, she was passing her excitement on to others.

Richardson was the glue that held Team USA together in the 1996 Olympics. Always positive, always enthusiastic, she knew how to inspire everyone around her just by being excited.

Enthusiasm can carry one a long way toward Greatness, and it's no secret that success seems to follow Richardson wherever she goes. She is a very talented and intelligent woman—you would have to be to accomplish all that she has on and off the field—but it's her attitude and enthusiasm that have made her into the incredible success story she is today.

Richardson made an incredible impact on her team, and not just with her glove and her bat. Her emotions and her love for the game helped motivate her entire team to play harder and cheer louder. Everyone else was fueled by the energy she created.

More from the Truly Great

It's amazing what a little bit of positive thinking can start. Consider Nancy Lopez, who was known for always wearing her emotions on her sleeve. One of the most successful golfers of the twentieth century, she helped to carry the Ladies Professional Golfers Association out of obscurity and into the national spotlight—and she truly felt every win and every loss.

Her infectious smile and good sportsmanship made her eminently likable, an important trait in a sport which, at that time, was still building a fan base and competing for media attention. Sure enough, Lopez's positive attitude and heartfelt excitement were hard to ignore, and the cameras soon turned to this future Hall of Famer.

Lopez always believed in staying focused on the positive in everything she did. When she retired from the LPGA tour, rather than dwelling on what she was leaving behind, Lopez chose instead to highlight her new pursuits of broadcasting, and designing courses and equipment. "I am at the beginning of a brand new chapter in my golf career," she said with her usual enthusiasm.

Her kind smile and real emotion helped build both a career and an entire sport. What can enthusiasm do for your goals?

To this day, the New York Mets' 1973 season is still an unmatched testament to the power of believing. Their season started with great potential, but as it progressed, the injury list grew longer and their confidence took a nosedive. Even their haplessly happy pitcher, Tug McGraw, was in a slump.

At the beginning of July, their record was an embarrassing 33–42—and the Mets had taken ownership of their division's basement. In search of some confidence, McGraw found himself having lunch with friend Joe Badamo. "You've got to believe in yourself," Joe kept saying, trying to boost the spirits of the struggling young pitcher.

And from that point on, when McGraw was asked about the Mets, his only response was, "Ya gotta believe!"

During a team meeting, with barely a month left in the season, Mets Chairman M. Donald Grant tried to offer the players a little motivation. The best he could do was tell the players that no one at the team's front office considered them a last-place club. Halfway through his rambling effort at encouragement, McGraw stood up. "Ya gotta believe!" he screamed, thrusting his fist in the air. "Ya gotta believe!" He looked every one of his teammates in the eyes as he repeated the phrase over and over again.

One by one, they heard him loud and clear. Between laughing at McGraw's performance, teammates began chanting those three words. Reporters heard about the incident and McGraw didn't mind encouraging others to join in the positive mind-set.

After four months of disappointing themselves and their fans, this crazy and illogical excitement found its way into the Mets dugout. With only twenty games remaining, they had to be optimistic and continue to believe that they could reverse their streak. To even get close to winning their division, the Mets had to win almost every game for the rest of the season.

They won one day, and then the next. Before they knew it, they were five games from first place. The team was on fire. Old injuries seemed to heal, and the fans packed the stadium yelling the new rallying cry.

Then, on October 10, 1973, the Mets won the National League Championship with a 7–2 victory over the Cincinnati Reds in the fifth game of the series. They ended the season with an 82–79 record and a .509 winning percentage. It remains the lowest winning percentage of any division winner or pennant winner in baseball history.

The Mets went on to lose in Game Seven of the World Series to the Oakland A's, but in New York, the rally cry "Ya gotta believe!" can still be heard today.

No other team has ever come back from that kind of deficit so late in the season. The season was not just about good baseball, but about the cycle of believing in oneself to deliver a positive outcome. In the end, McGraw's contagious enthusiasm was what the Mets needed to succeed.

Prior to the 1978 Orange Bowl meeting between Arkansas and Oklahoma, the media all but wrote off Lou Holtz's Razorbacks. After all, the Oklahoma Sooners had lost just one game all season to powerhouse Nebraska, and Arkansas had a much smaller team. In addition, Holtz had benched his top three offensive players for disciplinary reasons and had an All-American guard out with an injury.

Two days before the game, writes sports psychologist Gary Mack in *Mind Gym,* Lou Holtz gathered his Razorbacks and asked them why they thought they would win. In turn, each player offered a reason the team would be successful and as they did, the attitude in the room changed. Each player enthusiastically voicing a positive quality about his team began to pump it up as a unit, and Arkansas pummeled Oklahoma 31–6 in the matchup.

The pep talk didn't change the team's talent. It didn't make the All-American player well enough to jump into the lineup and save the day. It didn't convince Holtz to lift the suspensions of his three starters. But having the entire team contribute—out loud—positive examples of how they could overpower a heavy favorite inspired them to come together. They lifted their spirits and spread the enthusiasm, making themselves confident they could win.

Enthusiasm doesn't just have a place for teams in the national spotlight—but it can sometimes bring attention to Great winners who embody the trait!

No one at Greece Athena High School in Rochester, New York, was prepared for the media attention that resulted when Coach Jim Johnson put team manager Jason McElwain on the court for the final minutes of a game in 2006. The crowd went wild; his teammates started passing him the ball; and then J-Mac, as he is affectionately known, started to do the unbelievable: basket after basket, he scored 20 points in a matter of four minutes, hitting crazy shots from all over the court!

But what made this moment so special—besides the additional points that it added to the final score—is that J-Mac is autistic and had worked enthusiastically as the team's manager for the past two years just so he could be close to the sport he loved. He had been told his disability meant he was not likely to ever be on the team's roster and, in fact, that night was the first time he had ever slipped on a jersey. Regardless, his love for the game was undeniable, and his team spirit was infectious. "Usually you look for a player to be your team's heart and soul," Coach Johnson told me. "But on that team that year, J-Mac was the point of enthusiasm even though he wasn't playing. Every day he was at practice early with that big smile on his face. His attitude impacted us all."

J-Mac lived and breathed his team's success; his unbridled enthusiasm for Greece Athena's basketball team spread throughout the community—and it was returned to him in his final game before graduation. Hoping that Coach Johnson would substitute J-Mac into the game in the final minutes, fans showed up with signs and banners specifically designed to cheer on their hardworking manager. When Johnson signaled for J-Mac to hit the court, the crowd went wild, many of them holding up masks of his face. J-Mac's teammates went wild, too. Every time down the court, they passed him the ball and encouraged him to shoot. When the game ended, the crowd rushed the court and the boy who dreamed of playing was carried off on the shoulders of his teammates.

"I didn't tell them to do that," Coach Johnson explained. "I just told them I was going to try to put him in; they started passing J-Mac the ball on their own accord and they didn't want anyone but him to shoot."

But the story didn't end with Greece Athena's big win that night.

After he graduated, J-Mac came back to the high school to serve as an assistant coach with the Junior Varsity team. In 2011, Coach Johnson asked him to be an assistant with the Varsity. Together, Coaches Johnson and McElwain led the team to a 12–6 record all the way to the sectional finals.

"He's fully invested in basketball—there's no question," Johnson laughed, telling me how J-Mac's enthusiasm has only grown since graduating. "His goal is to become a college coach, and he has become a student of the game." He attends the school's Varsity, JV, and freshmen games, as well as several basketball camps in the summer. He exchanges text messages with a number of big-time college coaches that he has met since his "four minutes of fame" became national news. One of those is Steve Donahue, the former basketball coach at Cornell who is now the head coach at Boston College. Donahue, who has an autistic son, seems to relish J-Mac's enthusiasm for the game and tireless pursuit of Greatness.

In 2013, Coach Johnson and Greece Athena High School retired JMac's jersey, only the second time to do so in the school's history. J-Mac continues to assist with his old high school team. J-Mac has also become a long-distance runner, completing the Boston Marathon in 2014. Coach Johnson believes that J-Mac's can-do attitude and approach to the game will take him far: "He is the essence of what a team is all about."

Gabe is one of twelve children in the Marsh family, ten of whom are adopted. Ann, their mother, has determinedly taught every single child how to swim and encouraged each child to join the swim team in their town of Guntersville, Alabama. Gabe is unique, however, in that while he enjoys swimming and is every bit as cheerful a teammate as all his brothers and sisters, Gabe was born with only one arm and no legs—and yet, he swims every meet anyway.

Ed and Ann weren't sure at first if Gabe would be able to join their other children in the pool, but the determined little boy was quick to prove their doubts wrong. He made his way through the water to Ann the first time they were at a pool together. From that day on, she concentrated on giving him lessons just as she had the rest of the Marsh children. Before long, Gabe was suited up and on the starting blocks, ready to push himself off into the water at the sound of the starting gun. He loves the competition and he loves the training, working hard at every meet to better his time.

But Gabe's enthusiasm isn't confined to the swimming pool; he keeps up with his siblings running around the family house, playing video games and even climbing up into the barn loft by himself. His love for life is apparent to everyone around him as he relishes being every bit as much a part of his family's activities as any of the other Marshes.

Gabe's is the kind of spirit that makes everyone around him feel a little more encouraged. His determination and positive thinking doesn't just push himself forward toward Greater goals, but it also lifts up his family, teammates, and friends. And that is exactly what Greatness does.

And for the Truly Great in Business

With over seven million print copies sold, and a stay on the New York Times best-seller list of 186 weeks, Norman Vincent Peale's book *The Power of Positive Thinking* is one of the best-selling business books of all time. The book continues to sell by the thousands each year, and it remains a staple for leadership development programs.

The book's contents, which include chapters aptly titled "How to Create Your Own Happiness" and "How to Get People to Like You," are as important today as when the book was first published in 1952. Presidents, CEOs, physicians, scientists, and religious leaders have been influence by Dr. Peale's prescriptions for managing problems associated with everyday life, including self-doubt, stress, and negative thinking. His quote "It's always too early to quit" captures the essence of his approach to positive thinking.

What causes some leaders to give up during difficult times and others to forge ahead without hesitation? Simply put, it's a positive outlook. Leaders who are positive and enthusiastic see adversity as an opportunity to separate themselves from less like-minded decision makers who see challenges as prescriptions for failure. When faced with similar situations, positive CEOs seek opportunities to grow—negative CEOs look for ways to minimize harm.

For example, skeptics laughed at Richard Branson when he used proceeds from his music business to start Virgin Airlines in 1984. After all, running a music business and transporting people all over the globe are two very different things. Branson's schoolboy enthusiasm, which starkly contrasted with the prim, pompous demeanor of many CEOs, infused his organization, replacing "can't do" with "will do" employee attitudes. Today, Virgin Atlantic is England's second largest long-haul carrier.

Similarly, Jack Welch has been considered one of the most enthusiastic CEOs of all time. During his twenty-plus years as

General Electric's CEO, the corporation became the most highly valued company in the world and trained more future executives than any other organization.

Welch's recipe for such monumental success can be found in his doctrine: the four Es of leadership. Specifically, Welch describes "Energy" as the spark that gets people revved up to tackle difficult challenges and to stay focused on the task at hand when others would likely fade. Welch also noted the leadership importance of "Energizers," who through passion, vision, and positive thinking establish the buy-in needed to move ideas forward. "Edge" involves the ability to make difficult decisions that others shy away from, and "Execute" represents the ability to systematically bring tasks to fruition. These last two traits have little influence if divorced from a positive outlook. "Giving people self-confidence is by far the most important thing that I can do," Welch said. "Because then they will act."

Tops on *Fortune*'s list of best companies to work for is business and software company SAS, which provides benefits like inexpensive child care, unlimited sick days, a fitness center, and a summer camp for children. Employees are enthusiastic about the culture, which builds trust, according to cofounder Jim Goodnight. His company has the industry's lowest turnover, due in part to the positive atmosphere, *Fortune* says.

According to *Investor's Business Daily,* United Parcel Service has fostered a strong sense of corporate culture by sharing at each meeting a passage from their original company manual. This kind of unifying action helps to establish and maintain traditions while fostering a sense of unity. Identify the ideals of your organization and find a way to celebrate them with the rest of your team. This can encourage pride and focus while reminding employees of the excitement that should go into every project, client meeting, and customer interaction.

Finally, consider this: what would provoke a CEO to pay employees $2,000 after one week of work to simply walk out and never return? Would it be surprising that only a tiny percentage of employees would take the company up on its offer? That's what Zappo's CEO Tony Hsieh is counting on. This innovative strategy was developed to rid the online shoe, apparel, and housewares company of newly hired employees who don't have the same enthusiasm for the company and its customers as other self-described "Zapponians." Hsieh decided that getting rid of bad eggs early is better than letting them cause a stench as they age. Obviously, this tactic worked—Zappos experienced a 525,500% increase in sales from 2001 to 2007. Radical at its inception, the idea has spread, and other companies are implementing a version of this same strategy, including Amazon, Zappo's parent company since 2009. And in March of 2015, Zappos announced a complete restructuring of its corporate organization. The company made plans to remove managers and supervisors and create self-governing work circles. Tony Hsieh expected push back from the radical idea and offered an exit strategy to his employees. If they were dissatisfied with the change, the employees could follow the company's exit strategy with three month's severance pay.

The GREATNESS Challenge

Too often in the business world, an office is built around the opposite of positive thinking. Often times, negativity and stubbornness can be the most pervasive attitudes, which can limit a staff from reaching their goals or living up to their potential.

No matter the level of enthusiasm, the key is to stay positive. It is important to have people who are excited about where they are and what their contribution is to the goals of the overall organization.

That doesn't mean you have to bubble over with enthusiasm at every moment. Indeed, not everyone is the type of person to show their emotions on a grand scale...and that's okay. It would be uncomfortable if every member of a team was in enthusiasm overdrive all the time. No one wants to be in a room with ten people bouncing off the walls. The important thing is to remain positive rather than stuck in a gloom-and-doom mind-set.

One of the most important things about enthusiasm is that it needs to be genuine. Think about some realistic goals that you truly believe your company can achieve and then talk to others about the steps you think are necessary—and be sure to ask for their suggestions for reaching the same goals. Remember that part of fostering a team spirit is allowing everyone to feel they have a place.

If you don't think you know how to spread enthusiasm, stop by a playground and watch as children who have never met greet one another enthusiastically and welcome their new friends into whatever game is going on. Children are naturally enthusiastic, and adults can learn from them. Watch them live in the moment, finding joy in something as simple as a crayon, a dead bug, or an empty box. It takes little to excite them, and they're quick to share that excitement. You can't help but smile. What simple joys can you find in your everyday work life?

Consider small gestures you can make that will help create a positive environment. Anything from an encouraging word to donuts in the office to refusing to talk negatively about coworkers can help to boost morale and make those around you feel valued, proud, and united.

Be careful, though: just as enthusiasm is contagious, so is negativity. Many teams have a "downer" who refuses to look on the bright side of anything. If there is just one member who doesn't like their job and complains about it, their negative attitude can rub off on everyone else.

Choose to be optimistic. Financial guru Jean Chatzky says we're born with about 50 percent of our optimism; the rest is up to us. She suggests taking a moment to reflect every evening by writing three good things from the day. The events don't have to be big, and simply can be some positive thing you noticed or heard about rather than something that happened directly to you.

At the end of the week, Chatzky says to review the list. "You start to see a pattern of good things in your life," she said in an interview with *SUCCESS* magazine. "And that will make you over time more optimistic."

Is there anyone in your life who could use some encouragement? Make it a goal to send one card or note a week to someone, just to let them know that you are thinking of them.

Legendary University of Oklahoma football coach Bud Wilkinson believed in the power of positive reinforcement, choosing to encourage players to work harder rather than berating them for poor execution. "You can motivate players better with kind words than you can a whip," he insisted. Correction and discipline are necessary from leaders, but they should be done with an eye toward reaching the desired outcome next time and not dwelling on the missed opportunity past.

Think back to the best meeting you've experienced recently. What was it that seemed to energize everyone? What about the least productive meeting—what was the drain? See if you can pinpoint what it is that made the difference and try to embody those traits at your next meeting. Don't focus on dollar signs or ease of completion, since not all projects will generate the same revenue or interest. Think instead about how to create a sense of energy and enthusiasm about the end result or other possibilities the current project may introduce. If you're able to motivate others to consider these same ideas, you'll be creating contagious enthusiasm that helps both to bond a team together and to drive them forward.

Many things about a team aren't contagious, notes John C. Maxwell. Talent, practice, and experience can be cultivated but not caught. Enthusiasm, however, is infectious. "If you want great results, you need good people with great talent and awesome attitudes," the motivational speaker writes in *The 17 Indisputable Laws of Teamwork Workbook.*

Edward B. Butler, a founder of the Butler Brothers department stores, said, "One man has enthusiasm for thirty minutes, another for thirty days, but it is the man who has it for thirty years who makes a success of his life." Is your enthusiasm setting you up for success?

A positive attitude brings strength, energy, and initiative. To have someone in our lives who is filled with enthusiasm is a treat, and we are all the better for it. Why not be the one to embrace the role of encourager on your own team? It can take you a long way toward achieving Greatness.

PILLAR TWO

How They Prepare

CHAPTER 5

Hope for the Best, But . . .

The truly Great prepare for all possibilities before they step on the field.

Third-string fullback Sam "Bam" Cunningham wasn't even expected to play that night, but because he'd prepared, he wound up turning the tide of football in the South.

Back in 1970, Cunningham's University of Southern California football team was the only team in the nation with an all-black backfield, and Cunningham was a part of it—albeit, as a sophomore, quite a ways away from the starting lineup.

But five plays into the game against the all-white University of Alabama, USC head coach John McKay looked over and signaled Cunningham into the game at Legion Field in Birmingham.

Cunningham's performance that night was nothing short of spectacular. He scored two touchdowns and ran for 135 yards on only twelve carries. USC dominated Alabama 42–21, in a game that changed college football forever.

His performance made many in the stands finally recognize that in order to maintain its national prominence, Alabama would need to actively recruit African-American players, something Bear Bryant had been quietly advocating for years. Jerry Claiborne, one of Coach Bryant's assistants, is said to have jokingly remarked, "Sam Cunningham did more to integrate Alabama in sixty minutes than Martin Luther King did in twenty years."

While Claiborne's remarks may have been an exaggeration, it is impossible to deny that Cunningham's performance in that game made a lasting impression on many fans as he helped to open doors for African-American players throughout the Deep South. The following season, two black players wore Alabama uniforms and three more joined the team's freshman squad. By the time the '70s were over, Bryant had completed the most successful decade in college football, including three national championships in 1973, 1978, and 1979—all with integrated Crimson Tide teams.

"You just never know when opportunity is going to knock, and the difference between success and failure is being ready when that knock comes," Cunningham said. "I memorized the playbook. I studied. It wasn't just physical; it was mental. When I entered that game, I didn't do so with any fear or trepidation because I knew I was ready. I had prepared to succeed."

Cunningham had no promise of playing that night in 1970; in fact, the two players on the depth chart in front of him were both upperclassmen. He had little reason to prepare, but that didn't matter to him. His performance on that field—a direct result of preparation for success—made him a college football legend and future College Football Hall of Famer.

The Alabama game was just the beginning. Cunningham had a standout college career that he capped off with four touchdowns in the 1973 Rose Bowl, which helped push USC to a 42–17 victory over Ohio State and earned the Trojans the title of 1972 National Champions; the game earned him induction into the Rose Bowl

Hall of Fame in 1992. Cunningham went on to play ten years in the NFL and is the New England Patriots' all-time leading rusher.

"I didn't know that was going to be my opportunity to play, but I did know that when the opportunity came I had to be ready," Cunningham said. "In order for something good to happen, you have to be prepared. It's been that way every day of my life."

Now, Cunningham owns his own business in Southern California and continues to stress preparedness to his employees. If a major opportunity comes up at the last minute, will the company be in a place to step up and accept the challenge? If a "sure bet" falls through, do they have a contingency plan in place? These are the questions that he asks himself every day as he evaluates his business plan.

Sam Cunningham understood that preparation is not a last-minute scramble into position just before the whistle blows. It is the purposeful anticipation of what is to come, and the deliberate priming of one's mind and body for that moment.

More from the Truly Great

Todd Collins was a backup quarterback, plain and simple.

He was drafted by the Buffalo Bills in 1995 as their second-string guy and sat for two years before finally starting in 1997—only to be traded to the Kansas City Chiefs in 1998. He didn't take a single snap in regular-season games during his first three seasons in Kansas City, and he remained their backup through 2005.

In March 2006, Collins signed with the Washington Redskins, again as a backup, and finally took the field on December 6, 2007, when Jason Campbell's knee injury knocked him out of the game against the Chicago Bears.

But Collins's big shot wasn't the dream opportunity most athletes hope for. There were a number of injuries on the team at the time, but what was really hurting the Redskins was the fact that they were still mourning the murder of teammate Sean Taylor only nine days previously. The team needed someone to rally around, and Collins needed a chance to prove himself.

Completing fifteen of twenty passes to rack up 224 yards and two touchdowns, Collins helped guide the hurting Redskins to a 24–16 victory over the Chicago Bears and was named the NFC Offensive Player of the Week. The next three games were also victories for the team as they beat the New York Giants and Minnesota Vikings before punctuating their season with a 27–6 victory over their archrivals, the Dallas Cowboys. Under Collins's leadership, Washington finished with a 9–7 record and earned a spot in the playoffs.

What was Collins's secret as he launched himself from benchwarmer to the spotlight? Preparation. After Collins took Campbell's place to finish out the game against the Bears, teammate and Washington running back Ladell Betts told the press that the team had confidence in their quarterback's preparedness: "He's been learning the same offense for ten years, so we really didn't have to wonder whether he was mentally ready."

Redskins head coach Joe Gibbs told the Associated Press, "I don't know that I've ever had a better performance coming off the bench. Ever."

Cunningham and Collins each got their chance when an exceptional circumstance was thrown in their direction. But short of wishing a career-ending injury on the first-string player, what steps can you take to ensure that you are ready not just to fill in, but to step up? Are you ready to go at a moment's notice if there is an opening? Would you be a person people could trust to have a solution to a sudden complication?

Herb Brooks, the "Miracle" coach of the 1980 US Olympic hockey team, prepared for the team's toughest opponent, the Soviets, for more than a year before the Games. He studied film and analyzed the Soviets, trying to find out what made them so dominant. He watched game reels, and he even traveled to watch them play in Moscow and on the road. As the gold medal winners in five of the last six Olympic Games, the team from the USSR was unquestionably the best team in the world.

Before long, however, Brooks discovered that the Soviets' dominance wasn't due to a secret technique. Instead, he realized that their success was owed to the fact that they could out-skate their competition at the end of the game, when the stakes were the highest.

From that point on, Brooks changed his coaching to focus on conditioning, to prepare his team of college students in order to be ready to play the third period against the Soviet team.

"Coach pushed us harder than any of us had ever been pushed," US goaltender Jim Craig told me. "But he did it because he knew that the great strength of that Russian team was that its players were in incredible shape at the end of the game. They blew people away in the third period. We took that away from them by being in better shape. We worked every day in practice to be ready for that third period of that one game."

New Orleans Saints quarterback Drew Brees has high expectations of his performance on the field, and he's practiced hard in order to perfect his work. When the TV show *Sport Science* challenged him to throw the pigskin at an archer's bull's-eye—half the circumference of a football—Brees hit it ten times out of ten. By comparison, the 2008 Olympic archers hit less than 50 percent with their arrows.

In fact, Brees hit four of the ten passes on the dead center of the bull's-eye and was amazingly consistent in each of his throws. *Sport Science* reported he released each pass, thrown from twenty yards away, at fifty-two miles an hour and with a six-degree launch angle. Each pass was identical.

"It's muscle memory," the Super Bowl MVP said. "I'm just thinking to get rid of it quickly as I can to the spot I want to throw it."

Brees has dedicated hours to practicing his throw in order to perform in game conditions. When the defense is coming at him, he doesn't have to stop and think *Am I doing this right?* because he's practiced it so long it's an automatic response.

Each of John Wooden's seasons at UCLA started with an early lesson for the freshmen. Prior to the first on-court practice, Wooden would gather his new players and tell them to take off their shoes and socks. Each player in the room would look around, bewildered, but obliged. Wooden's first lesson went down to the basics: how to put on socks and shoes properly. "I want you to make sure that there are no wrinkles or gaps," he'd tell them. "Make sure your heel is full seated in the heel of the sock; run your hand over the toes and make sure to smooth out any bumpy areas."

Over the next half hour, he would show each player how to properly lace his shoes and tie them snugly so that there was no room for the shoe to rub or the sock to bunch up. "That's your first lesson." Wooden would then start to walk away, but, after about a dozen steps, he'd turn around and explain the life lesson to the puzzled players.

"You see, if there are wrinkles in your socks or your shoes aren't tied properly, you will develop blisters. With blisters, you'll miss practice. If you miss practice, you don't play. And if you don't play, we cannot win," he'd tell them. "If you want to win championships, you must take care of the smallest of details."

Think about the smaller steps you need to make sure you are properly equipped to take on that bigger task. Consider each goal on your list in its most basic form, and determine from there where you need to begin. Maybe it's something as simple as cleaning your desk so that you have a clear workspace without distraction. Take the time to smooth out all of the wrinkles that could cause blisters in your day.

And for the Truly Great in Business

FedEx CEO Fred Smith applied Wooden's illustration to his own business. Early on, when he sought funding during the oil embargo of the early 1970s, he brought in some potential investors from

Chicago to his Memphis operation. After touring the facility, the potential investors declined. Smith was crushed.

But the next day, the group called back, saying its members had changed their minds and would invest after all. Smith, elated, asked what had made the difference.

The leader told him that during the walk through the hangar, the group members had noticed how clean the floor was. "I could have eaten off the floor, it was so perfectly polished," Smith was told. "That's the reason we're going to invest."

Smith said that attention to detail in preparation for the visit—much like Wooden's shoes-and-socks example—is what got FedEx off the ground.

"We'd set the standards, but it was the guy that cleaned the floor that had the same influence that I did," Smith said. "It's the same principle—the attention to detail makes the difference."

This is true in any profession. Years before Captain Chesley "Sully" Sullenberger calmly told air traffic control, "We're going in the Hudson," and safely landed USAir flight 1549 in the Hudson River, he started getting ready for such an eventuality.

Sullenberger, a former Air Force pilot who'd flown commercial aircraft with USAir for thirty years, was also the president and CEO of Safety Reliability Methods, which provided technical expertise and strategic vision and direction to improve safety and reliability. He specialized in accident investigations and also taught flight attendants how to respond to crises.

So when his Airbus A320 hit a flock of birds that disabled the engines, Sullenberger kept his cool and did what he'd prepared to do: successfully land the aircraft and lead all 155 people onboard to safety.

"I was sure I could do it," Sullenberger told *60 Minutes.* "I think in many ways, as it turned out, my entire life up to that moment had been a preparation for how to handle that moment."

Planning in the business world can sometimes be especially difficult. Consider how quickly technology has changed over the past decade in computing, cellular phones, and even in the medical realm. Each year, it seems, some new advancement renders some other still-young product obsolete.

It can be overwhelming to imagine how to stay ahead of the curve in every facet of your company's work. But the key isn't necessarily being able to anticipate every single trend that might arise—it's always keeping a plan in sight to accommodate growth and changes to the market.

In 1966, Walt Disney remarked on the importance of innovation in an interview with NBC. Outside the main gate of Disneyland (which had opened just eleven years earlier), he explained: "There's a little plaque out there that says, 'As long as there is imagination left in the world, Disneyland will never be complete.' We have big plans. This year, we finished over $20 million in new things. Next June, I hope, we'll have a new Tomorrowland; and starting from the ground up, building a whole new Tomorrowland." For the Disney company, preparation for the next opportunity is always underway.

But smart businesses are not only preparing for what could go right; they also have plans in place to cope with the all-too-possible worst-case scenario. Consider the manner in which BP responded to the Deepwater Horizon oil spill in the Gulf of Mexico in 2010. Besides the tragedy of eleven lives lost in the explosion, with no feasible plan in place it took the company nearly three months to find a workable solution to cap the well. The delay resulted in 4.9 million barrels of crude oil gushing into the sea. Think of the billions of dollars of economic impact to the Gulf region, the impacted wildlife and ecosystems, and, of course, BP's own public image drop that resulted from a lack of preparation.

Strategic planning is a necessary part of any business's future, no matter the size of the company. A company develops an overall plan by starting out with a broad scope and then gradually specifying the components of each stage. First, the company must identify its mission in clear terms, then it must clarify each of its objectives. Policies, regulations, and strategies must then be defined for achieving success as well as identifying and reacting to possible problems; these must be followed by the programs and projects that will bolster such strategies. Finally, the company can determine the resources required (cost, time, facilities, manpower).

A truly Great business leader not only has their finger on the pulse of their field, but they also have a clear sense of how their company is going to move in the most desirable, lucrative, and sustainable direction. Only with a specific and detailed plan broken down into each level of action can a company begin to prepare not only for where it is headed, but also for where it *should* be headed and how it will be able to get there.

The GREATNESS Challenge

How long does it take you to get into a working mind-set when you sit down to begin a project? Is there any downtime ahead of your starting point that you can use to begin mental preparation for the task ahead? Use that time as a chance to study who or what you are going to be up against. Preparation isn't just about focusing on yourself but in understanding all you can about what you will be facing.

Take a few minutes during your morning commute to turn off the radio and mentally outline your day. Prepare your mind for the work in which you are about to engage, and weed out the other distractions that might steal your attention away from the task at hand. For some people, this kind of preparation is a methodical checklist; for others, it can be a prayer for or meditation on the day ahead. It certainly doesn't hurt to carry a pen and paper or a small handheld recorder in the car to jot down those thoughts that hit you on the road so you'll be ready to put them into action when you arrive at your destination. It's not profound advice, but it can have a profound effect on your performance.

You should look at those moments on the way to work as a warm-up—a chance to stretch your mental muscles for what you have to face that day. If you've allowed yourself the opportunity to consider your goals, you will be able to jump on them as soon as your day begins.

Motivational speaker Brian Tracy suggests starting out every morning by making a list of the least pleasant tasks a person has to accomplish that day and committing to having them finished by noon. In his book *Eat That Frog!* Tracy notes that by taking the time to identify those items, people can clear their mind of nagging worries created by undesirable jobs. Then, they can spend the rest of the day focused on those things they would rather work on. Those few minutes of preparation can also help to make sure that you finish each day on a positive note, rather than with a negative task.

Preparation doesn't start when the buzzer sounds to begin the big game; it starts with the first action at the first practice on the first day of the season. Greatness is not achieved in a moment—it is the result of hundreds of small acts of preparation along the way as you focus on the fundamentals of your goal.

Work on the basics. Coach John Wooden started each season's practices running drills without basketballs. Wooden recognized the importance of focusing on perfecting the drills. That way, Wooden knew, the player would focus on the drill itself, not whether or not the ball hit the net in practice. If the player executed the drill properly, the balls would drop through the hoop, so he took the time to make sure each drill was run to exactly like it should be run in a game.

We should take the time to work on the fundamentals of our jobs, too. We should strive to be so good at those basics that we can do them in all situations. If you're preparing a speech and the PowerPoint presentation you were counting on crashes at the last minute, you need to know your fundamental material well enough to be able to improvise on the special effects while not slacking on the message.

How prepared is your mind? Whether it's hitting the links, the court, the gridiron, or the corporate ladder, you need to have a game plan for your success and a clear vision of how you will get there.

First, try to identify what your preparedness needs are. Determine your goals, but also determine how much time you need to get into production mode. What is a simple thing you can do to prepare for the rest of the day and make it go more easily? It is important to remember that different people need different levels of preparation to be ready. If you know that you need thirty minutes to get in your groove, arrive to work or to practice thirty minutes early—or at least allow yourself that much time to get mentally prepared for whatever you're about to tackle. You would never start your warm-up with the game clock running, would you?

One of the most important pieces of advice that a job coach will offer a client is to always enter an interview with some degree of knowledge about the company. No one expects the applicant to be an expert, but some familiarity with the brand or procedures demonstrates initiative, intelligence, and intensity—all signs of a promising new employee. This kind of preparation allows the prospective applicant to ask informed questions and show a genuine interest in the company's goals.

Do you extend this same courtesy of attention to your own life and your own goals? Take the time to really consider what it is that you want to achieve, and dedicate yourself to taking all of the necessary steps to be ready when the right time finally comes.

Put in the hours. Studies estimate it takes ten thousand hours to become an expert at any skill. That's ten years of practicing three hours a day, seven days a week. "No one has yet found a case in which true world-class expertise was accomplished in less time. It seems that it takes the brain this long to assimilate all that it needs to know to achieve true mastery," says expertise specialist Daniel Levitin in *This Is Your Brain on Music.*

As an example, Malcolm Gladwell cites the Beatles in his book, *Outliers.* As a struggling band in 1960, the soon-to-be Fab Four got a gig in Hamburg, Germany, that required them to play eight hours straight for weeks. The all-night show, which they played seven days a week, gave them plenty of practice. "We got better and got more confidence. We couldn't help it with all the experience playing all night long," Gladwell quotes John Lennon as saying later. "In Liverpool, we'd only ever done one-hour sessions, and we just used to do our best numbers, the same ones, at every one. In Hamburg we had to play for eight hours, so we really had to find a new way of playing."

Think from different angles. For each project you tackle, try to consider all the possibilities you are likely to face and have an idea as to how you might react should any one of them present itself. Don't waste your time on a fully developed plan if the situation doesn't call for one; just having a sense of anticipation can go miles in terms of keeping you on your toes. Ponder and plan the worst-case scenario. What are the five worst things that could happen in your career? In your personal life? Come up with a list of options and courses or action.

Preparedness is more than just the first burst of energy; it goes beyond just the moment of opportunity. Readiness without sustainability is a waste of effort. Solid preparation should have foresight beyond the immediate circumstance and extend to the long-term goals that the first opportunity will usher in. Almost every great winner is legendary for his or her practice habits, and they would likely all tell you that it's not just about getting prepared, but staying prepared.

Before the game and on the sidelines, Sam Cunningham studied every potential play that could be called—he was ready even though he didn't know if he needed to be. Todd Collins didn't just sit the bench waiting on his chance; he studied and prepared for his chance at Greatness. Herb Brooks didn't hope for a miracle; he systematically studied his opponent to know to beat them, then prepared to win. And Drew Brees threw the ball until he couldn't do it wrong.

After all, it's not just a matter of answering the door when opportunity knocks. It's about knowing what that opportunity might bring and being ready for any situation. It's about taking the time to evaluate the circumstances and making the right steps in order to be ready at a moment's notice. Sometimes you'll know when your moment is coming; other times, you may be blindsided by it. Either way, it is essential to be prepared to seize it and make it your own.

Don't be content with waiting—be ready to be Great!

CHAPTER

6

What Off-Season?

**They are always working toward the next game.
The goal is what's ahead . . . and there's *always* something ahead.**

Hard work is the only kind of work the Tennessee Lady Vols head coach Pat Head Summitt knows. Growing up on a farm with one sister, three older brothers, and a father who didn't take no for an answer, Summitt didn't really have much of a choice. She heard it over and over again: "Cows never take a day off."

The cows had to be milked in the morning and afternoon, every day, no matter what. Chores didn't wait for anything, even young Patricia Head's sixteenth birthday. Some friends had planned a party for her and a friend, but Richard Head wouldn't let his daughter go until she'd finished her work.

"I spent my birthday sitting on a tractor," Summitt recalled in her book *Reach for the Summit.* "You can't pick and choose the days you feel like being responsible."

It was her mother, Hazel, who Summitt says worked even harder than any of the men in the family, who taught her hard work isn't always good enough. To be the best, she would have to outwork the rest.

"Growing up I never knew the changes in my parents' fortune. They worked just as hard when they were well off as they did when they were struggling," Summitt said. "They never rested. They understood that when you invest in and give to others, you are really investing in yourself."

It's no surprise then that Summitt never missed a single day of school from kindergarten through high school. Nor is it a surprise that shenever had a losing season in almost four decades as a coach. Her regular-season winning percentage of 84 percent matches her NCAA Tournament winning percentage, and the eight championships her teams have won is the third most under any coach in college basketball history—male or female.

She simply worked harder than everyone else.

She began coaching in 1974, and her teams accumulated 18 Final Four appearances. Three classes of players played in a Final Four each year of their collegiate careers. In 2009, she became the first Division I coach, male or female, to win one thousand games, and she finished her career in 2012 with 1,098.

Growing up, she held her own playing against her three brothers, and she practiced shooting hoops on top of the hayloft after finishing her chores. Summitt's father was the first to realize that together, his daughter and the game of basketball were something special. The local high school didn't have a girls' team, but Pat's athletic potential was enough for her father to move his family across county lines so she could play.

That determination paid off. Not only did she earn a scholarship for basketball, Summitt took over as head coach at Tennessee in 1974, when she was just twenty-two years old.

"It was an accident. I was supposed to be the assistant coach, but the former head coach left and suddenly the job was open," Summitt writes. "So they stuck me in it. We all get in over our head at some time."

Simultaneously, Summitt was rehabilitating her knee in order to compete in the Olympics, finishing her masters' degree, and teaching physical education as a graduate assistant at Tennessee. A

1998 *Sports Illustrated* profile highlighted her early days as a young head coach: a three-mile run at 6:00 a.m., the first of two personal workouts, teaching, taking classes, coaching, recruiting, working out again, and then arriving home around midnight to hit the books.

Summitt's work ethic led to an Olympic silver medal, a Master's degree in physical education, and a winning program for the Vols. Her vision and determination were clear, and her tireless dedication to improvement paved the way for what has become one of the most decorated coaching tenures in sports history.

After two or three championships, Pat Summitt could have traded her whistle for a lounge chair on the beach, but she didn't. She could have sat back and embraced her history among the best coaches of all time back in 2000, when she was inducted into the Basketball Hall of Fame—but she didn't do that, either. She continued coaching through the 2011 season, every season a winning record, and only after a diagnosis of early onset Alzheimer's disease did she decide to retire. Her illness has yet to stop her from living. She serves as Tennessee's coach emeritus, and she has written a book *Sum it Up* about her experiences with her disease. In 2012, she received the Presidential Medal of Freedom from President Barack Obama and the Arthur Ashe Courage award at the 2012 ESPYs.

Her motto? Never settle—not even for success.

"Anyone can be average. What separates out people?" Summitt asked *60 Minutes.* "People that are willing to work every day. People that are willing to do the things that aren't fun. People that are willing to look at all their faults, their weaknesses, then try and commit to a way to make their weaknesses strengths."

Pat Summitt represented the highest caliber of her profession because she worked harder than her competitors. She achieved Greatness through the same hard work and dedication that she demanded from her players, because true champions understand that nothing is given.

"When the NCAA championship tournament starts, some teams think, 'We've arrived,'" Summitt said. "You never arrive in this game."

More from the Truly Great

It's one the most memorable scenes in one of Hollywood's most memorable movies. A large African-American teenager named Michael Oher is walking down the street, hunched over against the cold, when an affluent family in a silver BMW pulls up next to him. The mother, played wonderfully in the movie by Sandra Bullock, asks where he is headed. It is the scene where everything changes—for the young man, for the family, and for the tremendous story that unfolds in *The Blind Side.* But as poignant a moment as that was, it didn't adequately shed light on what made Michael Oher truly Great.

Because the movie basically began with his "rescue," it was not able to fully convey the enormity of the nightmare that was his childhood, in which he was one of thirteen children born to a drug-addicted mother who raised him in one of America's most dangerous housing projects. When you look at Michael's upbringing, the real power in his story is that he spent the first sixteen years of his life—the years before he showed up at the Briarcrest School—making thousands of right decisions when most people around him were making wrong ones. If he hadn't made so many good choices, Michael would never have even been on that Memphis street that cold November day, in the path of the Tuohy family.

What Michael has explained to me was that he understood from an early age that life is about the choices we make. He knew that his only way to a better life was to "make the choice each day to work towards success." Yes, he had help getting there—but he had to make the right decisions along the way to put him in a position to get that help.

From his earliest memories, Michael said, he was committed to finding a way out of his situation, and he pursued that goal with tireless dedication. It was Michael's daily decision to show up to basketball practice early and to work harder than anyone else on his youth league team that caught the eye of the coach who helped enroll him at Briarcrest. It was Michael's decision to avoid involvement in the drug dealings and gang activity around him that kept him out of trouble. It was Michael's decision to be polite and have a positive attitude that helped the Tuohy family first notice him at school basketball games and track meets. It was Michael's decision to fight through his schoolwork, even though he'd never learned basic study skills that encouraged his teachers at Briarcrest to rally around him.

And it was Michael's decision to head to the school gym to work out, even on a vacation day, that put him on the side of the road when the Tuohy family passed him in their car that November afternoon.

Michael Oher is where he is today because of the choices he made every single day—choices about his career, his body, his health, and his life. And even after being selected by the Baltimore Ravens in the first-round of the 2009 draft and despite some of his setbacks from injury during his NFL career, he still shows that daily commitment to making the best choices for his own success, especially with a chance for new beginnings at his new position at left tackle for the Carolina Panthers in 2015.

One especially hot and humid July morning, I was standing in Vaught-Hemingway Stadium at Michael's alma mater, Ole Miss. As Michael went through his usual off-season workout routine, running drills up and down the field, I downed three bottles of Gatorade just standing there watching him; but Michael did not once complain about the heat. He was there to work—end of story. His conditioning coach remarked to me that a lot of professional players schedule practices at their old colleges: "But Michael is the only guy I've ever known who has never missed a workout. Not one."

Almost everyone works eight hours a day, but it's what happens outside those eight hours that will decide if you reach the highest level and whether or not you can keep moving up. Are you willing to put in the time to be the very best in your field?

Jerry Rice was. The legendary San Francisco 49ers wide receiver played college football at the little-known Mississippi Valley State.

He didn't have exceptional size or speed when he entered the NFL, but he practiced every day knowing that he had to outwork everyone else to be successful.

Now universally hailed as one of the best wide receivers as well as one of the best players ever to take the gridiron, Rice set himself apart by his dedication to constant improvement. He was on three winning Super Bowl teams, thirteen Pro Bowl teams, and he is the all-time leader in every statistical category that exists for wide receivers.

And the more his efforts paid off, the harder he worked. Rice achieved it through the personal drive to never see a finish line, but to keep pushing on to greater things. "I knew the day I stopped working, someone was going to pass me," Rice said. And for as long as he played—and worked—no one ever did.

With the NBA in a lockout in the summer of 2011, LeBron James took advantage during his busy off season, amidst camps and endorsement commitments, to improve his game. With the loss of the NBA Championship to the Dallas Mavericks still bitter in his mouth, James sought advice from former great NBA players, like Magic Johnson and Isaiah Thomas. Deciding he needed most improvement at the post position, James contacted Hakeem Olajuwon, two-time NBA MVP post with two championship rings of his own.

"He told me he has played basketball all his life," Olajuwon, the Hall of Fame center said to Mike Berardino of the *Sun Sentinel.* "Facing the basket, shooting threes, this and that, but to complete his game, he needed to get inside."

Olajuwon, still regarded as one of the greatest posts to ever play the game, invited James to his private gym in the Houston area for a week of training. LeBron James, with a few friends and a camera crew in tow, spent a week learning the classic spins and fade away moves that Olajuwon utilized in his career. The move paid off when James and his Miami Heat went on to win back-to-back championships in 2012 and 2013.

Are you prepared to do what it takes now to stay in it for the long run? Consider Cal Ripken Jr. He didn't break Lou Gehrig's MLB games-played streak by chance. He conditioned his body so he would be available to play in every game. Early in his career, Ripken heeded his father's advice to run, lift weights, and play racquetball and basketball in the off-season in order to show up to spring training in tip-top shape. He stayed sharp by hitting balls off tees and throwing against walls in an effort to keep his body ready for the next season.

"It seemed pretty simple to me," he recounted in his book, *Get in the Game.* "Take care of yourself and you will not only play your best, you'll also reduce the chances of injury."

During his twenty-one seasons in Major League Baseball, he always reported to camp in excellent shape, which allowed him to focus on the fundamentals of batting and infield practice. Keeping conditioned as the season went on, Ripken avoided suffering serious injuries, and he stayed in the lineup by being healthy enough to recover from other injuries quickly.

Walter Payton also understood the importance of conditioning. Off-season and outside of the Chicago Bears' practices, Payton, later a member of both the college and professional football Halls of Fame, trained on his own, running twenty laps up and down a steep, ninety-two-foot hill. In his thirteen NFL seasons, "Sweetness" missed just one game.

A commitment to constant conditioning kept both Ripken and Payton in the game when most others wouldn't go the extra mile. To the Great ones, being able to perform at a high level on a regular basis for their organization is worth it. They don't want to become complacent; they want to become better.

The Miami Dolphins didn't just happen on a perfect season in 1972. They were training long before preseason camp. The previous season, the team went 12–3–1 on its way to the Super Bowl, but fell

24–3 to Dallas in the big game. Players tell the story of Head Coach Don Shula's postgame talk to his players in the locker room. Rather than allowing his players time off at the end of a heartbreaking year, he told them, "Gentleman, we start today preparing for next season."

The next year, the Dolphins marched undefeated through the regular season, never giving up more than 24 points in a game and shutting out opponents three times. The team's perfect 17–0 season ended where it started—in a Super Bowl locker room—but on a different note. Because of Shula's year-round goal of improvement, his dolphins defeated the Washington Redskins 14–7 in Super Bowl VIII to cap off the perfect season.

This same drive is evident in Warren Moon. He wasn't a tight end or a defensive back. He was a quarterback—and he was determined to keep it that way.

During his Pop Warner days in southern California, it was clear that Moon had tremendous potential both on the field and off. It was also clear that his potential would never be fully utilized attending the inner-city school for which his family's home was zoned. Working with a friend of his mother's, he was able to secure admission to Alexander Hamilton High School, which could offer him much stronger academic and athletic programs. Moon was committed to make the most of this opportunity, and he worked constantly to maintain his grades so he could retain his eligibility for the football team—his ticket to a college education.

But when the college offers came in, many schools touted the same line: "We'd love to have you, but not at quarterback." It was the early 1970s, and Moon knew that many other African-American quarterbacks were still being urged to switch to other positions rather than to represent their teams in such a visible and prominent role. This was not an option for Moon. He knew that he was one of the best quarterbacks there was, and he was determined to show the world.

Rather than going straight to a four-year college, Moon enrolled in junior college and continued to push himself for better and better performance. That year, he wowed the crowd with his incredible arm—and secured a scholarship for the following fall at the University of Washington to play his beloved position.

At each level of play, Moon was a star athlete who won the respect of his teammates and coaches thanks to his cool head in the huddle, funny disposition, and the leadership he showed through his commitment to hard work and discipline. His senior year, he led the Huskies to a Rose Bowl upset over the University of Michigan, scoring two short-run touchdowns himself and throwing one 28-yard touchdown pass. He was named the MVP of the game.

Yet Moon came up empty-handed after the 1978 NFL draft. He'd been courted by several teams, only to have them try to persuade him to switch to tight end. Faced with that option, Moon decided instead to go to the Canadian Football League, where he knew that the playing time would only serve to make him a better quarterback.

He continued his tireless pursuit of improvement, pushing not only himself, but also his teammates. And his hard work paid off almost instantly when he led the Edmonton Eskimos to a record-breaking five consecutive Grey Cup championships from 1978 to 1982, and was named the MVP of the game twice.

In 1983, he reentered the NFL draft as a quarterback and this time, everyone paid attention. With several teams fighting for him, Moon finally signed with the Houston Oilers. He continued to develop as a player, growing and improving until, in 1989, the quarterback no team wanted in 1978 became the highest-paid player in the NFL. Before his retirement in 2000, Moon had been named to the Pro Bowl nine times, the NFL Offensive Player of the Year, the NFL's Man of the Year, and had his jersey number retired by the Tennessee Titans (formerly the Houston Oilers), among many other honors.

When Moon was elected to the NFL Hall of Fame in 2006, he became the first undrafted quarterback and the first black quarterback to receive the honor. He is also the only player enshrined in both the CFL and NFL Halls of Fame—an impressive legacy for someone whom no one wanted to give a chance.

Rather than sitting out until the next year or giving up on his dream altogether, Warren Moon decided to act, pursuing an alternative that he knew would put him in a better position in the future. He knew that hard work could get him back into the NFL draft, so he elected to take the route that allowed him to continue to improve—and to prove what could be done.

And for the Truly Great in Business

Thomas Edison was relentlessly pursuing new opportunities to expand not only his mind but also the possible applications for his inventions. "Genius is one percent inspiration and 99 percent perspiration" was the slogan by which he famously lived and worked. For Edison, it wasn't enough to simply create a product and then set it aside. Arguably America's greatest innovator, he refused to allow himself to simply coast by on reputation.

By the time of his death, Edison held 1,093 patents in the United States, as well as many others in Europe, including the phonograph, the first practical lightbulb for home use, and one of the earliest motion picture cameras. His dogged persistence toward Greatness led him not only to experiment and create but also to convert his inventions into commercially viable products, making him one of the most accomplished businessmen of the late nineteenth and early twentieth centuries.

Similarly, Steve Ballmer, former CEO of Microsoft, is worth an estimated $22.2 billion personally—and yet he hardly traded in his desk chair for a lounger on the beach. Until 2014, Ballmer stayed involved with the day-to-day goings-on of Microsoft's more-than-fifty-billion-dollar operations and eighty thousand employees. He personally made sales pitches to industry giants, and he kept himself and the rest of his executives not only involved in the growth of their company but also working hard to keep their product at the forefront of the field. "I think the output of our innovation is great," he said. "We have a culture of self-improvement. I know we can continue to improve." After his retirement from Microsoft in 2014, Steve Ballmer bought the Los Angeles Clippers.

Elon Musk has been described as a real-life Tony Stark, building companies in Silicon Valley that combine the finest minds of engineering and tech to tackle huge goals. Born in South Africa and educated in Canada and the United States, Musk started his rise to becoming one of the most talked about CEOs in business with three aims. According to his biography by Ashlee Vance, Musk decided the three things which would have the most positive impact on the world were: sustainable energy, the Internet, and making life multi-planetary.

He left college for the start up world, eventually becoming a co-founder of PayPal, a service which drastically changed the Internet by creating a safe way to exchange money online. When eBay bought his company for $1.5 billion in 2002, Musk used his new found fortune to invest in his other two goals, sustainable energy (TESLA and SolarCity) and muli-planetary life (SpaceX). While many tech companies focus on a social app or a distracting game, Musk wants his company to establish life on Mars. No wonder people see him as Iron Man.

Musk works 100 hour weeks, easily, between TESLA and SpaceX, and he does not simply throw money at his teams of engineers. Musk has made himself an expert in all areas of his companies. When he decided to build rockets, Musk focused his priorities on learning everything about rocket science. After failed launches at SpaceX, Musk often briefs the public as to what happened, pinpointing engineering flaws.

His critics see him as a "nanomanager," an extreme micromanager, having a say in every decision, even hiring the lowest level employees at one point. As a boss, he's known as tough and demanding. Both of his ex-wives have been honest about his personal life, that he's focused only on work. Recent critics note his unapologetic confession that he spends time with his sons by being in the room with them but checking email. Yet, people who have worked for him attribute this quality as intense curiosity and determination.

Dolly Singh, the former head of talent acquisition for SpaceX told *Business Insider,* "Diamonds are created under pressure, and

Elon Musk is a master diamond maker." He hires the best, and he expects the best from his employees, serving as the prime example.

What enabled each of these men to achieve success? It wasn't just their talent or shrewdness in business. Instead, each one recognized the value first of a personal investment *of* self, by never thinking they could get ahead by letting someone else do the work; and second, of a personal investment *in* self, by continually seeking out new areas of proficiency, competence, and skill.

The simple truth that Greatness never, ever stands still.

The GREATNESS Challenge

Everyone wants to experience success, but the truly Great—even when they seem to have it all—are looking ahead to the next thing. To them, being the best means something more than a trophy and a pat on the back.

Have there been times in your own career when disappointments have waylaid your progress? What did you decide to do? The Great ones keep moving forward, knowing that whatever new skills, experiences, and professional growth result will only serve to keep the momentum going.

Had he allowed himself time off, LeBron James's approach to the game would have been no different from his competition. By training with Olajuwon in the off season, he gained an edge that would prove invaluable.

Had he simply given up, Warren Moon might have never had the chance to make the impact that he did in gaining acceptance for black quarterbacks. By choosing to chase his dream in a different venue, he gained notice and notoriety—and became one of the most celebrated athletes of his generation.

The Great ones understand that there is no off-season; there should be no lapse in activity that can break your stride, because only further practice can lead to better results for the next go-round. Only effort can launch you into the realm of Greatness.

Do you have a clear idea of what your professional and personal goals are for the next six months? For the next year? For the next three to five years? What is your plan to attain each one of those goals? If you don't know, take the time to think about how you will get there from here. Are there any skills, proficiencies, or certifications that you will need to advance? What are you doing to gain those necessary requirements?

Even if it is not required for your job, taking continuing or community education programs can be a great way to expand your skill set. Learn another language, join a book club, or take a first-aid course. You'll meet new people, network, learn new skills, and keep your on top of your game.

If you happen to be faced with an unexpected break in your job, like a layoff or a furlough, see if there's something you can do to use the time to your professional advantage. Is there a course you could take to improve your credentials? Could you earn a certificate in a more advanced area, or something else entirely?

If you don't think you have the right tools, see what you can do to improvise. Growing up in Fiji, Vijay Singh didn't have golf balls with which to practice his swing. Rather than using this roadblock as an excuse, though, he found a way to practice anyway. "When we were kids we couldn't afford golf balls so we had to make do with coconuts," he said in an interview for *Pacific Magazine.* "My father used to say, 'Little Vijay, golf balls don't fall off trees you know,' so I found some that did!" Singh was determined to train in whatever way he could to learn his sport and become a master at it. Is there a creative solution to any obstacles that might be in the way of your growth?

It has often been said that the only way to truly learn something is to teach it. If someone is needed to give a presentation on a new project or company procedures, volunteer. This will force you to familiarize yourself with the concepts in a new way. Or, you could offer to teach a seminar on your area of expertise. If there isn't an appropriate opportunity within your company, you might be able to find a different venue. Community groups such as the Lions Club are often open to presentations on all kinds of unusual or informative topics. Simply by preparing a PowerPoint presentation or answering questions, you may come to a new understanding of the big picture, the process, or even your own expertise. It will also keep your communication and presentation skills sharp.

Year-round and constant preparation isn't just for athletes. Salespeople keep on top of trends, manufacturers constantly develop new products and improve existing ones, and service providers continually look for ways to better help their clients. Teachers, dentists, doctors, and attorneys all benefit from continued training, as well. Would you want to visit a surgeon who wasn't up-to-date with the newest techniques? Would you hire a lawyer who had no idea of recent court decisions? Good isn't enough. You want the Greatest working for you, so wouldn't you want to be the Greatest in your profession, too?

Famous running coach Percy Wells Cerutty shared this philosophy with his athletes: "I urge you to go on to your greatness if you believe it is in you. Think deeply and separate what you wish from what you are prepared to do." It's good advice to all of us: take some time to consider what it is that you are truly willing to do in order to accomplish your dreams.

Greatness of any kind requires hard work and dedication—not only to the final goal but to the process of attaining it. As Cerutty recognized, wishing for something is not enough to attain it. You need to have a realistic vision of what level of work is required in order to get there.

A number of years ago, Nike had a motivational poster with the message: "He's soft and he's fat and he's wearing my clothes and he's getting too old and he was born on my birthday and I'm afraid if I stop running, he'll catch up with me."

Don't let complacency or laziness or even just a sense of "good enough" catch up with you. The truly Great press on toward the next goal because it is that extra effort, that nonstop push towards something better, that can make the difference between good and Great.

CHAPTER

7

Visualize Victory

They see victory before the game begins.

All Shaquille O'Neal wanted was a fourth NBA championship and the opportunity to prove that the Los Angeles Lakers had made a mistake by trading him in the prime of his career.

But in 2007, three years removed from his third championship, he and his new Miami Heat team were pegged as too old to make an impact. Against the odds, they'd made it to the NBA Finals, but lost the first two games and all the momentum to a stronger, younger Dallas team.

It looked like the pundits were right. During the first two games in Dallas, the Mavericks wiped the floor with the older, slower Heat, taking control of the best-of-seven game series. During Game Three in Miami, it looked like Dallas was on the verge of going up 3–0 and putting the Mavericks on the cusp of a sweep. The Mavericks led by 13 points in the fourth quarter...but then Miami's offense started to click.

The Heat rallied to win Game Three, then Game Four, and even Game Five, all at home. O'Neal and the Heat were just one game away from becoming only the second team in league history to lose the first two games of a Finals series and come back to win four straight and the NBA title. All they had to do was head to Dallas and win one more game.

I have been lucky enough to know Shaq since he was a seventeen-year-old kid choosing a college, and each time he has had a chance to win an NBA Championship, Dale Brown, his coach from Louisiana State, has invited me to join him in witnessing Shaq's success. The 2007 series was no exception.

A few hours before Game Six, Coach Brown and I sat down with Shaq in his hotel room in Dallas, talking about the Heat's amazing season and reminiscing about Shaq's college days. Around 5:45, Shaq began to pack while we carried on with our conversation. The team bus, we knew, left for the arena at six o'clock, so Coach Brown and I didn't think anything of it as he picked up his bags and started to fold his clothes.

Suddenly, it dawned on us that Shaq wasn't just packing his gym bag; he was packing everything—suits, shoes, toothbrush—into his suitcase. As he continued to do so, Coach Brown shot him a puzzled look. "But this is only Game Six," he said. "If you lose tonight you're going to have to come back and unpack all that stuff."

Shaquille O'Neal's smile is the greatest grin in sports, and I saw it then, bigger than anything, as he explained: "Coach Pat Riley pulled us all together at the end of practice today. He looked at us and said, 'Gentlemen, I am so sure that we are going to win tonight, I have checked us out of the hotel. At six o'clock on the dot I want you in the lobby with your bags packed and ready to load the bus. We are going to the arena, we are winning the world title, and we are flying back to Miami tonight as champions.'"

Coach Brown and I exchanged glances, impressed, as Shaq continued: "That wasn't even the best part. Riley said, 'I want each and every one of you to go down to the front desk at six o'clock and I want you—not your manager, not your wife, not your running buddies—to hand your room key to that front desk clerk. I want you to say, 'Thank you so much for your hospitality, but I won't be needing my room tonight.' Got it?'"

At six o'clock, Coach Brown and I hurried to the lobby to witness the team's confidence play out. One by one, the likes of Shaq, Dwyane Wade, Alonzo Mourning, Jason Williams, James Posey, and the rest of the Heat handed their keys to the bewildered clerk, saying politely and confidently, "Thank you so much for your hospitality, but I won't be needing my room tonight."

I saw in the way O'Neal recounted his coach's words, in the way each player handed his key to the desk clerk, and in the way the Miami Heat played that game, that these were players who knew they were going to be successful before they ever walked on the court that night. Their vision of themselves had everything to do with how they played.

Pat Riley encouraged his team to visualize victory—and to win the biggest game most of those players had ever played—before their bus even pulled up to the arena to start the warm-ups.

More from the Truly Great

Visualization is a key aspect of sports psychology. An athlete who has a clear sense of the goal in mind and can imagine himself or herself sinking the basket or crossing the finish line or hitting the ball in just the right way will be able to channel both mental and physical energies toward accomplishing the task.

Consider Ted Williams, arguably the greatest hitter baseball has ever known. Even as a child he would train endlessly, swinging the bat and imagining how every pitch, real or imagined, would look as it ricocheted off into the outfield or over the fence. He once wrote about the hours he spent practicing hitting: "I swung a bat, my God; I used to take a heavy bat and swing it until I couldn't swing it anymore. Again hitting at an imaginary pitch and visualizing what I would do with it."

For Williams, the act of envisioning the goal was an integral part of the overall process of becoming Great. It was part of his practice and part of his playing. The same should be true of us—positive thinking and visualized goals in both our preparation and our action can have a huge impact on the effectiveness of our efforts.

John Wooden understood the importance of visualization, as well. At the beginning of each basketball season, the UCLA head coach would write down his prediction for how each season would go and place it in a sealed envelope in the bottom drawer of his desk. At the end of the season, he'd take it out and compare it with his team's record. "And I was almost always just about spot-on," he told me once. Considering that the Bruins won an unprecedented ten National Championships under Wooden's leadership, it's safe to guess that those predictions must have been very positive ones.

What Wooden understood was the importance of creating and maintaining a game plan for your life—knowing what you want to accomplish and clearly articulating what your goals are. This kind of thinking is the first step in being proactive, and the first step in seeing something out of reach as truly possible.

Boxing great Muhammad Ali always stressed the importance of seeing victory long before the moment of truth. In reflecting on his career, he looked back at his "downtime" and realized that there was no such thing. When he traveled, when he trained, when he rested—he always kept the goal in the back on his mind. Any moment that was dedicated to the task at hand should be fully committed to working toward that goal so he would be ready long before he was faced with the reality of it. "Before I get in the ring, I'd already won or lost it on the road," he explained. "The real part is won or lost somewhere far away from witnesses—behind the lines, in the gym, and out there on the road, long before I dance under those lights."

Visualization has become such a part of athletic performance, the *New York Times* published an article entitled "Olympians Use Imagery as Mental Training," during the 2014 Sochi Olympics.

Athletes like Emily Cook, an American free-style skier even simulated her visualization or, the more recent term, "imagery" process for one of her competition runs for the reporters.

"Visualization, for me, requires all the senses," said Cook. "You have to smell it. You have to hear it. You have to feel it, everything." Cook goes on to describe the benefits of using imagery to improve her performance by calming her nerves, helping her to anticipate setbacks, and to focus on the entire course.

The practice has become emphasized in competitive sport that Olympic teams from around the world have begun hiring sports psychologists on their staff, something America has done for a long time, employing nine psychologists for the Sochi Games.

This same philosophy was apparent even during NBC's coverage of the 2010 Vancouver Olympics. Before the Ladies' Downhill race, the camera showed Lindsey Vonn standing at the top of the hill, going through her prerace ritual in which she skis the course in her head, mimicking the movements her body needs to make over each turn and jump. Her visualization encompassed her mind and body, and it paid off when she captured America's first-ever gold medal in that event.

Curtis Strange, two-time US Open champion and PGA Player of the Year in 1988, believes in the simplicity of this strategy: "Visualization lets you concentrate on all the positive aspects of your game." In other words, positive thinking leads to positive results, and those results lead to Greatness.

Psychology Today points out that using imagery produces the same results as practice. When you imagine something happening, it trains your brain how to react during the real thing. The preparation can increase your confidence and motivation, and improve your performance—in sports or in business.

When you visualize your performance, whether it's teaching a class, closing a sale, or lining up a putt, be specific. As part of the same study, *Psychology Today* found it is helpful to imagine the scene as a picture and to employ all five senses in doing so. Do it just before going to sleep or just after waking up; repeat the scene and concentrate. If negative thoughts creep in, use an affirmation, like Muhammad Ali's famous mantra: "I am the greatest!"

Stopping negative thoughts is important, because visualizing failure is as effective as visualizing success. Don't gear yourself up for failure—only losers prepare to lose. We all know someone who constantly complains how nothing ever goes their way. They're usually right, aren't they? When an individual is stuck in a losing mind-set, failure and disappointment seem to follow them.

Returning to Shaq's experience, this point can easily be seen. During the NBA Finals, Dallas's coach, Avery Johnson, grew concerned when his team, which had been up 2–0 after those first two games in Dallas, lost the next two in Miami. Heat coach Pat Riley had no doubt his team would recover and win, but Johnson had an opposite reaction. He packed up his Mavericks and moved them to a hotel in Ft. Lauderdale, saying that there were too many distractions in South Beach. In essence, he doubted his team's ability to win, and the doubt rubbed off. Dallas lost the next game and returned home in a 3–2 hole.

Both Pat Riley and Avery Johnson visualized their destinies, but while Dallas's Johnson was unsure of his team's ability to stay focused on the game, Riley knew that he could use it as a moment to motivate. Both leaders got what they envisioned.

Former Clemson women's basketball coach Jim Davis had a team that didn't visualize victory. In 1996, as one of the least successful teams in the Atlantic Coast Conference, the Tigers entered the league's postseason tournament as a bottom seed and would have had to win games on four straight days if they were to win the title.

As they boarded the bus in Clemson to drive to the tournament, Davis sensed something was wrong with his team. He asked the driver to pull over and then asked each player, one by one, to accompany him to the luggage hold, take out her luggage, and show him what she'd packed.

Most of the team—including each of his starters—hadn't packed enough outfits for all four days. In other words, they didn't see themselves winning all the games they would need to hang in the tournament to the end. Davis benched every player who packed fewer than four outfits, knowing they hadn't planned on winning. His lineup went on to win two upset victories in the tournament and learned lifelong lessons about what it takes to be Great.

And for the Truly Great in Business

Many athletes use visualization as a means to picture themselves succeeding, but it's applicable to any business plan.

Will Smith is the one of the most bankable Hollywood actors and the first to have eight consecutive movies break the $100 million mark. He routinely pulls in $20 million per film, but it wasn't always that way. Smith's Fresh Prince rapper persona and *Fresh Prince of Bel Air* television program brought him fame to the younger crowd in the early 1990s, but Smith had a bigger goal: he wanted to be the industry's highest-paid actor.

Before Smith was a superstar, he wanted to *be* a superstar. So he sat down and mapped it out. "When I started in movies, I said, 'I want to be the biggest movie star in the world,'" Smith remarked in an interview. He and his business partner analyzed the top ten movies of all time, looking for similarities, and they found a pattern: "At that point, they were all special-effects movies." So Smith set out to act in movies that fit the formula. "*Independence Day* and *Men in Black* were really no-brainers," he laughed. He earned $25 million to star in *I Am Legend,* and subsequently eclipsed Johnny Depp to top *Forbes*'s annual list of Hollywood's highest-paid actors the following year. *Newsweek* proclaimed him the "most powerful actor on the planet."

It wasn't a surprise to Smith. He saw his Greatness in his future and made it happen. That's just how the Great ones operate.

In the 1970s, the American auto market was lagging. Lee Iacocca, a visionary who had risen to become vice president of Ford at age thirty-six, was named the chairman of Chrysler in 1979 in the hopes that he could somehow breathe new life into the company. In fewer than five years, Iacocca took Chrysler from the brink of bankruptcy to turning a $2.9 billion profit in 1984, which was higher than all of the company's profits in the last sixty years combined.

What was the secret of his success? Very simply, Iacocca had a clear sense of vision. He imagined where he wanted to see the company go, and with that clearly defined, took exactly the steps he needed to get there. By introducing both the minivan and the reliable, low-cost K-car, he turned the company around and sent sales through the roof. But his success didn't begin with the production of new types of automobiles. Instead, he insisted that goal had to be set in a real and tangible way: "The discipline of writing something down is the first step toward making it happen."

Visualization has wings. When Howard Schultz first pitched the idea of expanding a small-line coffee shop to a nationwide enterprise, the owners weren't interested. They figured they had a niche product of high-end brew that wouldn't appeal to the wider American public. Schultz had hoped that his vision would gain him the marketing position for the company, but instead, the owners decided it was impractical and impossible.

But Schultz could see that tremendous success was just out of reach of the small business, and he called the owners back in one last effort to make them recognize the very real opportunity that they considered too ambitious. The confidence Schultz demonstrated won over the others, and in 1982 he became the head of marketing for a small Seattle-based chain called Starbucks.

Now, after three decades and more than 16,500 stores worldwide, Schultz attributes his success to having a clear sense of his goals. "I believe life is a series of near misses," he said. "A lot of what we ascribe to luck is not luck at all. It's seizing the day and accepting responsibility for your future. It's seeing what other people don't see and pursuing that vision."

Vision paired with action is the surest way to achieve goals. Industry leaders are inevitably men and women who see where they want their companies to be headed and act accordingly; they are people who are driven by specific ambitions powered by a firm belief in the feasibility of their plan. Goal setting is about more than just making a sales figure—it's about really believing in the product and talents that will combine to accomplish something Great.

The GREATNESS Challenge

As you prepare for your next appointment, see it through in your mind from the greeting to discussion, and right up to the point that you get what you came for. If you haven't envisioned how you'll say thanks and exit, you haven't thoroughly prepared for the meeting.

It is amazing how many people could learn from this point. How many of us have lost before we've ever walked into a meeting? How many of us have convinced ourselves we're not going to get something we've said we're committed to?

Don't get caught in that trap of not visualizing but still expecting success. Instead, visualize your objectives and pursue them without restraint. When you visualize victory, you don't have to constrict yourself to modest goals. Go ahead and let yourself imagine the fullest impact of your efforts. Why not? If you limit yourself in your imagination, you'll limit yourself in real life.

Instead, use your imagination to your advantage. Peak-performance expert Dorothy M. Neddermeyer says if you're doing something for the first time, imagine that you've already done it successfully. Your mind doesn't know the difference between something you've imagined in detail and something that's real, she told *SUCCESS* magazine in an interview.

To give you a constant visual of your goals, write them down. Motivational speaker and author Brian Tracy suggests keeping them with you on a set of index cards, and continuously thinking about the next specific steps you can take to carry out your goals. To strive for Greatness, Tracy suggests reviewing your goals frequently and doing something each day to work toward them. When you look at the goals written on your index cards, take another minute to visualize them achieved. "Goals fulfill the greatest need of human beings—a sense of meaning and purpose in life," writes Tracy.

Remember, however, that although visualization is a key tool for improvement, you still need to practice. When an athlete uses imagery, she or he will often visualize a video of making the play. Serena Williams, for example, drapes a towel over her head before big matches and watch her previous victories on an iPod. But of course, that's not all she does. She goes to practice every day and puts her muscles through the motion. Visualization helps the brain remember the motions; but, just as a teacher needs to go over a lesson plan, an athlete needs to practice.

The key is combining practice with visualization. Using basketball free-throw shots, psychologist Alan Richardson studied the difference between practicing with just muscles or just visualization, verses using both. He worked with three groups of people, none of which had used imagery before. Over twenty days, one group shot free throws daily. A second group took shots on the first day and the twentieth day, but didn't practice at all in between. The third group shot free throws on the first day and the twentieth, like the second group, but utilized "mental practice" each day in between.

At the conclusion, Richardson, whose report was published in *Research Quarterly,* found that the group that practiced physically improved the most—by 24 percent. But the group that had practiced mentally improved by almost as much: 23 percent. Meanwhile, the control group, which had shot the balls on two different days but with no other practice at all in between the first and twentieth days, showed absolutely no improvement whatsoever. The group using visualization as a practice technique hadn't physically thrown the ball any more than the group that showed no improvement, and from this Richardson asserted that visualization occurs when the person is able to see and feel what he or she is imagining. His visualization group had practiced with the ball only on the first day, and but throughout their imaginary practices, they were able to see and feel the ball as they envisioned themselves holding it, and they could hear it bounce as they dribbled and hear it swish through the net.

When you visualize the situations, remember those details. Incorporate all the senses into your vision. Before the New Orleans Saints played in and won its first Super Bowl, Drew Brees visualized the walk to the field. The Saints had played at Miami earlier in the season, defeating the Miami Dolphins in a dramatic comeback—and Brees focused on the Sun Life Stadium's every detail, as it was to be the site of that year's Super Bowl. "Certainly, when we were coming here, knowing that this was going to be the Super Bowl site, we all talked about, 'Hey guys, let's visualize being here in February,'" Brees said. "Sure enough, we came up with a big win there. We felt that locker room atmosphere after the game and said we'd love to be back here and feel that feeling again."

From the locker room to the tunnel leading to the field, Brees took it all in. He wanted to be able to remember each detail for the rest of the regular season, knowing he wanted to be back in that same stadium for the big game. "I try to simulate the game as much as I can in practice and visualize every play and every defense we could see," Brees told the *Wall Street Journal.* "In essence I'm playing the game over and over so that no matter what situation happens, I've already played it and can anticipate what will happen." Visualizing those details helped make his dream a reality.

What do you want to accomplish? Make a list of goals that you'd like to achieve today, this week, this month, and beyond. Carve out a few minutes to really consider each one and what it might look like when you complete it. Take your time and really absorb how the scene appears. Try to engage each of your senses: What does it look like? How do the handshakes feel? What sounds can you hear? Walk yourself through the image and savor the details. The more real it becomes in your mind, the easier it will be to follow the necessary steps to living out the scene in real life.

Coach Pat Riley had his team check out of the hotel so that would be one less fallback plan that might make losing more convenient. Is there anything holding you back from going forward full force? Are there any Plan Bs that you're using as a crutch to keep you from Plan A?

Hold yourself accountable. Talk to people about your vision; not only can this generate excitement and momentum, but it may also cause people to hold your feet to the fire in order to accomplish what you've set out to do. Motivational speaker James Robbins suggests enlisting a friend as an "accountability partner" and meeting regularly. During the meetings, Robbins suggests you report the progress you've made toward your goal since the last meeting, and what you plan to commit to next. "If you are dragging your feet, it is the partner's responsibility to give you a kick in the butt," he says.

Do you visualize positive or negative outcomes? Challenge yourself to think only positive thoughts for one whole day. If you catch yourself slipping into negativity, quickly correct it. Use a positive affirmation to change your thinking. Say it out loud or write it down multiple times. It will bring your goals into focus, and you will likely find yourself accomplishing more and feeling better after only a few hours.

Why wait on history when you can write it yourself? Set your own course by determining to think positively, and follow that through to your goals. The truly Great can see victory before the game begins.

CHAPTER

8

Inner Fire

The truly Great use adversity as fuel.

I could spend the rest of my life looking and never again witness anything close to the Greatness I saw in Warrick Dunn during a visit to Angola State Prison in Louisiana. But I'm getting ahead of myself. Let me introduce you to Warrick Dunn first.

Dunn was born in Baton Rouge, Louisiana, the oldest of six brothers and sisters. They all idolized their mother, police officer Cpl. Betty Smothers. Though she worked several other part-time jobs to keep her family afloat, she always made time to nurture her children. In high school, when Dunn began getting attention from college scouts all over the country, his mother stayed by his side to ensure her son made the best decision for his future.

The day they met Bobby Bowden, Dunn and his mother enthusiastically agreed that playing at Florida State University was the best choice.

But just two days after Dunn turned eighteen, a call came that changed his life forever. His mother was shot and killed in the line of duty, ambushed while she provided security for a grocery store manager making a nighttime bank deposit.

Devastated, confused, and still a teenager, Dunn's new role was man of the house. Coach Bowden offered to let Dunn out of his verbal commitment to FSU, but Dunn knew his mom would have wanted him to go and improve his future. Choosing FSU had been among the last decisions they had made together, and Dunn intended to honor it by studying and playing football, even though he'd also be responsible for his brothers and sisters.

Incredibly, Dunn did it all. He raised his five younger siblings—oftentimes over the phone—while earning a degree at Florida State and becoming both a national champion and FSU's career rushing leader. His grandmother helped with the parenting back in Louisiana, but Dunn returned home every weekend he was able to dole out discipline, praise, and love to his brothers and sisters.

Dunn was taken in the first round of the 1997 NFL draft by the Tampa Bay Buccaneers and moved his three youngest siblings out to Tampa to live with him while they finished school. While the other players would go out after practice to enjoy the city's nightlife, Dunn would head home to make sure that homework and chores were finished.

And he did it all while maintaining an impressive career. No one ever thought a player Dunn' size—a mere five foot eight and 180 pounds—would have the strength to withstand twelve years in the NFL, much less become one of its all-time leading rushers. He's just the twenty-second player in the league's history to earn more than 10,000 career rushing yards, putting his name alongside NFL greats like Emmitt Smith, Walter Payton, and Barry Sanders.

However, for Dunn, it was—and is—the ever-growing numbers off the field that mean more than anything. At last count, the number was well over 140.. But it's not games, touchdowns, 1,000-yard seasons, or anything else related to football.

It's people. Specifically, it's single parents.

When Dunn joined his first NFL team, the Tampa Bay Buccaneers, he established a foundation to help single mothers like his own mom. He wanted those mothers to experience something his mother never did—home ownership.

"I always knew that if I ever got a shot in the NFL, I would use the opportunity to change the lives of other people," he recalled in his book, *Running for My Life.* "I wanted to change lives; I wanted to impact people for the long term—something that would help them on the path to better opportunities."

Dunn established his Homes for the Holidays program, which helps single parents take a big step in making the dream of home ownership become real. Each year, Dunn surprises deserving families by helping them purchase their first home. He delivers the keys to the house, which is filled top to bottom with furnishings, from furniture and appliances to a fully stocked kitchen, fresh flowers for the mothers, and toys for the children.

To date, the Warrick Dunn Foundation's Homes for the Holidays program has helped not only those single parents, but also their three hundred–plus children and dependents, earn homes of their very own for the first time, and the number grows every year.

But his hard work and concern for others didn't stop at his own front door or with the Homes for the Holidays program. In the aftermath of Hurricane Katrina, Dunn personally challenged his NFL colleagues to donate $5,000 each to raise money for relief efforts. In all, the league raised $5 million. In 2007, Dunn and a group of professional athletes (including Cal Ripken Jr., Jackie Joyner-Kersee, and Muhammad Ali) established Athletes for Hope, an organization that helps match athletes with meaningful and reputable charities. Dunn has earned both the Walter Payton Man of the Year Award and the Bart Starr award for his community accomplishments.

If the story stopped right there, Warrick Dunn would be among the Greatest winners I've ever known. But, while working with him on *Running for My Life,* Dunn showed me strength, character, and courage I never imagined. He invited me to join him the day he met, for the first time, with the man who had confessed to and was then convicted of murdering his mother.

Dunn had spent years in counseling dealing with the grief. That day at Angola State Prison, he was looking for answers—answers only Kevan Brumfield could provide. Dunn brought along a spiral notebook, filled with questions he wanted to ask the man who killed his mother. But the warden warned Dunn that Brumfield had filed an appeal with the United States Supreme Court, and Dunn might not get the closure he was looking for.

Dunn replied, "I didn't come here today for him. I came here for me."

The warden was right. No sooner had we had been seated than the inmate, who had confessed in court to killing Betty Smothers in the ambush, now told us he "didn't do it." Dunn sat patiently and listened to Brumfield's story for about twenty minutes. Then Dunn held up his hand.

He pushed aside his spiral notebook filled with questions, looked Brumfield in the eyes, and bared his soul to him.

Dunn explained that prior to his mother's murder, he had dreams of being a father, like the one he'd never had, and being a husband, like the one his mother had never had. But now, he was afraid to get close to anyone because he couldn't imagine losing love twice in one lifetime.

Dunn paused while tears ran down his face. "If you didn't do it, I don't know why you are here today, but I know why *I'm* here today. I am here because I need to forgive somebody."

As we walked out of the prison, past rows and rows of razor wire on the eighteen-thousand-acre penitentiary, I realized that Warrick Dunn was a living testament to the fact that if harnessed, adversity can fuel true Greatness. More than one hundred families who now have homes thanks to Dunn's dedication to his mother's memory can testify to that.

The truly Great find opportunity in the worst of times. Dunn will be the first to tell you that he would not have created a foundation to provide homes to single mothers if he hadn't lost his. "My mother used to tell me that adversity can make you bitter or better," said Dunn. "She always encouraged me to do better."

More from the Truly Great

Adversity can take many forms—and bring out Greatness within each of us that may have never even known that we possessed.

One of Dunn's Athletes for Hope partners, Mario Lemieux, has faced intense adversity in his life. Lemieux, whose last name means "the best" in French, has been nothing less for the Pittsburgh Penguins. Dubbed "Super Mario" even before being the National Hockey League's No. 1 draft pick in 1984, Lemieux turned the sad-sack Penguins into winners, scoring a goal on the first shift of his first game. He turned the Penguins around and led them to back-to-back Stanley Cup championships in 1991 and 1992.

But he didn't do it without adversity. Nagging back problems began in the late 1980s and escalated. By the time he earned his second Stanley Cup, he'd already undergone surgery for a herniated disk. The pain continued. Lemieux had a second back surgery and a rare bone infection in 1993. He couldn't even bend over to tie his skates, but he played through the pain.

In January that year, Lemieux was also diagnosed with Hodgkin's disease, a form of cancer. He wasn't going to let it stop him. He missed twenty-four games while undergoing radiation, returned to the ice the very same day of his last treatment. In Super Mario fashion, he scored a goal in his return and won the fourth scoring title of the year that season, even though he had missed two months' worth of games. For Lemieux, playing through adversity was the only way he knew.

"That's just the way I am," he told the *Washington Times.* "I have a strong will to be the best in the world. I drew a lot of strength from that."

Lemieux retired in 1997, unable to play up to the level he'd set for himself. At thirty-one, he'd suffered a lifetime of injuries and come back from cancer. He'd won six scoring titles, four MVP trophies, and two Stanley Cups, and had been named the MVP of the playoffs both times. The Hockey Hall of Fame waived the mandatory three-year waiting period for induction and welcomed him immediately in 1997.

A hockey hero in Pittsburgh, Lemieux missed playing. But when his four-year-old son asked his dad if he'd been any good, it was the reminder he needed that his pain could either rule him, or could make him stronger.

Lemieux returned after an emotional ceremony in which his retired jersey was lowered from the rafters. Reminiscent of his first NHL game, the player-owner assisted on a goal on his very first shift. From 2000 to 2005, Lemieux went on to score 77 goals and added 152 assists in 170 games. He also captained Canada's Olympic and World Cup teams to gold medals in 2002 and 2004.

Committed to Pittsburgh, the Mario Lemieux Foundation gave $5 million to the University of Pittsburgh Medical Center and $2 million to the Children's Home of Pittsburgh. The Foundation has also established playrooms for children at Pennsylvania hospitals.

Lemieux eventually re-retired at forty after dominating the sport for parts of three decades despite the adversity of multiple setbacks. He stepped away as a player seventh in all-time scoring with 1,723 points and eighth on the list with 690 goals. He's now owner of the team, and in 2009 became the first person to win the Stanley Cup as both a player and an owner.

His determination not to let circumstances defeat him have made him a Great player and given him an even Greater career the second time around.

Nick Springer was a typical fourteen-year-old growing up on Long Island. He loved playing hockey and spending time with his friends. But then tragedy struck in the form of bacterial meningitis while he was at summer camp in Massachusetts. Suddenly, his entire world changed.

After being airlifted from a local hospital to the Pediatric Trauma Unit in Springfield, Nick was administered last rites, as doctors were doubtful he would survive the night. The last thing he remembers was saying good-bye to his mother over the phone as his parents rushed to be by his side.

Two months later, as he faded in and out of consciousness while waking from a medically induced coma, his family tried to gently explain what had happened to him. Finally, when he was fully awake, they waited for Nick to realize his situation. It was important to the family that Nick be the one to feel ownership of his situation. But when he told them that he understood both his legs and hands had been amputated, his reaction shocked them. "I'm going to be okay," he assured them from his hospital bed.

"After something like this, a mourning period is natural," Nick's father explained. "We were always waiting for that." But it never came. Still every bit as energetic and positive as he'd been before the disease, Nick returned to his new life with humor and passion. When a family friend visited his hospital room, Nick jokingly greeted her with: "Quick—how many fingers am I holding up?" His main motivation for healing and rehab was to get ready for the upcoming hockey season. He didn't have time for self-pity; he was determined to embrace what the family called their "new normal" and get on with his life.

While sitting outside at the Boston Marathon, where some friends were running to raise money for his family, Nick started talking to a man in a wheelchair wearing a jacket with "Sled Hockey" emblazoned on the back. It turned out that the sport was a version of regular hockey adapted for people with physical disabilities. A few months later, Nick was playing on a local team and grinning like mad every time he took to the ice.

Not long after that, a teammate suggested that Nick try wheelchair rugby, another adapted sport. While he wasn't initially interested at first, since hockey was his first love, his family urged him to give it a shot, and it quickly became apparent that Nick had a natural talent for it.

But it wasn't just the physical activity and competitive drive on the field that helped Nick grow; he was also inspired by the challenges that his teammates regularly issued to one another with their fervor for living full lives. "So many people with disabilities are used to being coddled," Nick explained. "But on the team, everyone treats each other as equals." If one player took an especially hard hit, he would hoist himself back into his chair without any help. No one pulled punches or softened throws. The matches were a celebration of all that the players were able to do with no room for focusing on what they couldn't. After looking around, Nick noticed that none of the other players were in motorized wheelchairs, like the kind he had from the hospital, so he ditched his high-tech wheels ("Those are for *really* disabled people!") and switched to a manual chair.

Now, almost ten years later, Nick has an impressive résumé to back up his can-do attitude. In 2008, he traveled to Beijing, where he was part of the gold medal US Paralympic Wheelchair Rugby team in the Paralympic Games. His teams have also won the Canada Cup in 2006 and 2008; the North American Cup in 2006 (they came in second in 2008); and gold medals in both the 2005 World Wheelchair Games in Rio de Janiero, Brazil, and World Wheelchair Rugby Championships in Christchurch, New Zealand.

"There's a lot of good that came out of it...I don't know of many other people who would have gone to the Olympics. I sure as hell wouldn't," he said. And when people ask if he ever thinks about how his life has changed, he has a similar outlook. "It's really kind of hard to say what would have happened, but I'm pretty happy with the way my life is now, so why worry about it?"

And for the Truly Great in Business

Rough times can shape tremendous people.

One of the earliest employees of Intel, Hungarian-born Andrew Grove, suffered severe hearing loss as a result of scarlet fever as a child. As a young man of 20, he also lost his home and most of his belongings when his family fled their home country during the Hungarian Revolution of 1956. Starting his life over again in New York City, Grove went on to earn a Ph.D. in engineering and later helped transform Intel into an international leader in microprocessors. During his time as president and CEO, Grove grew the company to become the most valuable company in the world.

Despite the unlikely beginnings of this billionaire engineer, Grove insisted that it was the early adversity in his life that made all the difference. He credited his achievements on the mental alertness that he developed as a young man who knew how quickly circumstances could change. "Success breeds complacency. Complacency breeds failure," he explained in good humor. "Only the paranoid survive."

Patricia C. Dunn (no relation to Warrick Dunn), former chairwoman of Hewlett-Packard, knows a thing or two about battling adversity, too. In 2006, having already survived breast cancer, melanoma, and ovarian cancer, it was found that the ovarian cancer had returned and spread to her liver. At the same time she was undergoing surgery and renewed chemotherapy, felony charges were brought against her in an HP eavesdropping case. She resigned her position as chairwoman out of respect for the company; but rather than letting the legal proceedings take their course while she dealt with treatment, she decided to fight the charges and refused a plea bargain to take one misdemeanor in place of the four felonies levied against her. She'd already faced death so many times that a courtroom was hardly daunting.

In the end, as a result of her dogged determination to stand and fight, all charges were dropped and her name was cleared. Now, Dunn serves on the board of several international business research councils, as well as working as an advisory board member to the UC Berkeley Haas School of Business and as the executive director of a support program for Larkin Street Youth Services in San Francisco.

The challenges she stared down—and defeated—gave her the strength and experience to help others.

Sometimes, disappointing results can be turned around just by looking at them differently. In 1968, when Spencer Silver wanted to create a new, strong adhesive, he instead came up with a weak one that could only hold two pages together and pulled off easily. Many would have written it down as a failure, and Silver himself was initially bothered by his inability to solve the problem the way he'd wanted to, but the 3M scientist also mentioned it in his seminars for years, trying to figure out a use for it.

One day, a colleague named Arthur Fry, who'd been fed up with page markers that kept falling out of his books, attended one of Silver's talks. He thought about his page marker problem and tried Silver's adhesive on paper to use as a bookmark. The adhesive was strong enough to hold a bookmark in place, but weak enough to be pulled off again without tearing either the marker or the page. Spencer Silver's initial "failure" fueled Arthur Fry's creation of the Post-It note.

Adversity, be it in life, health, business, or any other realm, can be the distinguishing factor between a successful leader and an unsuccessful one. It can give us a different kind of insight, as it did for Andrew Grove. It can strengthen and embolden us to fight, like it did for Warrick Dunn. And it can teach us how to transform disappointments into Great success, like it did for Spencer Silver and Arthur Fry.

The GREATNESS Challenge

Adversity is one of the most potent forces in life, one that can bring out your best or your worse. Ultimately, it's up to you. How will you handle obstacles? Will they be roadblocks or springboards?

Consider this unlikely ascent to Greatness: In 1922, when Ernest Hemingway was still struggling to get published, a suitcase containing almost all of his drafts and manuscripts was lost on a train. Left with only two stories out of all of his efforts, Hemingway was crushed. But upon the advice of his good friend and already-established author Ezra Pound, he re-created all he could of what had been lost, and in so doing established one of his stylistic trademarks—bare-bones language and a simple, journalistic tone.

Hemingway later recounted that the event that had seemed so tragic to him at the time was actually a launching point for his career.

It gave him a chance to approach his work all over again, keeping only what was good and forgetting about the extraneous or mediocre parts that editors felt were keeping his stories from being Great.

Rather than throwing in the towel when he was faced with a seemingly insurmountable challenge, and thus robbing the twentieth century of one of its most important literary voices, Hemingway listened to Pound's encouragement and used the devastating situation as something to make his work stronger.

Has something similar ever happened to you? Think about a time when you've had a failure or difficult period in life. Can you think of three things you've learned from it? Does it seem as bad now as it did at the time?

Consider how many times you've dealt with a computer crash or an unexpected power outage while working on an important document. In the headache of re-creating your work, did you ever find you emerged with a new insight or a deeper understanding of it? In revisiting all of the information, did you ever come across a mistake in the data, such as some numbers being totaled wrong or a point that needed clarifying? Just as Hemingway's losing his suitcase helped him hone his craft, think about some of the minor challenges you encounter during the day that can actually serve to grow your knowledge or help you create a better finished product.

As the old expression goes, "That which does not kill us makes us stronger." Remember, muscles can be built up only by being worked, stretched, and forced beyond their current capacity. The process can be exhausting, but it is the only way to grow. Strength is born out of pain.

When adversity comes your way, look at it for the opportunity it may be providing you. A lost job can create a new career path… but only if you're willing to open your eyes to that possibility. Remember the words of Helen Keller: "When one door of happiness closes, another opens; but often we look so long at the closed door that we do not see the one which has been opened for us."

Every person faces all sizes and kinds of adversity every day, whether internal, like depression, disability, poor health, or a battle with addiction; or external, like a natural disaster, family difficulties, or even just a canceled flight. No matter how big or small your challenges may be, don't let them control and define your day or your life.

Think about one or two of the most difficult challenges of your life, and count how many positive things ultimately came out of the experience. Each may not have been evident immediately, but perhaps a broadened perspective, a new friendship, or a different opportunity resulted from what seemed to be a huge setback or devastating circumstance.

Everyone has big changes in their lives. The changes can be happy, like marriages and promotions; or difficult, like health problems and job losses. Everyone will experience three to nine of these turning points in their lifetimes, says Dick Biggs, a productivity consultant to Fortune 500 companies. Biggs explains that while some people have a "cease and desist" mentality, these turning points can provide perspective and the ability to look at those life changes within the bigger picture and let time heal. "By learning from your turning points," Biggs says, "you can grow at a deeper level within your career and life."

When you come face to face with setbacks, you must use your resources to create opportunities. Your problems have no minds of their own—so outsmart them. Think of one hardship that has been weighing on your mind lately and take it head-on.

Adversity is assured for all of us. It does not matter where you're from or who you are. It is the one thing we all have in common. You might not face the level of adversity that Warrick Dunn, Mario Lemieux, or Nick Springer went through, but something will come your way. How you deal with it, how you bring your inner fire to the forefront to push through—that is what measures your Greatness.

Your reaction to adversity shapes your character, clarifies your priorities, and can fuel your path to Greatness.

PILLAR THREE

How They Work

CHAPTER

9

Ice in Their Veins

They are risk takers and don't fear making a mistake.

For IndyCar driver Danica Patrick, putting everything on the line is just the way it goes. She was only twelve when she suffered her first real crash. Two years after she began go-kart racing competitively, Patrick was coming around the final turn of the national event in Charlotte, North Carolina. Relentless and gunning toward the finish line, she moved to pass the leading driver on the inside—the same driver who had bumped her off the course and from first place to third the lap before.

Patrick didn't win that race, and neither did her competitor, future three-time IndyCar title winner Sam Hornish Jr. But as Patrick hit the gas pedal, tagged his bumper, and soared up and over Sam before crashing on top of him, Patrick made one thing very clear: for her, backing down was never an option.

"I was going to get [the victory] or crash trying," she said. Patrick has been a fearless competitor ever since. Her need for speed and desire to win took her from kart racing as a girl to Rookie of the

Year in her first season as an IndyCar driver.

"My father taught me to do whatever it takes to win as long as it was within the boundaries of the rules," Patrick wrote in her autobiography, *Crossing the Line.* "He taught me to push the limits, so that I could break down barriers."

Pushing the limits doesn't come without risks—especially at speeds exceeding 220 mph—but for Patrick, it's all in a day's work. She has ice in her veins. Without risks, there are no rewards. It was a lesson she would have to learn again in the pros.

Racing in her first Indianapolis 500, Patrick became the first woman ever to lead the prestigious race. Afraid, however, that she wouldn't have enough fuel to finish the race, let alone win, she pulled off the throttle and settled for fourth.

"Not going for the victory in '05 is the single greatest regret of my life," Patrick said. "I promise you, I won't ever do that again. What's the point of putting yourself through a tiresome, grueling, four-hour race if you're not on the track to taste victory?"

Since then, amidst controversy and criticism in a male-dominated field, Patrick has spent most of her career testing the boundaries of her sport with plenty of crashes, accidents, and mistakes along the way. And in doing so, the five-foot-two, one-hundred-pound fireball has been called everything from "reckless" to "unworthy" by her critics.

"Male or female, there is no substitute for talent," said Bobby Rahal, the first team owner to take a chance on Patrick. "She not only wants the challenge, she looks for it. That's what champions do. They are not afraid and they don't shy from difficult times."

On April 20, 2008, Patrick finally broke through in Motegi, Japan, and became the first female driver in history to win an IndyCar race. She finished third at the Indianapolis 500 in 2009, the highest finish for a female in that race. Patrick shifted her career from the IndyCar series to the NASCAR Nationwide Series and NASCAR Sprint Cup Series in 2010. In 2013, she became the first woman to finish a NASCAR Sprint Cup Series Pole, and she also finished in eighth place at the Daytona 500 that same year.

Danica Patrick lives her life on the edge, and the road to victory wasn't easy. She's not reckless, she's not overly aggressive, and she's certainly not fearful. The key to her success is that she continues to take risks in spite of her failures. She continues to push the envelope.

She told me in an interview the only thing that would cost her a shot at victory was fear. Fear and failure often walk hand in hand. Without fear, you know no limits. But failure is not something to avoid. If you let it, failure can be a great teacher. Mistakes can be accounted for and learned from.

The truly Great, like Patrick, have ice in their veins. They are risk takers and don't fear making a mistake.

The key is that once you've realized you've made a mistake, you simply move on. Don't dwell on it. Fail fast and go forward. Risks are everywhere in life, and you won't get far without taking them. You may win, you may lose—or even crash—but if you want to be the best at what you do, you've got to go for it. If you ease off the throttle, others will leave you in the dust on their way to the checkered flag of your profession.

Everyone wants to experience the kind of success Great risk takers achieve when their gambles pay off, but few have the courage to face the failures necessary to achieve such Greatness.

More from the Truly Great

No one can dispute Brett Favre's lofty credentials as an NFL quarterback. The nineteen-year veteran won the Associated Press Most Valuable Player three consecutive times and led the Packers to seven division championships and two NFC championships. He was named to eleven Pro Bowl games and won one Super Bowl.

Widely considered to be one of the best quarterbacks of all time, Favre holds many NFL records, including most career touchdown passes, most career passing yards, most completions, most pass attempts, and most victories as a starting quarterback. But while the number of touchdowns Favre threw may be his crowning achievement, it's another league record that defines his path to Greatness.

Throughout the span of his long career, Favre threw over three hundred interceptions, the most in the league. But Favre didn't let the fact that he misfired more times than any other quarterback bother him: "If I hadn't set the interception record, there's no way I would have ever set the touchdown record. I was never the best player on the field, so I had to try the hardest."

Favre became successful because he was a risk taker. It was the interceptions as much as the touchdowns that made him a great player. He was a fearless playmaker who took chances on the field and, in turn, made a difference. For every mistake Favre made, he followed it with three or four outstanding plays. In an era of conservative and precise game-managing quarterbacks, it was his willingness to take risks that allowed him to lead the Green Bay Packers to a win in Super Bowl XXXI.

"If I had my way there would be no punting on fourth down; no throwaway passes," Favre said in a 1997 Nike commercial. "I would never be told to slide or step out of bounds. Safeties would learn to fear my footsteps."

And that was exactly how Favre played. Everyone wants to experience the kind of success he had, but few have the courage to face the failures necessary to achieve such Greatness.

Nolan Ryan never feared making a mistake, either. Ryan, who was drafted in the twelfth round by the New York Mets in 1965, grew quickly into a power pitcher whose fastballs often topped 100 mph—an incredible feat he was able to maintain well into his 40s.

Ryan went on to play a record twenty-seven seasons in the majors and finished his career as an eight-time All-Star selection. His 5,714 strikeouts, 7 no-hitters, and 6.56 hits allowed per nine innings are also tops in Major League Baseball history. He beat every team in both leagues and, among active pitchers, was first in wins, strikeouts, innings pitched, shutouts, and starts.

But the almost unanimously selected Hall of Fame hurler didn't accomplish these impressive feats by being a perfectionist.

Ryan also holds records of several less glamorous statistical categories, including most bases on balls (2,795) and most wild pitches (277). He is just one of two pitchers in MLB history to give up 10 career grand-slam home runs, ranks third all-time in losses, and ninth all-time in hit batters.

Through it all, however, Ryan will unquestionably be remembered as one of the Greatest and most dominant pitchers of his time. He was a strikeout pitcher whose big arm and "high risk, high reward" style put fear in the hearts of batters who hoped to touch Ryan's fastball, let alone hit it.

Targeting the strike zone with 100 mph fastballs against big-league hitters, Ryan came in knowing that any one of those pitches, when struck the right way, could easily find its way out of the ballpark. In a game in which every run has the potential to decide who wins and who loses, Ryan put himself on the line with each and every pitch.

And that's why Ryan crushed Major League Baseball's strikeout record—he wasn't afraid to make mistakes. He had the guts to put everything he had into every pitch, whether that pitch would result in a strike, a ball, a hit, or a home run.

Imagine the history that would be lost if Brett Favre had called it quits after his first NFL pass was intercepted and returned for a touchdown by the other team. What if Nolan Ryan had shied away from his fastball after giving up his first grand slam?

Favre and Ryan were able to throw more touchdown passes and more strikeouts, respectively, than anyone else in history because they were ready and willing to put everything on the line if it meant giving their team a chance to win. For them, it was never about their own personal failures, but the team's success. You don't want to be the guy who throws the most interceptions or the most bases on balls, but if by taking chances your team racks up more wins than losses, so be it.

Facing the possibility of failure—and embracing the challenge anyway—is the stuff of truly Great winners, like Michael Jordan. As a high school sophomore, he got cut from the varsity basketball team; he was 5foot 11 at the time, and the coach opted to keep a 6-foot-7 player named Lamar Smith instead. Stung, Jordan went home and began practicing in earnest the next day. He promised himself he'd never make an excuse for finishing second, and he spent the next year getting ready to make the team as a junior.

The rest is, quite literally, history. Over his fifteen-year professional career, Jordan racked up 32,292 points and holds more NBA records and team records than any other player in basketball. When he joined the Hall of Fame, he made sure Lamar Smith attended the ceremony. During his acceptance speech, Jordan thanked Smith and said he wouldn't have had such an illustrious career had he not been driven to succeed as a sophomore.

It was Jordan's early introduction to pushing past failure that inspired him to victory. "I've missed more than 9,000 shots in my career," Jordan once said. "I've lost almost 300 games—26 times, I've been trusted to take the game winning shot and missed. I've failed over and over and over again in my life, and that is why I succeed."

Bethany Hamilton may be one of the Greatest examples of a person who doesn't shy away from risk. On the morning of October 31, 2003, the thirteen-year-old surfing champion was catching some waves with friends when a fifteen-foot tiger shark bit off her left arm only two inches below her shoulder. After losing 60 percent of her body's blood and spending seven days in the hospital for surgery and recovery, Bethany was committed to making a full recovery.

Less than one month after the shark attack, she was back in the ocean with a custom-made surf board designed to help her relearn how to balance and maneuver. Whereas most people might have been too afraid to ever venture near the beach again, Hamilton knew that the only way to achieve her dream of going pro was to get back out there and try again without letting fear stand in her way. "Courage, sacrifice, determination, commitment, toughness, heart, talent, guts," she wrote in her book *Soul Surfer,* which was released as a movie in 2011. "That's what little girls are made of; the heck with sugar and spice."

Consider the long list of Great ones who embrace this same fearless attitude:

Babe Ruth always swung big. Going into every at bat, Ruth knew he was going to hit big or miss big—and he was okay with that. He wanted to live life as fully and with as much drive as he could. And, to this day, Ruth remains one of baseball's Greatest icons.

Jerry West learned early on in his career that he wouldn't get much done in life if he only worked on the days he felt good. One of the best players in NBA history, West knew that to be successful he had to have a short memory. If he took a bad shot or his jumper simply wasn't falling, he forgot about it and moved on to the next play. He worked harder to get open, took better shots, and got to the foul line but—most important—he never stopped shooting.

Phil Mickelson has made plenty of mistakes, but he never shies away from attempting the difficult shots that could make or break his round. He may drive it into the trees or end up in the deep rough, but he always gives himself a chance and he's almost always in contention. He's confident going into every swing and he doesn't fear making a mistake. And why should he? The aggressive play that has left him in the hazards so many times has helped him master his short game and perfect the shots he needs to save par.

Dan Gable finished his collegiate wrestling career at Iowa State with a record of 118–1, and every match he had a target on his back. He was the guy whom everyone wanted to beat, but Gable was famous for never worrying whether or not his opponent could do it. Instead, he focused on whether or not he would allow himself to lose by playing it safe. Gable went on to win a gold medal wrestling in the 1972 Olympic Games in Munich, Germany, and did so without giving up a single point to his opponents.

Chris Moneymaker was a nobody, but he won his way to the World Series of Poker through a series of online tournaments. With an aggressive approach, Moneymaker bluffed and gambled his way all the way to the final table and found himself playing heads up for the title and a $2.5 million dollar prize with poker pro Sam Farha. In the game's defining moment, and with an absolutely worthless hand, Moneymaker went all in on a bluff and stole the pot. A few hands later, his courage to risk it all on poker's biggest stage was rewarded with a WSOP title bracelet and a place in poker history.

Annika Sorenstam is often criticized for her attempts to make it on the men's PGA Tour. Sorenstam never did make the cut, but that never kept her from trying or discouraged her in the face of what so many media pundits determined to be almost certain failure. A dominant player in the LPGA, Sorenstam could have been content as one of the best women's golfers in the world—but she wasn't. She was brave enough to make a pass at an even Greater challenge.

And that's exactly what one coach did with the big game on the line. Down 10–6 at halftime in Super Bowl XLIV, New Orleans Saints coach Sean Payton took a chance. When the Saints kicked off to open the third quarter, Payton made the call for an onside kick, and the Saints recovered it. New Orleans scored on the ensuing drive and took the lead for the first time in the game.

"Our head coach is unbelievable," Saints quarterback Drew Brees said. "An aggressive play caller, a confident play caller, a guy who can instill those things into his players."

As the second quarter wound down, New Orleans was close to the 1-yard line on fourth down. Down by a touchdown at the time, most coaches would have been content for the easy field goal. Instead, Payton called for a running play, but the Saints got stuffed and didn't move the ball. The risky move failed, but Payton refused to give it up. New Orleans got the ball back and scored a field goal before the end of the half, and Payton came out with the onside kick call.

Payton wasn't afraid to take a risk, and even when he failed, he tried again. The onside kick surprised the Colts and the spectators, but it wasn't an uncalculated move. Payton had researched Indianapolis's coverage and knew he had a good chance to get the ball, take the lead, and change the momentum.

Payton's gutsy call was the first time an onside kick had been used outside the fourth quarter of the Super Bowl. The Saints stole the lead, gained momentum and went on to win the game, 31–17, over the favored Indianapolis Colts. The coach wasn't afraid to take a risk—even when he'd previously failed. Taking a risk lead to Super Bowl Greatness.

And for the Truly Great in Business

Media mogul Ted Turner is known for his exceptional willingness to embrace risk. Already a savvy local media provider, in December 1976 he launched the nation's first superstation by broadcasting from a $750,000 transmission antenna based in Atlanta. It was a gamble, since cable television was a brand-new technology and the number of homes wired for such a service was limited. But Turner calculated the risk and knew it would pay off if he was at the forefront of the next wave of media technology. His station's signal could be picked up by other television stations across the country; in eight years he had 36 million viewers, and Turner Industries was worth an estimated $70 million. At that same time, he also purchased the Atlanta Braves baseball franchise in order to ensure that his stations always had sports programming to air.

In 1980, he launched the Cable News Network. CNN was an enormous financial investment, and most experts predicted the experiment would fail. Americans were used to their evening news—who would want it twenty-four hours a day? But Turner's risk paid off, and his empire continued to grow as he acquired more networks and teams. In 1986, against the advice of all his advisors, he purchased Metro-Goldwyn-Mayer's film library, which would allow him to broadcast the movies on his stations. And in 1995, Turner Broadcasting merged with Time Warner for a deal that was worth $7.5 billion for Turner's company. By the end of the decade, Turner's risk-taking had resulted in him being the largest private land owner in the United States and a personal net worth of $2 billion.

Ford Motor took a great risk when, in 2009, it refused the government bailout money offered to the major American auto manufacturers that were famously deemed "too big to fail" in the struggling economy. It was a tremendous risk to bypass the loan that would have meant an immediate infusion of cash for the company, but the current Ford CEO at the time Alan Mullaly (retired in 2014) knew that public perception mattered. Though turning down the loan was a gamble, it sent a message to consumers that Ford was not in dire straits like its competitors General Motors and Chrysler. It also sidestepped the political backlash from many Americans who were unhappy about the taxpayer-funded program. The risk paid off and, in February 2010, Ford's sales moved ahead of GM's for the first time in more than ten years.

T. Boone Pickens is as famous for his failed aspirations as his successful ones. A leader in the oil and natural gas industry, he became a popular figure in the media in the 1980s for his aggressive attempts to purchase at least six other competing companies, as well as fostering presidential ambitions. Though many of his efforts failed, the deals he was able to broker were highly lucrative investments, which he was able to parlay into even bigger producers.

Now, with speculative mineral and water rights purchases, as well as being an outspoken proponent of alternative energies such as solar and wind power, Pickens is respected as one of the most vocal and innovative thinkers in the energy industry. Bold and unpredictable decision making is a large component of his success, he insists: "I've always believed that it's important to show a new look periodically. Predictability can lead to failure."

The GREATNESS Challenge

Are you afraid to fail? When given the chance, do you have the courage to pursue opportunity and leave your comfort zone behind? As an employee, are you willing to put yourself out there with new suggestions or creative techniques? As an employer, are you willing to let your employees try their hand at something new and, if necessary, learn and grow through their mistakes?

Think of a time when an opportunity presented itself and you *didn't* take it. Why didn't you? What were the circumstances? What would you do differently if you could do it all over again?

Great winners hate to lose, but when they do, it's never in vain. The fact is that you can learn more from a loss than you do from a victory. Mistakes translate into experience, and those who gain valuable experience early in their careers will have the potential to be more successful in the long run.

Just as he pushed past disappointment when his ideas didn't work, Thomas Edison also embraced the possibility of failure. In his efforts to create the lightbulb, Edison is said to have experimented 586 times before he got it right. But when his assistant told him it was a shame they tried so many times and failed, Edison countered, "No, we have only found 586 ways that won't work and won't be tried again." Edison didn't see a setback as failure at all; he saw it as a learning opportunity. "I am not discouraged, because every wrong attempt discarded is another step forward," he said.

Is there a risk you've taken in the past that paid off? What prompted you to make the decision to go for it? How about a risk you took that failed? Would you take that risk again?

Start-up companies often prefer a leader who has a failed business venture on their résumé rather than one who does not. Those who have failed know how to avoid future failures, while those with a perfect track record may not recognize the dangers that lie ahead.

And the ones who have failed understand that there is life on the other side of it. Pick yourself up from failure quickly. Sometimes, risks don't pay off—but don't ever let that keep you from trying again. Get up as soon as you can and dedicate your energy to moving on to the next goal rather than dwelling on past mistakes, and don't be afraid to take a risk on something you believe in.

Thomas Watson, founder of IBM, once said, "If you want to increase your success rate, then double your failure rate." The first step to finding more success is trying new and innovative things. Doing that, he said with confidence, will almost assuredly produce record failures.

How you deal with failure is ultimately what will help you succeed. Once you've failed, running right back onto the field with confidence is the key to success. The question is, do you have the courage to face failure and learn from your mistakes?

Think of courage as a muscle. The more you develop and strengthen it by putting yourself out there, the more willing you will be to fail. The more you are willing to fail, the more success you will find.

If you have an idea that you believe will improve the way you do business, give it a try. If it fails, try something else. It sounds simple, but most of us are so afraid of failure that we never act on innovative ideas.

Risks are everywhere in life and cannot truly be avoided. As explained in an anonymous quote: "To love is to risk not being loved in return. To hope is to risk pain. To try is to risk failure, but risk must be taken because the greatest hazard in life is to risk nothing."

Simply put, to avoid risk is to avoid life. There are times when we have to take risks. We often have to take action or make decisions based on the information at hand. We're never going to have all the answers, and, as a result, we're going to make mistakes. Hindsight is 20/20, as the cliché goes, and it's absolutely true. But in reality, there is usually more gray area than the comfortable clarity of black-and-white.

Try new ideas around the office just to see if they work—especially if they come from a promising employee or colleague looking for a chance to be more involved. Everyone wants to feel like they are a part of the team, and when given the chance, people will surprise you.

"Those who dare to fail miserably can achieve greatly," John F. Kennedy once said. "There are risks and costs to action, but they are far less than the long-range risks of comfortable inaction," he later added. Don't allow yourself to fall prey to the temptation of comfortable inaction.

But, remember, taking risks doesn't mean taking shots in the dark. There are times when risks will pay off and times when they won't. Renowned author and sports psychologist Bob Rotella says there's a fine line between taking risks and playing recklessly. "A player who's playing to play great loves a great drive more than he fears the rough," Rotella says. "He likes making putts more than he cares about three-putting." But it doesn't mean taking shots you know you can't make or firing at sucker pins you know you can't hit.

Search for and evaluate areas in your life and in your business where you could afford to take more chances. Maybe that means taking a chance on a potential hire or trusting someone with a project you would normally handle yourself. What might you lose? What could you gain?

It may seem like a tough concept to grasp—the window of opportunity in which to take risks—but as you gain experience and become more comfortable with failure as a stepping stone to success, you will benefit more by taking calculated risks in your quest for Greatness.

CHAPTER

10

When All Else Fails

The truly Great know how—and when—to adjust their game plan.

Any athlete who's ever played in a best-of-seven series knows the hardest game to win is the fourth. It's the clincher. Without it, there is no championship.

Even with three wins, nothing is guaranteed. So when the Chicago Bulls led the Utah Jazz three games to two in the 1998 NBA Finals, the team knew it couldn't take anything for granted.

The Bulls were not only one game away from a win, but also two losses away from losing the series and championship, and the five-time NBA champions trailed 86–83 with fewer than forty seconds remaining in the game.

Michael Jordan took the inbounds pass, went straight to the basket, and hit a lay-up over the Utah defenders to cut the deficit to one. The Jazz took the ball downcourt and passed it to all-star forward Karl Malone. Although Dennis Rodman was guarding Malone, Jordan slipped behind him and swatted the ball away to come up with the steal.

Calmly, Jordan dribbled the ball upcourt. At the top of the key, he paused momentarily. He eyed his defender and, with fewer than ten seconds left on the clock, made his move.

With complete grace, Jordan dribbled to his right before crossing over and stepping back to his left. He cleared his defender, now off balance, with his left hand before pulling up from the top of the key. With pure perfection, the ball soared up and in, hitting nothing but the net. As the horn sounded, the Bulls won their sixth NBA title and Jordan his sixth Finals MVP.

Today, Michael Jordan is a living legend. His clutch performance in the game against Utah was just one of the many times Jordan's late-game heroics saved the day and left his opponents helpless.

But it wasn't always that way. Yes, Michael was always talented. He was always considered one of the most athletically dominant players of his era, and he was always able to dunk on nearly any defender. But for him, that wasn't good enough. He chose to take his game from good to Great.

Some fourteen years before, a twenty-one-year-old Michael came into the league at 210 pounds, seemingly able to fly through the air—and hang there. He became an instant celebrity and was named Rookie of the Year. But it wasn't until seven years later that he won his first NBA championship, and he was in his mid-thirties by the time he beat Utah in 1998.

Jordan learned that high-flying dunks brought fame but not necessarily wins. He learned that he could score forty points a game, but in order to win a title he would need to get more out of himself and his teammates.

"Talent wins games, but teamwork and intelligence wins championships," Jordan would often say as he matured.

The turning point came in 1991. The previous three seasons, Chicago's archrival, the Detroit Pistons, had knocked Jordan and the Bulls out of the playoffs. But by the 1991 playoffs, Jordan had adapted. Through constant practice, he had developed one of the most deadly jump shots in the league. He had also learned how to use his teammates, and he knew what he had to do to make them better.

This time around, Detroit's defense was no match for Jordan's new-and-improved arsenal. He picked apart their double teams by finding open teammates, and when they didn't double him, he stepped back and hit tough shots.

By changing his game—giving his teammates what they really needed rather than what looked great on television—Jordan took his game, and his team, to the next level. That year, he won his first championship ring.

Yes, Michael Jordan could still dunk with the best in the NBA, but for the Bulls to begin their championship run, it couldn't be the center of his game any longer. To win, the Bulls needed a floor general, and Jordan took on the challenge. When his team needed him most, Jordan adapted. He turned weaknesses into strengths and elevated his game—and his team—to an elite level.

Jordan knew every season and every game would require him to do something different from before. His talent was tremendous, but it was Michael's ability to adjust his game plan that truly made him the Greatest basketball player of all time.

Because, when all else fails, the truly Great know how and when to adjust their game plan. Adapting yourself and your skill set to meet new challenges is similarly important. In a fast-paced world that changes by the day, you can't afford to be one-dimensional, or to simply do the things you were good at last year.

More from the Truly Great

When he began his career in 1986, Andre Agassi was a rebel. A young gun with a mullet instead of a clean-cut look, Agassi's wardrobe looked better under a black light in a techno club than it did on the tennis court or in a country club. Rather than following a strict regimen of healthy eating, he boasted that the staple of his diet was the cheeseburger.

On the court, Agassi was known for an aggressive style in which he tried to overpower his opponents with sharp-angled shots. His extraordinary reaction time and hand-eye coordination allowed him to play the ball inside the baseline and put his opponents on the defensive.

He was good back then—good enough to dominate a young Pete Sampras—but he was also naïve. After the match, Agassi said he felt sorry for Sampras because he was never going to make it. Sampras proved otherwise when he upset an overly confident Agassi in the 1990 US Open final and went on to become the No. 1 player in the world. He would also become Agassi's biggest rival.

But the turning point in Agassi's career came after the 1997 season in which Agassi didn't win a single major title and sank to a world ranking of No. 122 to end the year. Humbled, Agassi was forced to reevaluate his game and his mentality. He emerged as a better player and a better person, winning five titles in ten finals and earning a newfound respect from his peers. By season's end, Agassi ranked No. 6 in the world, the highest jump into the top ten by any player in a calendar year in the history of tennis.

Over the course of his career, Agassi's game continued to evolve into something better. As a young rebel, Agassi looked to end matches with flashy moves. As a rising star, Agassi developed a backhand drop shot and became more tactical and more consistent. As a seasoned veteran, an oft-injured Agassi committed to an exhausting off-season conditioning program that allowed him to both outplay and outlast his opponents.

By 2005, 35-year-old Agassi was again among the world's best. An improbable run in the US Open led Agassi to another tournament final—three years after his archrival Sampras had hung up his racket and retired—where he would face a top-ranked and increasingly dominant twenty-three-year-old named Roger Federer.

"I've been motivated by overcoming challenge and overcoming the hurdles and obstacles that face me," Agassi said during his run at the year's US Open. "There still is plenty out there to get motivated by."

Although Federer won the well-contested final, Agassi's legacy had already been set in stone. With eight Grand Slam titles and sixteen seasons of top-ten finishes, he achieved Greatness because he grew to understand how and when to adjust his game plan.

"I question myself every day," Agassi once said. "That's what I still find motivating about this. I don't have the answers, [and] I don't pretend that I do just because I won the match."

Instead of attempting to win points with a single swing, Agassi learned to pass up dramatic, game-winning power shots in favor of more conservative shots that kept his opponents on the run and reduced his own unforced errors. An experienced Agassi no longer saw Sampras as a bitter rival, but as someone who enhanced his career by pushing him to play his best tennis.

"I think I've always had the shots," Agassi explained, as his career began to peak, "but in the past, I've suffered too many mental lapses. Now, I'm starting to get away from that and my mental discipline and commitment to the game are much better. I think I'm really taking a good look at the big picture. That's the difference between being around for the final or watching the final from my sofa at home."

Andre Agassi made major adjustments to both his approach and his game plan over the years that allowed him to be a contender for two decades.

The 1985–1986 Louisiana State University Tigers' leap from No. 11 to make the Final Four—the first of only two teams ever to make it so far from such a low ranking—is a perfect example of how adaptation can lead to Greatness. After a season plagued with injuries and illness, coach Dale Brown needed to figure out a way to make the most of his players' talents, even though the constantly shifting lineup made it difficult to practice one specific approach.

What resulted came to be known as the Freak Defense—changing strategies from zone to triangle-and-two in the blink of an eye. Virtually every type of defensive strategy was employed depending on the situation on the court; the players just had to learn to read one another and the game. It was unconventional, but it worked.

Brown, an avid reader, was particularly intrigued by a line from Sun Tzu's *The Art of War*: "When the enemy prepares everywhere, he will be weak everywhere." He decided to employ this technique to his team's needs and found it to be true: their opponents were too concerned about which defensive strategy would be used next that they were unable to play effective offense.

Instead of trying to force the players he had to fit the traditional approach, Brown was willing to adapt his approach. The team's unlikely success demonstrated that the Freak Defense adjustment was exactly what the Tigers needed to navigate through the tournament and grab the attention of their competitors and the media.

In fact, the world of sports is filled with examples of athletes and coaches who adapted to become or remain successful. Greg Maddux was able to be a dominant pitcher well into his forties because he knew how and when to adjust his game plan, which often varied from one batter to the next. For Maddux, every pitch had a purpose. As he grew older and lost velocity on his pitches, he instead relied more and more on pitching to situations and pitching to what each hitter was showing. By doing so, Maddux earned four consecutive Cy Young awards and boasted a Major League record of 17 straight seasons with at least 15 wins.

Jack Nicklaus won his first major championship when he was 22 years old. At 46, he became the oldest player to ever to win the Masters. Breaking the record for the most major championship victories, Nicklaus showed time and time again why he is considered to be the best golfer who ever played. In his prime, Nicklaus was one of the longest and straightest hitters on the PGA Tour; but as he grew older, Nicklaus relied on his tremendous course-management skills and a more conservative approach to continue vying for championships.

Bobby Bowden had a winning program at Florida State, but when quarterback Charlie Ward took over the offense, he struggled. A tremendous athlete, Ward showed an innate ability to make plays with his feet, but bad reads and interceptions also showed he was having a hard time getting a handle on FSU's pro-style offense. So Bowden and the Seminoles devised a system that would better fit Ward's athleticism. They called it the Fast Break, and it allowed Ward to work out of the shotgun where he was free to find open receivers or open running lanes. The adjustment was exactly what the team needed and, in 1993, Ward ran all the way to a National Championship and was awarded the Heisman Trophy.

And for the Truly Great in Business

Steve Jobs understood the importance of adjusting the game plan. The CEO of Apple since 1997, he helped resurrect the computer company by not only rethinking their branding but also by adapting their focus to include not only computers and software, but pioneering in the field of portable technology such as iPods, iPads, and iPhones. This wildly successful line of product has helped to launch Apple to the forefront of the industry precisely because it was willing to look outside the traditional boundaries of that industry.

But Jobs's willingness to adjust with changing markets also led him to help grow Pixar Studios. Recognizing that computer animation was poised to become the new standard, Jobs negotiated a partnership to distribute its films. The small studio that had been struggling to succeed as an independent company soon took off, producing such iconic animated films as *Finding Nemo; Monsters, Inc.; Cars; The Incredibles;* and the *Toy Story* franchise.

Jobs once famously quoted Wayne Gretsky when attributing the secret to his success to the manner in which he constantly adapts to changing circumstances: "'I skate to where the puck is going to be, not where it has been.' And we've always tried to do that at Apple since the very, very beginning. And we always will."

Toys "R" Us adapted, as well, when it faced a challenge struggling against discounters Target and Wal-Mart in the early 2000s. When a group of investors took the No. 2 toy retailer private in 2005, they turned it around and shifted its focus. Instead of competing on price, Toys "R" Us now focus on its true customers: not children from infants to age twelve, but their mothers.

The store doesn't attempt to undercut the big box stores' prices but, instead, works to enrich a family's experience both in the store and a home by offering products that appeal more to parents, such as educational toys and learning-oriented video games.

Sometimes, changing the game plan means challenging deep-rooted beliefs. When Marty Homlish left Sony to become the chief marketing officer at the software company SAP in 2000, he found the company so entrenched in its engineering culture that it had never bothered to learn how to talk to its customers. As a result, SAP, a business-to-business marketer, never really explained its complex products or communicated its fundamental value proposition.

"I knew SAP was a marketer's dream. We already had great products and a strong history of innovation," Homlish said. "All we needed to do was transform marketing." The man who had launched Sony's PlayStation went on to form SAP's global marketing plan and gave SAP a consistent message about its brand. Under his guidance, the company realigned and changed from an engineering-focused company to focus on its marketing and customers. Had Homlish just stuck to the status quo, the multinational software development and consulting corporation would never have grown to be the world's fourth-largest software enterprise.

Not all adaptations are about branching out in new directions, however. Sometimes, a company can adjust its game plan successfully by realizing that a new direction or product is not answering the demands of the market. Consider, for example, the colossal failure of New Coke in the 1980s. When the Coca-Cola company launched its new product in an effort to boost sales and recapture a bigger share of the market, the push-back from angry consumers was overwhelming. The flavor itself did not seem to be the main issue, as it continued to win taste tests against the classic Coke recipe and Pepsi; the issue that raised the ire of consumers was the fact that the company had tampered with an iconic product. Within three months of launching the new Coke, the Coca-Cola company announced it would turn back the clock and return to the original formula due to the outpouring of consumer fury.

While many maintain the whole thing was a publicity stunt, Coke executives have staunchly denied it. It was merely a case of forging ahead with consumer support, they insist, and what they discovered was that they had to reevaluate their plan to modernize and update the product by changing their marketing, not the product itself. After abandoning the New Coke line, they focused on celebrating what made Coke a classic American product. Rather than sticking by their vision for the brand, they had to respond to the market, and that meant going backward in order to move forward.

The GREATNESS Challenge

Can you recall a time when you had to change your plan to make your team successful? Is there something like that staring you down today? Businesses must adapt and grow. If they don't, they remain stagnant or worse—they lose their customer base. Think about how business industries have changed through the years: airlines offer online check-ins; hotels and fast-food restaurants promote their Internet access as much as their products and services; safety features on cars have improved drastically; many companies offer online bill-pay.

And it's not just how companies relate to customers. Over time, employers have adjusted their game plan on how they work with their employees, too. No workplace is the same as it was fifty years ago, and employees today have conveniences no one could foresee in the 1950s. Now, many workers can opt for flex time, free child care, reimbursed continuing education, and even health club memberships. In order to remain competitive, companies have to remain open to changing both how they approach their services and products as well as their workplace.

In the same way, individuals must be open to adapting to meet new challenges. What role do you play at work? Could your team benefit if you took on an additional responsibility or delegated one of yours to someone else?

Think about the last meeting or interview you had or the last time you had to pitch something to a client, customer, or committee. Review the game plan you had and think about if everything went accordingly. Looking back, consider if you could have made any additional adjustments, given those unique circumstances, to gain better results.

On their road to success, the truly Great find a detour that bypasses each roadblock. When all else fails, Greatness finds a way to be successful. Whether that's through trial and error, through extra preparation, or by working to gain a mental or physical advantage over the competition, those who want something bad enough will stop at nothing until they find the winning combination.

Are you adaptable, or are you too stubborn to change your game plan? Are your policies and procedures flexible enough to account for change? When the pressure is on, can you make adjustments on the fly to keep your ship from sinking?

Randy Pausch, author of *The Last Lecture* and former professor of computer science at Carnegie Mellon University, faced a tremendous roadblock in his life in the form of pancreatic cancer. With three young children and an adoring wife, he could have given up and surrendered to his disease or spent his last days in the comfort of a hospital bed. But he didn't. Instead, Pausch decided to give a last lecture at Carnegie Mellon that would show his kids who their father really was. He wanted to give them a lifetime's worth of fatherly advice through a collection of short stories that they could always refer to—stories that exemplified his values and the lessons he learned.

Randy Pausch changed his game plan. He found a way to influence his children's lives in a positive way even though he regretted he couldn't be there to see them grow up or teach them himself. And, in the process, he inspired millions of people around the world with the same stories, which were published in his *New York Times* best-selling book.

If change is needed, ask your colleagues or employees for suggestions. That's what Lexus does with its Pursuit of Innovation. The program annually awards up to $400,000 to dealers who submit new ideas for good service. Lexus reviews the ideas and implements the best, sometimes on a national scale. "The Lexus Pursuit of Innovation program was created to use the expertise of our dealers and their associates to uncover ideas with sustainable value that would enhance the customer experience in our dealerships," said Marv Ingram of Lexus Planning, Business Development, and Marketing.

Life is not easy. If it was, as Mike Ditka has said, then everyone would be great at what they did. The real world is constantly changing. The real world doesn't care what you want or what you are good at. The only thing you can do is take life as it comes and adjust as needed.

If you're willing to be flexible and adapt to changing circumstances, those circumstances will seem a whole lot less daunting. Embrace change and stay open-minded about making adjustments—that's what the Great Ones do.

CHAPTER 11

The Ultimate Teammate

They will assume whatever role is necessary to win.

In his program's darkest hour, Mike Pressler never wavered. He stuck with his team, knowing success would be synonymous with the truth. The former Duke University lacrosse coach stood behind his players in the midst of a public outcry and media frenzy resulting after three members of his team were accused of rape.

As a coach, Pressler united his players and proved himself to be the ultimate teammate as he entered the bottom floor of the Murray Building on Duke's campus to deliver the news. Pressler informed his team that their lacrosse season had ended and he had resigned, effective immediately.

What had begun as an off-campus team party with two hired strippers had accelerated into a rape investigation—one that would expose prosecutorial misconduct, sloppy police work, an administration's rush to judgment, and the media's blatant disregard for the facts. The events divided a prestigious university, as well the city of Durham, and were played out in an ugly story on cable television talk shows and on covers of national magazines.

Hysteria erupted as Pressler talked to his team. For the next thirty minutes Pressler, a three-time ACC Coach of the Year, put his personal situation aside and encouraged his players to stick together. Pressler also made a bold promise to his team that one day they would get the opportunity to tell the world the truth. And, in essence, that truth would be their victory.

It was.

The case never went to trial. The stripper's story lost its credibility when she continued to revise her statement, and DNA tests showed no evidence supporting her claim. The three indicted Duke lacrosse players were proclaimed innocent of charges by the North Carolina governor; the Durham district attorney involved in the case was disbarred and found guilty of criminal contempt.

Pressler won a wrongful termination settlement from Duke and has resumed his stellar coaching career at Bryant University in Smithfield, Rhode Island, where his team posted an 11–4 record and won the Northeast-10 conference regular-season title in his first year.

Those who know Pressler are not surprised by his success. He understands the importance of accountability, loyalty, and setting a high standard.

Pressler encouraged his team to stick together and demand the truth, even when the truth wasn't popular in Durham and beyond. Despite the facts being in their favor, the odds were stacked against them as the prosecutors and the media seemed out for blood. But Pressler, his team, and his family always believed that the truth would win out. Together, they remained committed to seeing that truth through to the end, and Pressler remained committed to leading his players in the fight even when he was no longer their coach.

Pressler first learned and implemented these traits as a player and team captain while he was a student at Washington and Lee University in Lexington, Virginia. He further demonstrated the significance of these qualities in 16seasons as the men's lacrosse coach at Duke University.

A head coach has to wear many hats, and they all seem to fit nicely on him. Pressler is proof teamwork is necessary to accomplish goals. And in that framework of teamwork, there needs to be a person willing to take a role that helps teammates solve problems and succeed. That approach translates into board room meetings in the business world or to the dinner table in your own home.

Even in times of turmoil, Pressler made personal sacrifices to help his Duke University lacrosse players move forward and move on. While it was a case that cost him his job and life at Duke, and nearly cost him his coaching career, Pressler remained committed to team, family, and friends. That same approach can help you face daily issues at the office and in your life.

By shifting immediately from a focus on the sport to a focus on standing up for his players and fighting for his team, Pressler demonstrated that he understood a fundamental fact about being the Ultimate Teammate: in order to be Great, you have to be ready to assume whatever role your team needs you in to succeed.

More from the Truly Great

Mike Flynt is another great example of someone who lived out this principle. As one of the toughest linebackers in the Lone Star Conference and a team captain for the 1971 Sul Ross State University Lobos, Flynt found his leadership niche in his toughness. Often uniting his team through his willingness to scrap at the drop of a hat, this trait also broke his team apart when he got into one too many fights. On the eve of his senior season, coaches kicked Flynt from the team and out of school. Not only did the fight end Flynt's college career, it led to the unraveling of the Lobos' season.

For more than three decades, he carried the burden of letting his teammates down because he couldn't control his fists. At a team reunion more than three decades later, he confessed to his former teammates that letting the team down was the biggest regret of his life; they suggested that Flynt check to see if he had any remaining eligibility in order to play for one last season.

The rest is history. At the age of 59, Flynt suited up for the Lobos once again, and became the second-oldest player ever to take the field in a college football game.

But this time around, Flynt knew that his place on the team would be a very different one from before. No longer a hothead ready to settle disagreements with his fists, Flynt used the perspective and wisdom gained from his own life to reach out to his much younger teammates.

One particular incident first opened his eyes to his purpose for the team. Before practice one day, Flynt noticed that Jeremy Cartwright, a wide receiver with great speed, size, and work ethic, was not mentally prepared for the workout. Cartwright explained that after a racially charged confrontation with another student the day before, he was thinking of leaving the team and quitting school. "After what they said I didn't fight. I just turned and walked away," Cartwright told Flynt. "I was so depressed I've just stayed in my room."

Memories of how Flynt would have handled the situation in his younger days flooded his mind. He knew he would have flown into a rage in 1970—and that was exactly why he lost his scholarship and was kicked out of school so many years ago. He grabbed Cartwright's shoulders. "Don't you see?" Flynt said. "The decision you made was in the best interest of you and your teammates. We need you out there, and if you would have fought those guys it would have been selfish and you'd be gone. You did something I was never able to do. You walked away and I'm so proud of you. Who knows—you may go on to become an All-American because of that one right decision!"

Cartwright suddenly smiled from ear to ear. "Mike, you're an angel," he said.

Throughout the rest of the season, Flynt mentored many of his teammates. Instead of being the fiery on-field leader he had been in his previous playing days, Flynt became the heart of a Division III team that overachieved in the 2007 season.

Mike Flynt arrived in Alpine, Texas, to play his last year of college football with one purpose in mind. He left having fulfilled a different, deeper purpose. And by both standards, he had a very successful "senior" season.

Times change, people change, situations change. And as they do, so does your responsibility within an organization if you aspire to be part of something bigger than yourself. The Great ones recognize that the most important thing is what the organization—the team—needs from you. It is your responsibility to take on whatever role necessary to lead your team to success.

What the 2008 USA Olympic Basketball Team needed from Chris Paul was to be a bench player behind Jason Kidd. Sports analysts questioned how a player with Paul's impressive statistics could be happy as a second-string player, but Paul put the team ahead of his own ego, and never challenged the coaches' decision.

That's not to say that he didn't make an impact anyway. In fact, despite not being Team USA's starting point guard, Paul still had plenty of playing time, finishing the Olympic basketball tournament with the third-highest amount of game time on the team, behind only LeBron James and Kobe Bryant.

Individual skills are essential for a team's success, but only as far as they lift the entire team with them. When a person becomes obsessed with the attention and accolades of being a superstar, they can often damage their overall winning record by damaging their team's cohesive chemistry. By engaging those same skills to elevate the team toward a common goal, the individuals are ultimately doubly honored, both for what their team accomplished and for how they each helped to move that team towards victory.

Consider Shane Battier, who during his career was not a top scorer. His plays rarely made highlight reels, and he never had any high-profile national endorsement deals. But as any fan of the Miami Heat, the Houston Rockets, the Memphis Grizzlies, or the Duke Blue Devils would tell you, Shane Battier won games.

As one of the most highly decorated and sought-after high school recruits in the country in 1997, Battier won a National Championship and numerous awards his senior year at Duke and then was drafted in the first round of the NBA draft in 2001. By all counts, he was poised to become one of the next great stars on the court, making headlines and chasing championships.

Instead of sinking basket after basket to light up the scoreboard, though, Battier's professional career took a much lower-profile route. He was an incredibly smart individual, clean-living, and with no shortage of talent. Why wasn't his name splashed all over the headlines or the king of endorsement deals?

The answer is simple: Battier wasn't playing any worse; he was simply playing a different role on the team.

The value of Battier's presence wasn't in his scoring abilities, but in his record as one of the best defenders professional basketball has ever known. In game after game, Battier guarded the league's superstars and would shut them down. Afterwards, players like Kobe Bryant would insist they had an off night. But the game video and the numbers would prove that many of the most significant moments of play came as a result of Battier's incredible ability to block shots, as well as his tendency to pass the ball to teammates with a better line to the basket rather than taking shots himself.

During his three years with the Grizzlies, Battier helped lift their record from one of the lowest in league history to 50–32 three years later and a place in the play-offs. When he was traded to the Rockets in 2006, he once again helped lift their record from a losing one to 52–30 in his first year and 55–27 the following one, including an incredible twenty-two-game winning streak such as the NBA hadn't seen in more than three and a half decades. Battier moved to the Miami Heat in 2011, and helped lead LaBron James, Dwyane Wade, and company to two championships as well as a twenty-seven game winning streak in 2013.

Every season, every game, Battier deflected the flashier star status just as he deflected the opponents' balls. He was on the court to contribute to his team's success in whatever way helped the most. And that strategy served him well.

Michael Phelps understands that principle, too. He stars as an individual in swimming, but he takes more pride in being part of a successful team. He admitted to me in front of a live audience that although he had found his niche in a sport that is largely dominated by individual performers, more than anything else he enjoys being a member of a team.

It's why he gets more joy out of victories in relays, in which he's only a part of the success, than he does in the individual golds that he achieved. He said it before, but I, like most of America, saw it vividly when he and his teammates, Jason Lezak, Cullen Jones, and Garrett Weber, beat the French in the 400 freestyle relay, in one of the closest races in the 2008 Summer Olympics in Beijing and in swimming history.

Michael Phelps's excitement on the pool deck was almost childlike, and certainly not like anything you would expect of a man who is now considered among the most elite Olympic athletes ever. He was real. He was raw. If you watched his reaction and his celebration when Jason Lezak kicked it in and passed Alain Bernard, the trash-talking Frenchman, it clearly wasn't about Phelps securing his own place in history. It was about winning as a team.

In postrace interviews from Beijing, each of his fellow American swimmers said that Michael Phelps was one of the Greatest teammates they could ask for. He never sought the spotlight—though the spotlight was always shining on him. He shared praise, he knew how to contribute his part—never considering it more valuable than his teammate's—and he performed at the highest level when the highest level was required.

Phelps would not have won eight gold medals, setting a bar no one may ever match, without competing in relays. In order for him to set this new standard—surpassing the record seven gold medals won by American swimmer Mark Spitz 36 years earlier—he was forced to rely on the success of his teammates. And if he was going to be part of a team, he was going to completely immerse himself in the experience. He understood that his role was not only to swim as fast as he could, but to encourage and inspire his teammates to do their best, as well.

His passion for his teammates was real. His enthusiasm for their collective achievement was real. They all felt that, which made Team USA even the more enthusiastic about helping Phelps reach his individual place in history.

At the 2012 Olympics in London, Phelps was chasing another Olympic record: to become the most decorated Olympic athlete of all time. He tied the record at 18 with a disappointing silver medal finish in the individual 200-meter butterfly. To break the record, he would need the help of teammates Ryan Lochte, Conor Dwyer, and Ricky Berens. And he got it. His team handed him a four second lead as Phelps entered the pool for the last leg of the race, adding his total medal count to 19 and his name to another place in Olympic history.

"I thanked those guys for helping me get to this moment," Phelps told ESPN. "I told those guys I wanted a big lead. I was like, 'You better give me a big lead going into the last lap,' and they gave it to me. I just wanted to hold on. I thanked them for being able to allow me to have this moment." Phelps finished the Olympics with a total of 22 career medals, 18 of them gold, and he finished as the most successful athlete for the third Olympics in a row, a feat he would not achieve solely on his own.

And for the Truly Great in Business

Jack Welch, former CEO of General Electric, is an avid believer in the importance of supporting the overall vision of the team over seeking a personal goal. "Numbers aren't the vision," he explains. "Numbers are the products." His management model puts the success of the company, or the team within the company, first. This keeps the shared goal in mind, but doesn't make it the only object. With teammates focusing on how to combine efforts to achieve the desired end, the desired numbers will naturally follow.

In the case of Michael Dell, he stepped aside for the betterment of his company, then returned when he was needed again. In 2004, he recognized that the company he helped found needed new leadership in order to continue its growth as the largest personal computer company in the world. Agreeing that some fresh blood might help Dell Computers become competitive in new and innovative ways, he willingly turned over the role of CEO for three years. In 2007, Dell was invited to pick up the mantle again and did so without harboring hard feelings or old grudges. His primary concern was not what move would stoke his own ego, but what actions he could take that would be best for the team as a whole.

Ursula M. Burns is another leader who made a sacrifice for her team when she was wary of accepting the job of executive assistant to an executive at Xerox. She had been working for several years in product development and was afraid that the new job might be the end to her rising career. However, senior management needed someone with her business smarts and intimate understanding of the company to keep the executive team organized and in top form, so she took the job. Quickly, she became the assistant to the company's CEO, then was named the vice president of global manufacturing before becoming a senior vice president. In 2009, Burns's willingness to embrace whatever role would help the company the most in the long run won her the position of CEO, making her the first African-American woman to hold that position in an Standard & Poors 100 company.

Greatness is assuming whatever role is necessary for the team to win. By placing the needs of teammates above their own desires or preferences, the Great ones are willing to take on different responsibilities in order to positively affect the desired outcome of their team's aspirations.

The GREATNESS Challenge

If you are ever to achieve Greatness, you must realize that that highest level of success can never be accomplished alone. Your team includes not only your boss and colleagues, but your friends, significant others, parents, or even the neighbor who always gives good advice. And the only way to ensure that those around you will continue to look out for your best interest is to share your enthusiasm for them and share your success—and credit—with them.

Do you take an active interest in the lives of your coworkers? Get involved. Ask how they are doing, how their family is, how their golf swing is coming along—anything that shows you listen to them and remember what is important. This can help to relieve stress, help people to feel more plugged in to their work community, and shows you value their place on the team.

Set a goal to reach out to one coworker each day. It could be something as simple as just stopping for a few minutes to ask about the family photos on their desk, or maybe you could offer to bring them lunch. Small gestures like these can go a long distance in creating an atmosphere of connection and unity.

Voice your appreciation for them as often as possible. Most of the time this is as simple as saying "Thank you" or offering to take more than your share of the workload when they've had a rough day. Shift your energies in a more beneficial direction, if this will further your common goal. And though most team players would never admit it, they almost always appreciate when they're publicly acknowledged for their role in your shared success or achievement. Sometimes that means making a grand announcement in front of the company. Sometimes it's giving them a small gift or award. Sometimes it's just a handshake and a smile. But it is always appreciated.

Strong teams have trust in each member to do his or her part. Foster a culture of trust by making promises and following through, whether it is something as small as simply arriving to a meeting on time, following up on a co-worker's e-mail, or something larger, like making a deadline. If each member demonstrates that they are dedicated to fulfilling their individual roles within the group, you will be helping to create a strong unit and a strong product that maximizes the talents of all its contributors.

Brainstorm with your team. Ideas usually don't first appear in their final form; they're best bounced off others. Don't be shy about talking to other people about your ideas, and listen to theirs. Build on each other for the betterment of the team.

Examine your own role on the team. Are you even clear about

what it is? If asked, how might your teammates view you and describe your contributions or value? If you don't have a clear role, perhaps you should consider defining one for yourself. If you do have a clear role, make an honest evaluation as to whether or not it is really meeting the team's needs at the moment. If you find that the current situation may be calling for a slightly different contribution, adjust your actions accordingly so that your energies and resources are always being maximized for the team's benefit.

Being able to step aside for the good of the team is a sign of Greatness, and many entrepreneurs face the challenge. Founders of small businesses often have a hard time letting go of their life's work and want to stay involved in every aspect of the business they've begun. It takes a Great winner to recognize that someone else can do it better and to accept a different—and maybe even lesser—role in their organization.

In his book *Joe Torre's Ground Rules for Winners,* the manager of the 1998 World Champion New York Yankees used a baseball play to illustrate sacrifice. "Giving yourself up for the greater good—that's the essence of sacrifice," Torre said in his book. "In baseball—and in business—sacrifice is not just a bunt." The team's end result is more important than the batter's particular at bat.

Like baseball, businesses are made up of individuals working toward a common goal. Sometimes, employees feel that if they sacrifice themselves for the company goals, their own personal goals will suffer. But Torre says that's not the case, citing his 1998 World Championship Yankees as an example: "When you reach heights of achievement, glory rubs off on everybody."

When was the last time you reevaluated your vision? Do it today. Rather than making the end result your only goal, try focusing on how to support your teammates so that the group itself is stronger. Mike Pressler masterfully steered his team through a crisis in the immediate to get them through to a place of vindication on the other side. Mike Flynt used his unique wisdom to mentor his team. Chris Paul, Shane Battier, and Michael Phelps understood the importance of supporting their teammates rather than elevating themselves—

and helped their teams rise to new levels of success.

Henry Ford, the father of the assembly line, once remarked: "Coming together is a beginning. Keeping together is progress. Working together is success." Teams are the sum of a group of individuals who have different strengths and weaknesses. The Great ones know how to combine individual strengths for the team's goals.

Industrialist, business mogul, and philanthropist Andrew Carnegie succinctly expressed his belief in this philosophy when he wrote, "Teamwork is the ability to work together toward a common vision...It is the fuel that allows common people to attain uncommon results."

How well does your office work together as a team? Is it only when the project requires it, or is there always a feeling of unity and shared purpose? If there's something hampering that spirit, try to identify the causes. And if there's something that brings positive feelings to your team, see if there is something you can do to keep it going.

When you get the ball, it's sometimes in the team's best interest to pass, not shoot. In his book *The Team Member Handbook for Teamwork,* Price Pritchett points out that sacrifice is the "price you pay for membership in the group." If you hold on to the ball instead of passing once in a while, your teammates—and your coworkers—will start to question if you'll be there when you need them. Basketball coaches want players who can shoot; they also want players who know when it's best to step aside and get the ball to someone else, or to play defense.

Look out for your team. Show appreciation. Share the burden of your team's challenges and celebrate your achievements with the ones who propel you forward. In other words, be the ultimate teammate—and you'll be one step closer to Greatness.

CHAPTER

12

Not Just About the Benjamins

They don't play just for the money.

The summer of 2015 marked another career milestone for power forward Tim Duncan of the San Antonio Spurs: the NBA named him the 2014–2015 Twyman-Stokes Teammate of the Year. Beginning in 2013, the award was created to honor the ideal teammate. To select a winner, the league chose past NBA stars to create a candidate pool from which 300 current players then voted.

The vote should go toward the athlete who best embodies a teammate: one who represents loyalty and friendship, someone who sacrifices ego or individual success for the good of the team. It is an honor based solely on character rather than achievement. "That's what makes it the most special," said Duncan, during a press conference concerning the award, "knowing that people from around the league, and teammates, those guys voted me and chose me for this award. It's an amazing honor."

The award's name stems from the friendship between teammates Jack Twyman and Maurice Stokes, two former NBA players. In the last game of the regular season in March of 1958, Stokes drove to the basket, made contact with another player, fell, and hit his head. He lost consciousness but was revived with smelling salts and finished the game. Three days later on the plane back to Cincinnati after a playoff game with the Detroit Pistons, Stokes became violently ill. An ambulance awaited the plane to transport Stokes to a hospital. There, he dropped into a coma, and when he woke up, he was paralyzed. Diagnosed with post-traumatic encephalopathy, Maurice Stokes lived the rest of his life mentally alert but very limited in his physical condition.

"How would you like to be one of the premier athletes in the world on a Saturday?" Jack Twyman once said. "Then, on Sunday, you go into a coma and wake up, totally paralyzed, except for the use of (your) eyes and brain. I mean, can you imagine anything worse?" Twyman stepped in to care for his friend. He became his legal guardian, taking care of medical bills and hosting an annual charity game for his friend. Twyman and his family took care of Stokes until his early death in 1970.

The same summer of 2015 when Tim Duncan received the Twyman-Stokes award, he was also up for contract renewal and salary negotiations with his only team, the San Antonio Spurs. Duncan, born in 1976 on St. Croix of the U.S. Virgin Islands, did not even play basketball until his freshman year of high school. Until then, he had been a competitive swimmer, but after the 1989 Hurricane Hugo destroyed his community pool and training center and the death of his mother from breast cancer shortly after that, Duncan decided to try something new. By 1993, he grew nine inches and headed to Wake Forest University, where he played as an All-American and was the NCAA Player of the Year. The San Antonio Spurs chose him for the first overall pick in 1997, and he has spent his entire career there.

After leading his Spurs to the playoffs for 18 seasons and five NBA championships, after 15 All Star Games, 15 All-NBA Team and 15 NBA All-Defense Team recognitions, Tim Duncan left approximately $5 million sitting on the table in his 2015 salary negotiations. This was nothing new; he cut his salary in half just two years before.

In the 2011–2012 season, Tim Duncan was the third highest paid NBA player in the league, trailing only Kobe Bryant of the LA Lakers and Kevin Garnett of the Boston Celtics. With the chance for a Championship run in the next year, Duncan willingly slashed his salary in half to allow the Spurs management to keep his team together and to add more talent. By doing so, Duncan dropped from being the third highest paid player in the league to the fourth highest paid player *on his own team.* The Spurs lost the Championship by one game in 2013, but then beat the Miami Heat in five games for the Championship in 2014.

In contrast, Kobe Bryant has remained the NBA's highest paid player from 2009 through the 2015 season. The Lakers won two Championships in 2009 and 2010, yet the years following 2010 have been a disappointment. The LA Lakers haven't even reached the playoffs since 2013, when the San Antonio Spurs beat them in four games.

The summer of 2015 was filled with free agency negotiations and drama. The LA Lakers, along with the Miami Heat, Phoenix Suns, New York Knicks, and the San Antonio Spurs, were all courting LaMarcus Aldridge, a free agent leaving the Portland Trail Blazers and the hottest player on the 2015 free agency list. Negotiations fell flat on team after team because of poor organization or salary cap issues, which left no space for Aldridge – except for the Spurs.

With Duncan willing to take another pay cut, the Spurs could get Aldridge and keep Duncan's teammates Kawhi Leonard, Danny Green, and Manu Ginobili on staff. Duncan's negotiations allowed more than just money to entice Aldridge. Aldridge would be able to return to his home state, work within an organization with the legacy of five Championships and seeking a sixth, as well as play with a deep and talented roster, including Duncan.

Facing his 19th season, Duncan will more than likely have less playing time, but his role as a leader will not change. Teammates look to him for guidance and direction, and Duncan knows that as he faces retirement within the next year, his team will need help to continue their Championship Tradition. He understands that a teammate has more important value than money.

Everyone wants to believe they are the reason their team is experiencing so much success. But those who truly understand the bigger picture are those who want to make sure their teammates and their employer can also be successful. It's only then that Greatness can be achieved.

In an era where everyone talks team first, Tim Duncan demonstrated true Greatness.

More from the Truly Great

The Great ones don't just work for the money. They know you cannot achieve Greatness if your only concern is financial.

Brett Hull and the Detroit Red Wings together made a similar choice as Duncan when Hull, an unrestricted free agent, signed with the Red Wings for the 2001–2002 season. Hull, coming off a 39-goal season with the Dallas Stars, took his time choosing a team that was right for him and ripe for the Stanley Cup. The sniper shopped around but hadn't signed weeks into the off-season, waiting for the best opportunity instead of the largest paycheck.

"It's not about the money, whatsoever," Hull told Booth News Services. "I've played long enough to have saved some money. It's about the opportunity to play for a great organization, with great players, and to win the Stanley Cup."

General Manager Kenneth Holland approached several Detroit players and asked them to defer their salaries in order to free up cap money to make Hull part of the team. For the other players, it was a no-brainer. They knew Hull, as a teammate, would help their team compete at a higher level, and it was worth it to them, whatever the personal inconvenience.

"I called some players to see if they would pitch in," Holland said. "They immediately said, 'Absolutely, if it's going to help us bring in another great player.'"

Rather than chase the team that would give him the highest paycheck, Hull signed with a like-minded team: the one that was willing to forgo immediate financial gain in order to compete for the ultimate goal.

Truly Great athletes recognize that there is more to the game than which team will write them the biggest check. They make decisions based on what is best for the people around them, for supporting the organization and for achieving the ultimate goal.

Former dual-sport athlete Deion Sanders wanted to win a Super Bowl. Coming off five seasons with the Atlanta Falcons, the then-free agent had his choice of teams. He listened to pitches from New Orleans, Miami, Detroit, San Francisco, and Atlanta, recalling in his autobiography that media reports called his choice "the biggest move in the three-year history of [NFL's] free agency."

Although he had a four-year, $17 million offer from the New Orleans Saints, he wanted to be surrounded by a team with a good chance to win the big game. Money wasn't as important to him as were strong teammates who could compete for the Super Bowl. Sanders could have commanded a salary and contract on his own team, but he decided instead to sign a one-year contract with San Francisco at a bargain rate because he knew he had a good opportunity to win the NFL's ultimate prize with the 49ers.

"I've said all along my main concern is to win a Super Bowl. I think the tradition of the 49ers exemplifies is they don't come second to anything," Sanders said. "And that's just where I want to finish up—first."

With players like Jerry Rice, Steve Young, Brent Jones, and others already in the locker room, Sanders knew the 49ers offered the best chance to make it to the big game, and he could be a part of the team who had a good chance of winning it all.

Sanders could have demanded more money, but being a part of a championship team was more important to him than a bigger, long-term contract. He explained, "[Owner Eddie Bartolo] said they didn't have much money to give me, but I realized that if I could make the sacrifice and go out there, I could fulfill one of my dreams. I think the main thing I wanted to accomplish with that tour was to sign on with a team that really had a chance to make it to the Super Bowl, and I knew the 49ers had about a good a chance as any."

The 1994 season turned out to be Sanders's best in his fourteen-season NFL career. He finished as the Associated Press's top defensive player, intercepted six passes and returned them for over 300 yards and three touchdowns, and earned NFL Defensive Player of the Week in his first start for the 49ers. And Sanders wasn't the only standout on the well-rounded 49ers. Eight other players joined him to compete in the Pro Bowl, including Rice, Young, Jones, and Merton Hanks, who were all named starters.

But the best part, in Sanders's view, was that the talented team won Super Bowl XXIX, 49–26, earning Sanders and his teammates their ultimate goal. Sanders had a fourth-quarter interception in the game, but he told the media afterward he was just a part of the victory: "The game plan didn't revolve around me. I took care of the man in front of me, and my teammates kicked butt."

He chose to play with a high-level team and be a part of the ultimate goal, deeming the team's collective goal more important than his wallet. Sanders could have signed for more money elsewhere, but it was more important for him to be a small piece of the larger puzzle to win a championship.

As any baseball player, statistician, or fan will tell you, it's no small feat to pitch a no-hitter and it's even rarer to pitch a perfect game. Yet Roy Halladay of the Philadelphia Phillies did both those things. On May 29, 2010, he threw only the 20th perfect game in MLB history, and on October 6, 2010, he became only the second pitcher ever to hurl his way to a no-hitter in the postseason.

With numbers like that, one could easily assume that Halladay was near the top of the league's pay chart for pitchers. But in reality, he actually took a pay cut for the 2010 season to leave the Toronto Blue Jays and play for the Phillies, who had won the National League pennant in 2009.

In the four years prior to his move, he averaged 233 innings, the highest in all of Major League Baseball. His fastball and cutter were considered among the best as well, and most experts ranked him as one of the top three or four pitchers in the league. In short, Halladay was a standout player in a crucial position, which meant he could have commanded just about any salary he wanted. But he wanted to play for a team he felt was a better fit for him, and the choice he made shocked the baseball world, when he signed a contract that many pundits believed was worth $60 million less than he could have demanded.

Clearly, Halladay recognized that there was something more important than money at stake, and his decision seems to have paid off for him, even if the checks were smaller. As the Phillies advanced in the playoffs, it was clear that some things were just worth more to him than a fat salary—like surrounding yourself with the best group of people as possible.

Even after his remarkable postseason no-hitter, Halladay celebrated the work of his team and their shared goal more than he did his own achievement: "It's just one of those special things I think you'll always remember. But the best part about it is the playoffs take priority. It's pretty neat for me to be able to go out and win a game like that and know there's more to come for us and more to accomplish."

For some, being Great means sticking with an organization that's on the right track, regardless of the salary involved. For instance, Martin Brodeur, the National Hockey League's all-time leader in wins, minutes played, and shutouts, did it all with the same team for twenty-one years—the New Jersey Devils.

Within his career, the goaltender signed three contract extensions with the Devils, an organization with a history of keeping its players. And as a result, the Devils competed as a unit, playing for the Stanley Cup four times since 1995 and winning it three of those years.

"I always did things a certain way because I really appreciate what was going on here," Brodeur said of his longtime employer.

Brodeur realized that taking less money during his 1997, 2001, and 2006 contracts gave the Devils a better opportunity to win, because it allowed General Manager Lou Lamoriello to commit more money to other players.

"It was mutual," Brodeur said after signing his last contract, on which he acted as his own agent. "We looked at different possibilities in helping the organization."

Though he finished his career in the middle of the 2014–2015 season, playing seven games for the St. Louis Blues with the promise of a future coaching position, his tenure with the Devils cannot be overlooked.

And for the Truly Great in Business

John Mackey, CEO of Whole Foods, runs his business under the philosophy of "conscious capitalism," which unites civic and environmental responsibility with a commercially viable and profitable business model. One of the things he emphasizes is a limit on how much executives in the company are paid. Rather than hiring people who are motivated by a paycheck, Whole Foods seeks out employees who are dedicated to the mission and are willing to work for a little less in order to be part of a stronger team. If the company's higher-ups are willing to accept a slightly smaller check so that the company can afford to pay the rest of the workers a little more, Mackey reasons that the business becomes more unified and offers consumers a better shopping experience.

Costco's former CEO (retired in 2011), Jim Sinegal, operated with a similar mind-set. "Our attitude is that if you hire good people and pay them a fair wage, then good things will happen for the company," he explained. And in order to make such opportunities possible, he limited his annual salary to $350,000, plus stock options and a small bonus. For a company that did almost $60 billion worth of business each year, it might seem shocking that Sinegal worked for so much less than his counterparts in other similarly-sized companies. But a higher salary meant lower pay for other employees—which often would lead to an unmotivated or a weakened team...and that was not a sacrifice he was willing to make.

Some CEOs even go so far as to decline a salary or to accept a $1 salary for a year's worth of work. Known as an unofficial, yet exclusive club, CEOs of some of the most profitable companies would rather put money back into the company rather than adding to their personal wealth. *Business Insider* profiled some of these CEOs, including John Mackey of Whole Foods, Elon Musk of TESLA and SpaceX, Mark Zuckerburg of Facebook, and Google co-founders Sergey Brin and Larry Page. Granted, these CEOs are hardly scratching out a living, each worth millions and billions of dollars in personal wealth, but this gesture impacts the overall morale and perception of the top executives and sets a precedent for others to follow. Mark Zuckerburg told *Business Insider,* "I've made enough money. At this point, I'm just focused on making sure I do the most possible good with what I have."

No one would deny that a company's CEO deserves adequate compensation for the stress, responsibility, and accountability that go along with the job. But what Great leaders like John Mackey, Jim Sinegal, and Mark Zuckerburg understand is that leaders are only as good as the team they lead; and a strong, productive team is infinitely better for a company's growth than a CEO with padded pockets.

The GREATNESS Challenge

Compared to the corporate world, the earning career of a professional athlete is relatively short. In the business world, careers can span over forty years, but a professional athlete's career peters out in a few years—unless injuries end it sooner. Therefore, many athletes utilize their earning power while they can. But that's not the route that Great winners take.

Tim Duncan Brett Hull, Deion Sanders, and the rest are living proof that the great ones don't play just for the money. As Duncan told me, "If you're doing what you're doing simply for the paycheck, you'll never be happy."

At work, a paycheck factors in, but it's not the main thing around which these athletes built their lives, nor should it be for you. They each loved their different sports but put something other than money first. Sanders and Hull wanted to be surrounded by teammates who could propel them to championship status. Brodeur's longtime loyalty stems from being a part of an organization that's been cohesive for years and succeeded because of it.

For the truly Great, the pursuit of money is secondary. It's not about how much you make; it's about goals; succeeding as a unit, a team, and a family; and enjoying what you do.

Look at the organization for which you work and make sure you understand that the most important thing must always remain the team. Success is fleeting, and you cannot hold onto it alone. The proven path to success goes through your colleagues and through your business. What are you doing to make sure you have the best colleagues possible?

Professional athletes aren't the only ones who are willing to sacrifice for their teammates. In these hard times, many companies have been forced to cut back in order to make ends meet. Most of the time it means employees are laid off, but some employers work hard to find a way around breaking up their team because they recognize the value of each member of their staff.

Rather than being forced to lay off a team member, many companies have opted for furloughs. The unpaid time off can be a few days or even weeks or months. The payroll saved is enough to stave off cutbacks and keep all of the company's employees in their jobs.

When Arizona State University faced a budget cut of almost $90 million, the educational institution opted to furlough staff instead of announcing massive layoffs. "Had we not done this, we would have had to lay off about one thousand administrative personnel," Matt McElrath, ASU's former chief human resource officer, told the *Wall Street Journal.*

Universities, newspapers, state governments, and automotive and transportation suppliers are just some of the industries that used furloughs or across-the-board pay cuts as a way to cut costs but still keep as many as people as possible with their organizations.

Companies—and employees—recognize the importance of each team member and are willing to sacrifice their own paychecks so colleagues can continue to work. Others recognize that money isn't the most important factor in a job.

The truly Great want to surround themselves with people who make their place of business a Great environment. What would happen if something threatened the cohesion of your Great environment? Rather than wait until an employer asks you to make a sacrifice to keep your team together, think about it now. Would you be willing to make it? How would you have to alter your lifestyle? If you were faced with a two-week furlough or a 10 percent pay cut, how would it affect you? Would you be willing to accept it to keep your team together? Now, think about your colleagues—would they say the same thing?

What is your job situation? Have you ever had to decide between your own financial goals and that of your team's? Have any of the choices you've made gone against your personal interests for the sake of the people around you? If you're doing your job just for the money, the truth is you'll never truly achieve Greatness doing it. Being wealthy doesn't make you bad; being well compensated is not a bad thing. But if that's all you're in it for, you can be good but you can never be Great. Considerations that carry a higher value, like the people you work with or what good you achieve through your job, are more important to Great winners than money.

It is imperative to remember that even the most talented athlete shares the same win-loss record as the rest of his or her team. A team sport is not about self; it's about how the group is able to blend their abilities to achieve victory. The same is true off the field, too. In order to reach a goal, the members of a team cannot just look up to where their own ambition might take them. They have to be able to look laterally and recognize the needs of those around them because they are ultimately a unit.

Rudyard Kipling wrote in the poem "The Law of the Jungle,"

which appeared in his 1892 classic, *The Jungle Book*: "For the strength of the Pack is the Wolf, and the strength of the Wolf is the Pack." In other words, a team is only as strong as the people who make it up, and the team members together are only as strong as the team of which they are a part. What are you giving to make your team stronger? What does your team give back to you?

The Great Ones realize that they're just one color on the canvas. Without that color, the painting would be incomplete; but one color or one shade cannot covey the full picture. As long as you understand that, you won't be playing just for the Benjamins—you'll be working toward Greatness.

PILLAR

FOUR

How They Live

CHAPTER

13

Do Unto Others

They know character is defined by how they treat those who cannot help them.

Walter "Sweetness" Payton never refused an autograph, and he never let the requester get away with just a signature, either. Payton always chatted personally with the fan—he said it meant more that way.

The Chicago Bears Great treated everyone the same, whether he knew them or not. He liked people and he just wanted to make a difference in their lives. Everything he did came from the heart.

"Too many of us only take. We don't give. Fame is what you have taken, character is what you give," Payton said. "I wanted to have character because football already gave me fame."

During an emotional news conference in February 1999, Payton announced to the sports world he had a rare autoimmune liver disease and would die without a liver transplant. In April, he made what would be his last public appearance as he threw out the first pitch at a Chicago Cubs game at Wrigley Field.

That same year, Payton contacted me about writing a book with him—but he made clear it wasn't going to be about his football legacy. He wanted to focus on the importance of organ transplants, which he had been promoting since his news conference.

When I first met with him he told me the latest: His cancer of the bile duct had spread, and a donated liver wouldn't save him. He had been taken off the organ donor list and told he would die in the upcoming months. At the time, Payton weighed only about 155 pounds but remained upbeat, joking, "You better write fast."

He laid out a time line that noted important dates since his diagnoses. I studied the dates as Payton explained them to me, noting when he'd first been diagnosed, the date of his February news conference, and the date the doctors had told him a donated liver would no longer save him—essentially the date he'd been given a death sentence. Payton talked about other entries on the calendar as well, including notable dates in his organ donor campaign. And I saw he'd spent an entire day filming public service announcements.

Then I looked again, not believing what I had seen. The day the doctors told him a donated liver wouldn't save him was three days *before* the day he spent a full day filming the PSAs. One day, the doctors told him he had just a few precious months left on earth to spend with his family, loved ones, and friends and he was being removed from the life-giving donor list. Three days later, he forfeited one of those special days to promote the very list that would no longer save him.

When I asked him about it, he shook his head and said, "You don't get it. We all get something in life. It's not worth a nickel if you don't give it back."

Payton spent his entire football career giving back to those who had no way to repay him. He quietly sowed seeds of good all around him, from taking over a shift from one of the Bears' customer service representatives so she could tend to personal business, to cheering up underprivileged children who had no idea who "Sweetness" was.

At one such party, a child took one look at him and burst into tears. "I can't believe it," the boy said. "I can't believe Santa Claus is here and that Santa would come all the way from the North Pole just to see me." Payton, who had arrived in costume alone with Mrs. Claus, Frosty the Snowman, and the Easter Bunny, was so touched by the boy that he went on to establish the "Wishes for Santa" program.

The year he died, the Walter Payton Foundation gave 50,000 underprivileged kids a Christmas of their very own. No one outside of the Foundation knew where the thousands of $100 gift bags came from until after Payton had passed.

On the field and off, Payton's life was about showing kindness to people from whom he wanted nothing in return. He ran as hard as he could every season, every game, and every down. He said he did it for the hard-working man who spent everything he had to take his family to the top of the stands and watch the one and only Bears game they could ever afford. He wanted that man to be able to say he saw Walter Payton at his very best.

Payton ran with the motto "Never die easy." He never quit running, choosing instead to bounce off, over, and through what were always "attempted" tacklers. He never went down or out of bounds voluntarily, and at times seemed invincible—sitting out just one game in 13 NFL seasons, he almost was. He was a nine-time Pro Bowler, took the Bears to a 1985 Super Bowl title, and broke Jim Brown's all-time record for career rushing yards. He viewed every game as a gift to him, and as a gift that he shared with whoever might be cheering him on. The respect he had for each and every fan was incredible.

The truly Great, like Walter Payton, know character is defined by how they treat those who cannot return the favor. They make it their mission to touch the lives of those around them every day by extending courtesies, kindness, and respect.

"[My father] told me when I was young that it was your responsibility, once you've had some success, to reach back and bring someone with you," Payton said. "You cannot achieve great success without being helped along the way. Someone gave to you. That's why it is your job to give back. Do anything that might make the world a better place for someone."

More from the Truly Great

Roberto Clemente was another man who understood the true meaning of character. Growing up in Puerto Rico, he knew hard work in coffee and sugar plantations; his professional statistics show he knew a few things about baseball, too: four-time National League batting champ, two World series rings, the 1966 MVP award, twelve Golden Gloves, and 3,000 hits. But Clemente knew something more important than any of that. He knew that kindness was more important than celebrity.

During his major-league career, his humanitarian work was well known, even if Clemente himself didn't talk about it much. It wasn't something he did for the fame. He did it for the sake of lifting up people who just needed a hand.

On December 23, 1972, a catastrophic earthquake hit Nicaragua, wreaking devastation upon the capital city of Managua. As soon as news of the disaster reached Clemente, he scrambled to assemble aid packages and send them on relief flights into the country. When it became clear that corrupt government agents had confiscated the aid, Clemente decided to charter a flight and go himself to see if he could personally straighten out the problem and get supplies to the suffering people.

Tragically, Clemente never made it to Nicaragua. On December 31, 1972, just minutes after takeoff, his plane crashed into the ocean. There were no survivors.

Walter Payton and Roberto Clemente both lived lives that mattered. They did not consider themselves too important or too busy to reach out where they saw a need. In fact, it was quite the opposite. These great men recognized that they had a responsibility to create something out of the circumstances of their life, fame, and resources—*and they did.* Payton and Clemente died far too soon, and their loss is felt all the more keenly because of what they represent to us. They didn't just see a need. They took action, and did so expecting nothing in return.

But they are not alone. There are many Great ones who have dedicated themselves to helping others. Paul Newman used his status as an actor and a businessman to establish a network of charity programs that have lived on after the founder's death. All profits from his grocery store brand of products, Newman's Own, are earmarked for over a hundred charities.

"I'd like to be remembered as a guy who tried—tried to be part of his times, tried to help people communicate with one another, tried to find some decency in his own life, tried to extend himself as a human being," Newman wrote on the Newman's Own Foundation website.

Arguably Newman's most popular charitable venture, the Hole in the Wall Gang started in 1988 as a summer camp for children with life-threatening diseases. It was designed, in Newman's words, to give them a chance to "raise a little hell." Today, there are eleven member-camps worldwide, and over two hundred thousand children—from every state and 45 countries—have attended a camp or an affiliated program free of charge.

Newman didn't care that the kids had no idea who Butch Cassidy, Cool Hand Luke, or Fast Eddie were. "The most striking thing about Paul Newman," former camp counselor turned journalist Dahlia Lithwick wrote, "was that a man who could have blasted through his life demanding 'Have you any idea who I am?' invariably wanted to hang out with folks—often little ones—who neither knew nor cared."

LeBron James, without question the greatest basketball star currently in the NBA – a man on a mission to establish his place in NBA history – remembers his roots. He knows his athletic ability allowed him to rise above the circumstances of his upbringing but that many others helped pave the way. In establishing the "Akron I Promise Network" as part of his LeBron James Family Foundation, James will help 2,000 underprivileged students in Akron, Ohio, attend the University of Akron in 2025.

James grew up in Akron, the son of a young, single mother. With the help and encouragement from not only his mother, but also his teachers and coaches, James escaped poverty and the road to delinquency so often paved for others in the same situation. Using his current status and wealth, James will be able to provide the same escape ticket to students from his hometown. By identifying at-risk students and enrolling them in programs for educational support, the LeBron James Family Foundation provides these students with skills and encouragement along with the promise of a future in education. "He was one of these kids," said Michele Campbell, executive director of the James Family Foundation, in an interview with *USA Today.* "He feels the need to share that with other kids that are just like him."

And for the Truly Great in Business

Target has long been involved in community service. For years, the company has donated five percent of its income to community outreach, which amounts to about $3 million each week to promote education, the arts, and social services, among other causes. Every month, individual Target stores put aside discretionary funding to benefit their local communities.

Home Depot follows a similar community-awareness path, but theirs is directed at activism and volunteerism. Former CEO Robert Nardelli told *BusinessWeek,* "There's good will. We've seen it time and again. It's not why you do it, but it's a benefit. I would challenge anybody to say, 'Here is a hard return-on-investment on why you do it.' You do it because it's the right thing to do."

During Nardelli's time as CEO of Home Depot, he encouraged its 350,000 employees to volunteer to build homes and playgrounds, established the Home Depot Foundation, and donated $25 million to KaBOOM!, a nonprofit organization Home Depot helped create that is dedicated to building safe activity areas for children. The actual cost Home Depot—or any company—outlays for social responsibility isn't reflected in the bottom dollar. Nardelli says people ask if the costs are a burden. "I say, 'No, that's a responsibility,'" he told *BusinessWeek.* "It's something we do willingly."

Mary Kay Ash founded her company on the principle behind the Golden Rule that brought out the best in everyone. "I have learned to imagine an invisible sign around each person's neck that says 'Make me feel important,'" the founder of Mary Kay Cosmetics said in an interview once. "I never cease to be amazed at how positively people react when they're made to feel important." Ash thought that there was a certain dignity about selling as a profession, and along with this came a certain dignity with which everyone was meant be treated. "Everyone wants to be appreciated," she said. "So, if you appreciate someone, don't keep it a secret."

Following the Golden Rule made business sense for Mary Kay Cosmetics, too, because people invariably want to do business with people who show them respect and treat them well. "Some might consider the Golden Rule corny and old-fashioned, but no one can deny its simple truth," she noted. "Imagine how much better our world would be if everyone lived by this creed."

The GREATNESS Challenge

A popular series of commercials for Liberty Mutual Insurance ran a few years ago that showed one individual picking up a dropped toy for a child, another holding an elevator door, and a third helping up a person who has tripped on the sidewalk. Each time an act of kindness took place, someone else saw it and then paid it forward. That's how Walter Payton, Roberto Clemente, and Paul Newman operated. They didn't receive any benefit from their actions, but they inspired countless others.

We can't all sponsor after-school programs, charter aid planes, or establish camps for terminally ill children, but we can volunteer at a school or help an elderly neighbor or support a local charity. If you're waiting for an opportunity to volunteer, you're wasting your time. There are thousands of needs in every community each day. Find one and get involved.

If you don't know how to start, try searching websites like Volunteer.org and Idealist.org for ideas. Join a weekend fix-up project or contribute a few hours a week. "Volunteer vacations" are another way to give back, either locally or globally. Many local churches and community groups take groups offer volunteer opportunities to teach at camps, fix up buildings, or do other projects. The United Nations even has an Online Volunteer program for those who want to contribute but aren't able to travel.

If you feel drawn as a global citizen, research groups such as Cross Cultural Solutions, Habitat for Humanity, or Global Volunteers to find out how to serve on an international stage. Go alone and meet like-minded people, or attend with your family and set a good example for your children.

Make a list of what your particular interests and concerns are. See if you can find opportunities that are local or more far-flung to act upon. For example, if you enjoy gardening, you could contact a local after-school program about helping children to plant some trees. Not only are you reaching out, but you're modeling that behavior for another generation. Enjoy shopping? Maybe you could fill up a gift box for a holiday charity. Alternately, you could find a cause that moves you. If you grew up in a single-parent household or are a single parent yourself, you could make contact with another single parent and offer to bring over dinner or watch the children to give him or her an evening off. The most important thing is to identify what speaks to your heart because that is what will keep you involved.

Martin Luther King said, "Everybody can be great because everybody can serve." Greatness can come from volunteering to help others. There's little, if any, money involved; however, anyone who's volunteered can vouch that not only does the act help the community, but the person volunteering gets a fantastic pick-me-up, too. Those who volunteer learn new skills, expand their social network, and explore new interests and hobbies. Working for free can lead to benefits at work, too. The Oregon organization Hands On says that 73 percent of employers would recruit a candidate with volunteering experience over one without.

Pay attention to your emotions after you give something of

yourself. Psychologists have identified something they term a "giver's high." This is a positive, optimistic feeling that people tend to get after they have donated time or resources to a worthy cause. Chances are good that you'll begin to notice this natural lift yourself once you begin to reach out. Use these good feelings as momentum to find other opportunities to give.

But as nice as those benefits are, that's not the reason to do it.

Think of the old expression, "My good deed for the day." Now throw it out the window. Don't limit yourself to just one good deed each day; actively look for opportunities to help others, even if it's as simple as holding a door or pointing out an untied shoelace. Small acts of kindness for our family, friends, and colleagues go a long way. Clean out the refrigerator at work, bring in cookies for the office, or fold the laundry at home. See what kind of a change that makes in the day of the people around you.

Doing unto others is perhaps the simplest thing we can do on our way to being truly Great. It costs nothing, takes little effort, and yet makes a world of difference for the people involved—including the doer.

Think about how you felt the last time you were in a hurry to get home but faced a long line of oncoming traffic—when, all of a sudden, someone stopped and let you in front of them. It cost the driver nothing but perhaps 15 seconds of his or her life, but you certainly drove away less stressed. You'll likely never be able to see that person again, so you can't repay the favor. It's just a little thing that can mean the world to someone else.

Brighten a stranger's day by taking time out to do a favor for them. At the grocery store, allow the hurried person with three grocery items in front of you and your cartload. Hold the door open for someone else. Compliment a hairdo or tie on a stranger. You'll not only give that person a lift but perhaps, like the Liberty Mutual commercial, inspire someone else to do a similar kindness.

Remember the basics of the Golden Rule. Treat everyone with respect, no matter their age, income, status or any other variable. "Please" and "thank you" are always appreciated. Instead of rushing your order for a coffee and bagel while chatting on your cell phone, hang it up and greet the server. Say "Good morning" to the parking attendant. Learn the names of your company's maintenance and janitorial staff. Show respect to those around you; it's amazing how uncommon "common" courtesy has become.

People want to feel good, about themselves, their friends and colleagues, their world, and even the companies they do business with. These days, people gravitate towards socially responsible companies, both as potential places of employment and as customers. It is in businesses' best interest to be aware of their relationship with their clientele and community.

It is up to each one of us to determine if we are going to look beyond our own lives to see the countless people whom we can help or encourage, or if we are going to be content with lives focused only on our own interests.

The question that each of us needs to consider very carefully is whether we are going to be people of apathy, selfishness, and blind ambition, or if are we going to strive toward being people of action, people of kindness—people of Greatness.

CHAPTER

14

When No One Is Watching

The great ones live their lives with integrity.

Dick and Rick Hoyt are a father-son team who together compete almost every weekend in some backbreaking marathon. And if they're not in a marathon, they are in a triathlon—a daunting combination of 26.2 miles of running, 112 miles of biking, and 2.4 miles of swimming. Together they have climbed mountains, and once trekked 3,735 miles across America.

It's a remarkable record of exertion and discipline—all the more so when you consider that Rick can't walk or talk.

Over the past 30 years, 65-year-old Dick has pushed and pulled his son across the country and over hundreds of finish lines. When Dick runs, he pushes Rick in a wheelchair. When Dick cycles, Rick is in a seat on the front of the bike. And when Dick swims, he pulls

Rick in an inflatable dinghy.

Rick's fight started at birth when he was diagnosed with cerebral palsy. "The doctors told us that Rick would be a vegetable for the rest of his life," Dick said. "They told us to forget him. Put him in an institution. On our way home, my wife and I cried." But the Hoyts refused to abandon Rick and, much to the surprise of doctors and others around him, Rick responded. "When you looked in his eyes and he was looking right at you, you could tell there was a lot going on up there," said Dick.

At 12 years old, Rick proved doctors wrong when he found his voice through a computer called the Hope Machine. Soon after, Rick learned of a five-mile charity race for an athlete from his school who had been paralyzed in an accident. Rick told his father he wanted to show his support. Dick doubted that he, a self-described "porker," could run five miles while pushing his son in a wheelchair, but he gave it a shot.

"That first race almost killed me," Dick remembers. But none of that mattered when Rick told him, "Dad, when we're running I don't feel like I'm paralyzed anymore."

That was all Dick needed to hear, and he knew what he needed to do. That sentence changed their lives, and countless others, forever. Team Hoyt was born.

Today the duo is embraced by all who meet or even hear of them, but it wasn't always that way. In the beginning, Dick remembers, "Nobody wanted Rick in a road race. Everybody looked at us. Nobody talked to us. Nobody wanted to have anything to do with us." Even the Boston Marathon, which Team Hoyt now competes in every year, wouldn't let them enter until they completed another qualifying race in record-setting time.

For most of Team Hoyt's running career, almost no one knew what Dick was doing. It wasn't some kind of a media stunt or bid for fame. It was simply a father and son spending time together in a way that made them both feel more alive. After more than two decades of quietly sharing this joy within their family, Team Hoyt became worldwide celebrities when someone noticed them at a race, and put a video of the pair on YouTube. That video, translated into half a dozen languages, is still one of the most watched in the history of YouTube. Team Hoyt is now regularly invited to participate in races around the world.

But that's not why Dick Hoyt did it. He didn't start running marathons with his son to become a famous face or even to generate inspiration for others. He did it because he loved his son and wanted the best for him.

It's not about winning—they've never finished first in a race (though Dick is proud to note they've never finished last, either). It's not about attention—they've been pretty anonymous for most of their running career. It's about doing the right thing—the thing that would give them both a new purpose in life and forge an incredible bond. And despite all of the attention in recent years, they still tackle each race for the same reason: because it is how they continue to grow...together.

Dick was determined never to give up. His motivation is singular and selfless. He is determined to give his son a better life, a life that transcends the limitations of his body.

"He is not just my arms and legs," writes Rick. "He's my inspiration, the person who allows me to live my life to the fullest and inspire others to do the same."

Dick and Rick Hoyt are living proof that the decisions we make when no one is watching are the ones that truly define us. The duo never set out to become famous, but the tremendous love that has propelled this father-and-son team to pursue something extraordinary has become a story that has captured the hearts of countless people.

The desire simply to win isn't enough to get you to the finish line every time. There has to be something more that inspires you to start each race and see it through. Integrity is about more than just choosing right over wrong; it is about living in such a way that your actions are consistently rooted in a genuine desire for something Greater.

Rick showed this with his request to run that very first race—

he had a selfless desire to support someone else. Dick showed this when he agreed to a difficult task—he knew it would be a beneficial experience for his son. And together, both have lived this kind of day-in-day-out integrity with every race they've run, and every challenge they've overcome.

Consider today what motivates you each morning. What decisions are you making that no one else may see but that determine the course of each day, the direction of your career or hobbies, and even your relationships with the people around you? Why do you do what you choose to do?

When no one was watching, Dick Hoyt made the right choice. That's Greatness.

More from the Truly Great

Fame and honor are not the same thing. Fame is just recognition—anyone hounded by the paparazzi can attest to that. Honor is much more difficult to cultivate and much more rare to witness.

Every year, numerous athletic organizations present awards to honor athletes and coaches who exemplify the ideals of sportsmanship and character. Some of the honorees are famous, some are local names, and some are hardly known outside their schools or leagues. But so many of the stories that emerge from programs stand as reminders that doing right is infinitely more important that winning.

Take, for example, Teresa Clark. Now retired, she coached volleyball at Cedarville University for ten years and was named the NAIA Coach of Character in 2006 for the success she brought to the program. Her secret was to teach her athletes integrity. If a player touched the ball before it went out of bounds but was not called for it, she would inform the officials in what Clark termed an "honor call"—even if the call cost her team the game. Her players developed not only as athletes, but as citizens—and Clark never had a losing season in her coaching career.

Another great example of integrity was modeled by the Edwardsville High School wrestling team. When they defeated

Granite City High School in a nail-biter of a final round in the regional finals in 2008, the team celebrated their half-point victory and the trip to the state competition.

There was just one problem: the half-point advantage wasn't theirs. A friend quietly informed Edwardsville coach, Jon Wagner, that a scoring discrepancy had skewed the final tally in Edwardsville's favor. When Coach Wagner recalculated the score, he discovered the error and knew that the only thing to do was to contact the Granite City team and work to get them the title that was rightfully theirs.

The Illinois High School Association initially upheld its decision, despite the agreement between both teams as to the real results of the meet. But the Edwardsville coaches and wrestlers, along with the parents and school administrators, would not accept their unearned victory and appealed a second time. Granite City was finally awarded the title and the place at the state competition that was fairly theirs. The young men on Coach Wagner's team learned an incredible lesson in how to live a life of integrity. The wrestling team of Edwardsville High School was honored in 2008 by the National Federation of State High School Associations for their conduct—recognition of real Greatness.

With fewer than 100 fans watching from the stands, Sara Tucholsky hit her first career home run when it counted: late in the season as her Western Oregon University team fought Central Washington toward the conference championship.

Tucholsky's shot went out of the park, and in her exuberance she missed tagging first base. Realizing her mistake, she turned back quickly but tore her ACL in the process. In agony, she crawled back to first but couldn't go any farther. And if she didn't round the bases, the point wouldn't count, nor would she be able to meet one of her collegiate goals: to hit a home run.

Her coach, Pam Knox, asked if another Western Oregon player

could help her around the bases, but the umpire explained it was against the rules—if a teammate touched her, she would be called out.

First baseman Mallory Holtman, who happened to be Central Washington's career home run leader—walked up to the umpire and asked if she, as an player from the opposite team, could help Tucholsky around the bases. He said there was no rule preventing it, so Holtman and shortstop Liz Wallace asked Tucholsky if it was okay to help her around the bases.

"I said, 'Thank you,' and she said, 'You hit the ball over the fence, you deserve it.'" Tucholsky told ESPN. "I have a lot of respect for her and her teammates, and I can't thank her enough."

Holtman and Wallace—whose Central Washington team lost the game, 4–2—showed true integrity by acting against their own team's goal because it was the right thing to do. There weren't huge crowds or television cameras to celebrate their decision. Holtman and Wallace weren't acting for headlines, but because they wanted to do what they felt should be done.

Holtmon later remarked that she didn't understand the fuss that followed. She looked up in the stands as the trio rounded the bases and saw tears, but maintained the help she and Wallace provided was nothing special: "Granted, I thought of it, but everyone else would have done it," she told ESPN. For those young women, it was not about impressing the scant crowd at their game; it was about doing what was right.

"It's a great moment when someone has character to step up and do the right thing at the right time," said Western Oregon coach Pam Knox.

And for the Truly Great in Business

In the corporate world, it's the same thing. Employees with integrity bring that sense of honor to the workplace. Those who aspire to be Great put their focus on the job at hand and don't allow themselves to get distracted from their purpose. Even when their managers are away, they stay on task and don't get distracted by access to the Internet or free phone calls on company time. That's not to say they don't have fun and enjoy their work, but they get the job done.

On a much larger scale, companies made up of people with integrity will put doing the right thing ahead of the convenient or profitable thing.

For example, in 2001, two patients in Spain died within hours of receiving dialysis from Baxter products. The company teamed up with an independent testing company to launch an investigation but found nothing wrong. Still, the death toll continued to rise.

Even though Baxter couldn't determine a link between the deaths and its products, they voluntarily recalled and then stopped manufacturing the product worldwide. They then shut down the plants that made the filters and settled with the families involved. In addition, Baxter Chairman Harry Kraemer voluntarily took a 40 percent cut in his bonus and reduced the other executives' bonuses by 20 percent.

Baxter couldn't be proven to be at fault, but the company stuck to its values and accepted responsibility. Kraemer agrees that articulating the vision throughout the company is key. "I always say that we're fortunate to be in a business where you can do well by doing good," he told the *Harvard Management Update.*

A similar situation occurred in 1982, when seven people in the Chicago area died after taking Tylenol products that had been tampered with. Within days of the first death, Johnson & Johnson CEO James Burke issued a nationwide recall of the approximately 31 million bottles of his company's products, at a cost of more than $100 million. He also issued warnings to hospitals and launched an ad campaign urging consumers to cease the use of all Tylenol products.

Even though it was quickly determined that the poisonings had taken place in the retail stores themselves and therefore outside of the Tylenol facilities, Burke pulled all of his company's products anyway. To him, the issue was no longer about his company's reputation or profit but about making sure no further lives were lost.

Although the culprit has never been apprehended and it remains an open case in the FBI files, Tylenol recovered its losses quickly thanks in large part to the integrity it showed during the tragedy. Now, with anti-tampering packaging and other safety measures put into place, Tylenol is once again one of the largest and most trusted brands on the market.

Maintaining integrity in the face of pressure separates the good from the Great. Too often, good people get caught up chasing the wrong standard of excellence and lose their way. Take Martin Winterkorn, former CEO of Volkswagen. Rather than build a company that everyone connected to the brand could be proud of, Winterkorn decided he wanted to preside over the "largest automaker in the world."

In 2011, Winterkorn presented a bold vision for Volkswagen – he wanted to overtake Toyota by 2018 as the world's leading automaker in production. This plan, though ambitious and seemingly great for his company, led to twisted decisions and sketchy tactics to circumvent standards. Why? Winterkorn's ambitions centered around one piece of technology – clean diesel. Like Toyota's hybrid-electric Prius, Volkswagen looked to clean diesel to provide a fuel efficient and inexpensive solution to America's growing consumer demands for higher gas mileage while meeting the government's stricter control on emission levels.

However, clean diesel, as yet, has proven to be a myth. In September of 2015, Volkswagen admitted to installing software in 11 million diesel cars to deceive emissions testers and Winterkorn was forced to resign. Ironically, the revelation – and the resignation – came just months after Volkswagen had achieved his grandiose goal, passing Toyota years ahead of schedule.

Though Winterkorn continues to claim he had no knowledge of the tampering, integrity begins with leadership.

In an era where transparency is essential to survival and where news shifts to scandal with one viral post, most companies are far more aware of their ethical responsibilities. Many major corporations, including Boeing, Nike, and HP, have established a code of ethics, by which each employee must abide. It's not a public relations move; these creeds are not paraded out for the public to see. They are in place because these companies understand that how they operate when no one else is watching determines who they really are.

For example, Chevron worked its values into a pledge called "the Chevron Way." Employees take the pledge seriously, and the company works to conduct itself in a socially responsible and ethical way and strives to respect the law, support human rights universally, and protect the environment and communities.

The GREATNESS Challenge

How is your character guiding you? Legendary UCLA basketball coach John Wooden once said, "Be more concerned with your character than your reputation, because your character is what you really are, while your reputation is merely what others think you are."

Can you name one action or decision from today that was driven by your character, versus your reputation? What about this week? This month?

How do you would handle yourself in a place where no one knows who you are or what you're doing? As Rick Warren describes in his book *The Purpose Driven Life,* there are the people who carelessly throw trash out the windows of their cars and then there are the people who walk by and pick it up. When no one is looking, which person are you?

It all comes down to this basic truth: integrity is who we are, and who we are determines what we do. "Our system of values is so much a part of us we cannot separate it from ourselves," John C. Maxwell said in *Go for Gold: Inspiration to Increase Your Leadership Impact.* "It becomes our navigating system and guides us."

The convictions that you hold most dear can be spiritual, professional, or communal—whatever steers you. Imagine that an outside observer was doing a study of your life. Would they note the same convictions, or do you think they might get a very different impression of your values? What does your walk say about your talk? What decisions have you made privately that have come to shape who you are and what you pursue? Would people describe you as someone who strives always to make the best choice, or as someone whose motivation is more externally driven?

In Gary Mack's book, *Mind Gym,* he adopts former NFL and college coach John McKay's "mirror test," in which McKay says what matters "is if you can look in the mirror and honestly tell the person you see there that you've done your best." That's integrity.

Try that this evening. Can you honestly face your reflection and say you were the best person you could be today? If so, congratulations! Keep it up! If not, consider what you can do differently tomorrow.

If everything about you and the way you do business became transparent, would you be comfortable if anyone could see how you really operate—your parents, spouse, children, and close friends included? Take an honest assessment of your conduct over the past month. Is there any decision you've made or action you've taken that you would do differently if it were to be brought to light? Do you find that you tend to be a different person in public than you are in private?

If the answer is yes, decide who it is that you want to be, what qualities you'd like to be known for, and what mode of living gives you the clearest conscience at night. Make a list of "integrity goals"—ways of behaving that you feel are a more accurate and honorable reflection of who you want to be. Set one integrity goal for the next day, week, and month, and pay attention to see how your outlook and sense of peace increase as you achieve each one.

Pick a person whom you admire for their leadership and integrity qualities. Make a list of qualities the person possesses. Which of those qualities do you feel you possess, and do you practice those qualities regularly?

In *The Winning Spirit,* Tom Mitchell and Joe Montana suggest looking at the list again, selecting a quality from the list that you don't have, and focus on practicing it for the next thirty days with the intent to display it so much that someone comments on your newfound quality.

It is one thing to act with integrity when circumstances call for it, and another to live with it each and every day of your life. Through challenges, tragedy, or triumphs, when everyone is watching or when no one is around, integrity is living with honor and respect, and acting for all the right reasons.

Integrity isn't just about honesty. It isn't always righting a wrong—though that's certainly something a person with integrity does. Integrity is simply holding oneself to a high standard and consistently adhering to it no matter the circumstances. It is unwavering standards that don't change with the circumstances—audience or not, public or private. A life of integrity is honest, good, fair, and consistent. It is rare, but it is powerful. In short, it is Great.

CHAPTER

15

When Everyone Is Watching

They embrace the idea of being a role model.

His father left his mother two days before Dale Brown's birth, but that abandonment taught Brown an important lesson. From his father's departure, the future Louisiana State University basketball coach came to value loyalty and a strong example above all else.

As a young boy, Brown lived in Minot, North Dakota, in a one-room apartment. Yet despite the fact that his mother was a single parent working and making ends meet with welfare, on more than one occasion she braved the frigid North Dakota temperatures to return extra change a grocery store clerk had given her by accident.

His mother became an extraordinary role model for Dale, and in turn he would become a standout role model for countless others. To this day, players like Shaquille O'Neal and John Williams say "unquestioned integrity" was the greatest lesson they ever learned from Coach Brown, and that "honest" and "loyal" are still the two words that most accurately describe the winningest coach in LSU basketball history. In a world full of scandal, gambling, and steroids, Dale Brown has always focused on doing what he believed was right because, as a coach, he knew that his players would be looking to his example.

He wasn't afraid to set an example for his bosses, either. In 1972, when Brown was just a little-known assistant coach at Washington State, he received a call to interview for the head coaching position at Louisiana State University—the chance of a lifetime. But instead of answering their questions with what he thought they wanted to hear, as he sat before the interview committee Brown announced: "I think you should know before you interview me that I am not going to be dictated by a kid's ethnic status, color, or religion. I'm recruiting human beings first and basketball players second. It makes no difference to me what they look like. That's the way I operate."

People said he was crazy for declaring he would aggressively work to more fully integrate an LSU basketball program that had only one black player by 1972. But Dale Brown got the job and he stayed true to his principles as his team captured the national spotlight. He built from the ground up a basketball program at a football school, and he continued to run a clean program—and foster a clean reputation—throughout his twenty-five-year career at LSU.

But even before he became a big name, he understood the importance of being a solid role model. In 1964, Brown was teaching physical education at Garfield Junior High in Berkeley, California, when he was introduced to a young troublemaker who was on the verge of getting kicked out of school.

The boy was tiny, tough, and tired. He was very dirty and obviously quite poor. Other teachers wanted nothing more to do with the boy, but Brown could see that he just needed a mentor. "I know what it is like to be poor," Brown explained, "but poverty doesn't mean you have to be dirty. People don't respect you if you don't respect yourself."

Soon after, the boy had cleaned up and started to take pride in himself. He told Brown the thing he liked to do most was playing baseball, but admitted he didn't go out for the team because he didn't have a glove. So the following weekend, Brown took him shopping to fix that.

The boy stared at his glove for a minute before breaking down in tears and asking his teacher to sign it. Brown declined, explaining to the boy that the glove belonged to him. "I know, but I want your name on it," he said, wiping his eyes. "You're the first person to ever care about me."

That day, Dale Brown did something that would be a part of his career for the rest of his life: he became a role model to someone who needed him. He was able to make a difference when no one else was willing to try.

Greatness cannot be found in a win-at-all-costs approach. Dale Brown led by example. He taught life lessons and he proved to everyone watching—even in the dog-eat-dog world of college basketball—you don't have to sacrifice your morals to be successful. The truly Great embrace the idea of being a role model and act accordingly.

Honesty and loyalty will translate into longevity and success for anyone in any field, but more important, they are qualities that can influence others and make a difference in people's lives.

There are the choices we make quietly each day, and there are they choices we make because we understand that we have a responsibility to model right living. "The supreme quality for leadership is unquestionably integrity," Dwight D. Eisenhower once said. "Without it, no real success is possible, no matter whether it is on a section gang, a football field, in an army, or in an office."

More from the Truly Great

Have you embraced the idea of being a role model? Because, like it or not, there is always someone watching. Your attitude and your actions can and will have a profound impact—positive or negative—on the lives of others.

Consider how the following Great ones inspired others by embracing the idea of being a role model when all eyes were on them:

If anyone has ever felt like everyone was watching, like the weight of the world was on his shoulders, it was Jackie Robinson.

"He knew he had to do well," said Dodger teammate Duke Snider. "He knew that the future of blacks in baseball depended on it. The pressure was enormous, overwhelming, and unbearable at times. I don't know how he held up. I know I never could have."

On April 15, 1947, Robinson jogged onto Ebbets Field before twenty-six thousand spectators to start for the Dodgers at first base. By stepping on that field, Robinson was attempting to integrate the famed pastime of a nation whose own government had yet to legislate full desegregation. Robinson's major-league debut marked the beginning of one of the most trying journeys endured by a single man in American history.

"Jackie, we've got no army. There's virtually nobody on our side. No owners, no umpires, very few newspapermen. And I'm afraid that many fans will be hostile. We'll be in a tough position," Brooklyn Dodgers general manager Branch Rickey told him. "We can win only if we can convince the world that I'm doing this because you're a great ballplayer, a fine gentleman."

Robinson lived and played under a microscope. He endured every cheap shot imaginable. Pitchers threw at him, base runners spiked him, and he was bombarded with hate mail and death threats. All his life Robinson had never been one to turn the other cheek, but now he realized the choice was no longer his.

Robinson embraced the idea of being a role model for a cause much bigger than his own. He sacrificed to make an impact that reached well beyond major-league ballparks.

"He was taking us over segregation's threshold into a new land whose scenery made every black person stop and stare in reverence," baseball great Hank Aaron said in *Time* magazine. "We were all with Jackie. We slid into every base that he swiped, ducked at every fastball that hurtled toward his head. I'm still inspired by Jackie Robinson. Hardly a day goes by that I don't think of him."

After sixteen years of professional golf, Brian Davis found himself on the verge of his first PGA tournament title. But in a sudden-death playoff with PGA great Jim Furyk, the unthinkable happened.

While hitting onto the green, Davis felt his 7-iron brush a small reed in his backswing. Immediately, he called the tournament director over, explained what had happened, and insisted that he be penalized the standard two strokes under PGA Rule 13.4, which prohibits "touching or moving a loose impediment."

The violation was barely discernible, even in slow motion. But after reviewing video of Davis's play, officials were able to confirm that a tiny twig had, in fact, been disturbed by his backswing. The penalty assured Davis he would finish second—and lose $411,000 that was the gap between the first- and second-place checks. But no one—not even Furyk, for whom this victory at the Heritage was his fifteenth on the PGA tour—considers Davis to have been the loser that day.

Tournament director Slugger White praised Davis's honesty, insisting: "That will come back to him in spades, tenfold." And in some ways, it already has. Almost immediately, Davis started receiving voice mails, text messages, and e-mails thanking him for his honesty, remarking on his integrity, and above all, congratulating him on being a solid role model.

Brian Davis could have easily let the violation slide, since no one else had noticed it or called a penalty. But Davis knew what the rules of the game dictated, and he knew that his character was more important than a win. To be truly Great, his life must set an example.

Had he won the tournament, Davis would have commanded a lot of media attention. But he knew he'd broken the rules—as unwittingly as he had—and therefore didn't earn the title. It hurt him to lose the match, but it would have hurt him more to win under the circumstances. "You're not playing for second, but playing to win. But I can hold my head up high," he explained.

Similarly, on the sporting world's list of "good guys," Ken Griffey Jr. was one of the best. A former American League MVP who was also one of the best home-run hitters baseball has ever seen, he's currently ranked sixth on the list of most career home runs (though he should be fourth, considering both Barry Bonds and Alex Rodriquez were accused of steroid use) and tied with Don Mattingly for the most consecutive games with a home run. But Griffey placed something other than his career first.

He didn't have an arrest record; he wasn't splashed on tabloid covers for outrageous antics; his name was never inked to any discussion about performance enhancing substances. That's just not who he was. In fact, during his thirties when Griffey was facing injury after injury, the MLB was enamored with power hitters, Griffey was facing a string of injuries. He resisted the temptation to use performance enhancing drugs, though and ultimately retired with fewer homeruns and fewer games due to injuries. Buthe also left with his integrity.

A former teammate recalled: "You know what? He even got injured the right way. Meaning, during that era, people were taking stuff and other people were turning a blind eye. Junior was on the field busting his butt to play and freaks of nature happened. He got injured. He never traded in his integrity for self-promotion, so to speak."

A dedicated husband and father, Griffey switched the number 30 he'd worn on his jersey for the entire duration of his professional career to the number 3 in honor of his children. His family was always his top priority, along with the foundation that bears his name and supports a number of children's hospitals, as well as working with Boys and Girls Clubs across the country.

In short, Griffey understood that developing a personal life was not about stealing headlines. But the tremendous fan base he developed over the years was always quick to point out that he was a man who managed to do both. Griffey himself believed that living quietly as a family man and a solid role model was his most important priority. In retirement, he lives up to this reputation, spending most of his time supporting his children's athletic careers, most notably as a photographer for his son's football games.

Billie Jean King was already a role model in her own right, but one of her most crowning achievements came from accepting a challenge outside of the traditional tennis circuit on September 20, 1973.

In the so-called Battle of the Sexes, King made a stand for women's sports when she defeated male chauvinist and former top-ranked men's tennis player Bobby Riggs in front of 30,000 spectators and another 50 million television viewers from 37 different countries. Knowing that a loss would doom women's athletics in the court of public opinion, King stood up to Riggs's sexist remarks and scored a victory that was felt all over the world. What was more, her example set the stage for a new generation of female athletes to become popular figures in the mainstream.

Consider the doors King opened for athletes like Mia Hamm. Hamm's gender and style of play put her on a platform to be noticed by young athletes, and she embraced that platform, using it to inspire girls to be a tough, fierce competitor in soccer.

"I grew up always good at sports, but being a girl, I was never allowed to feel as good about it as guys were," Hamm told *Sports Illustrated.* "My toughness wasn't celebrated."

It wasn't long before Mia Hamm was the best, and, in the process she inspired young girls all over the country to be their best. At North Carolina, she led the Tar Heels to four national championships and an impeccable record of 95–1. Internationally, she helped the US national team win two FIFA Women's World Cup Championships, and her 158 career goals are second to no one—man or woman—in soccer history.

"Every little girl's dream is to be like Mia," said teammate Carla Overbeck. "They want her autograph, they want their picture taken with her—they're screaming her name throughout the game. There's no better role model out there than Mia Hamm."

While Hamm accepted the daunting responsibility of being a role model and the face of women's soccer—and, to some extent, women's athletics—she humbly refused any notion of celebrity status and directed the national spotlight to her sport and her teammates. In doing so, Hamm helped draw the largest audience for a women's sporting event in history. In front of an unprecedented ninety thousand fans at the Rose Bowl and another 40 million viewers on television, the US national team defeated China to win the 1999 FIFA Women's World Cup.

"She was the definitive face of the sport, and that was not a responsibility that she took lightly," University of North Carolina coach Anson Dorrance said in an interview with ESPN. "She knew she was carrying the torch, and never forgot how important it was to represent herself and her teammates well."

When the world was tuned in and the pressure was on, Mia Hamm was an inspiration to girls all over the country who were unsure of themselves and their dreams. She embraced the idea of being a role model, helped put women's sports on the map, and made believers out of all of us.

"She has changed the face of sport for girls," said Lauren Gregg, a former assistant coach for the US national team. "[Now] it is acceptable for girls to be beautiful, be athletic, be smart, and be professional athletes."

When everyone was watching, not only were Dale Brown, Jackie Robinson, Brian Davis, Ken Griffey Jr., Billie Jean King, and Mia Hamm willing to be role models, but they were willing to take on causes much bigger than themselves. And, as a result, their successes inspired people to pursue dreams of their own.

"Without heroes, we are all plain people, and don't know how far we can go," Bernard Malamud, the author of the baseball novel *The Natural,* once said. More than anything, people need someone they can look up to—someone who will raise the bar and redefine what is possible.

Being a role model, especially to children, is important to many athletes and entertainers. They're in the spotlight, and the world sees what they do. But that's not why they do it; the Great ones do it because it's the right thing to do.

And for the Truly Great in Business

Katharine Graham understood the challenge of working without a professional role model. When she took over as acting publisher of the *Washington Post* in 1963 (she wasn't given the full title until 1979), there were almost no other women in similar positions anywhere in the world. With no professional peers, and while still struggling to make inroads in what had long been considered a boys' club, she was determined to be one of the toughest publishers out there, not only for the sake of journalistic integrity but also to set the stage for women who might want to follow in her footsteps.

Her masterful management of the newspaper, her grace and strength in the face of personal tragedy, and her extensive philanthropic work all helped to make Katherine Graham one of the most respected figures in her field and a legend to generations of reporters and publishers alike.

Taking a very different path, Dave Thomas, the founder of Wendy's and a huge supporter of foster care and adoption, recognized the fact that people will emulate those who are successful—even their flaws. Thomas, a high school dropout, was worried that his success despite that choice might encourage others to drop out, as well. Knowing he was a role model, he earned his GED in 1993—when he was sixty-two years old. He didn't want anyone looking up to him to make the same bad decision he had.

Carlos Gutierrez, former CEO of Kellogg's and secretary of commerce under President George W. Bush, is known for being one of the hardest-working—and most down-to-earth—people in corporate America and Washington, D.C. His family was driven out of Cuba by the revolution and found themselves starting over in Miami with nothing. Faced with such circumstances, Gutierrez was determined early on to become not only a success in business but also a role model to Hispanic youth.

Studying business in Mexico as a college student in order to gain a broader perspective on North American markets, Gutierrez joined Kellogg's upon graduation and rose rapidly through the ranks to become the company's youngest CEO in its 100year history, as well as the only Latin-American CEO of a Fortune 500 company at that time. But his successful business career, as well as his presidential appointment, never went to his head. The entire Gutierrez family, including his wife and two children, are well known for being approachable, accessible, and outstanding ambassadors to the next generation of immigrant business leaders.

Leaders like Katharine Graham, Dave Thomas, and Carlos Gutierrez enjoyed tremendous success in their areas of work, but at the end of the day their influence reached well beyond their workplaces. When the whole world watched, they stuck to their principles and sought to make the unique experiences in each of their lives positive examples of what it means to be Great.

Role-model status can change in the blink of an eye, however. Consider the sharp turn around in Bernie Madoff's career from being a celebrated investment advisor with a well-respected company to being an almost universally despised scam artist who cost his clients—many of whom were retirees and philanthropic foundations—millions upon millions of dollars. A similar thing happened to Tiger Woods, who went from being arguably the most popular golfer of all time for both his talent and his clean-cut image, to being outed as a serial philanderer.

Being a role model is not a part-time job. It is not only understanding but embracing the scrutiny of others' eyes, knowing that one's life, ethics, and leadership decisions can not only stand the test but inspire others to reach higher, too.

The GREATNESS Challenge

Are you ready to make a difference? What is it about you and what you have accomplished that could be an inspiration to others? What kind of example are you setting with your life? When the stakes are high and you know that people are looking up to you, how do you act? Could the battles you have fought and the challenges you have overcome serve as encouragement to someone if you only took a minute to share your experiences?

Author Mark Twain said that the truly Great "make you feel that you, too, can become great." We all need someone in our lives whom we can look up to. Without Great men and women to follow, we would not question our limitations or dream as big as we do. Whom do you look up to? What is it about that person that makes him or her a role model? What have you learned from him or her?

Role models are more than childhood heroes. Even as we grow up and grow old we still need people to inspire us, to believe in us, and to push us toward greatness. Never stop looking for role models, and never doubt your ability to have an impact on others.

If today was your last day on Earth, what advice would you give your family, friends, and colleagues? Could they learn those same lessons by simply watching you in your everyday life?

Joe DiMaggio gave his all in every game because he was motivated by the thought that there was always a kid seeing him play for the first time. He felt that he owed each kid his best. "A person always doing his or her best becomes a natural leader, just by example," DiMaggio said.

If you are looking for another reason to strive to be the best you can be, DiMaggio offers a compelling thought. It is also an important reminder that being a role model is easier than you think, and the number of people you influence without even knowing it would probably surprise you.

Do you actively strive to be a role model in your field and within your community? What steps could you take to increase the positive impact you have on others? Is there a colleague, friend, or family member you could take under your wing?

Remember, every time you make the right choices you are encouraging others around you to do the same. And when you can, take a break from your own goals to push others toward theirs. Embrace the idea of being a role model and realize the potential you have to be a positive influence in the lives of many.

Dale Brown had an athletic director at LSU who supported

his philosophy and encouraged him to stay his course. Try to find those kinds of people to work for, and then strive be that person of integrity in your office. Stay true to yourself, and in doing so, be a role model to your children, your colleagues, and your community.

Taking risks and working for a competitive advantage doesn't mean taking shortcuts. Your character is the Greatest thing you have. More often than not, it's the foundation of your best sales pitch.

Build positive images into your corporate image, and live up to that image. Many companies use their public face and market clout to help raise awareness or to inspire others to reach out, too. For example, Dawn dish soap boosted its environmental image when it ran a commercial campaign focusing on how it was used to clean wildlife victims of oil spills. Likewise, TOMS Shoes created its business model around the concept of social responsibility. For each pair of shoes sold, the company donates another to an underdeveloped country. As of late 2009, 140,000 pairs had been distributed in Argentina, Ethiopia, and South Africa.

Live as if you're being watched, because you are. Every day, you put yourself in public and on display. How you react to the world around you is witnessed, both by friends and strangers alike.

Think about the office culture you've helped create. Does it represent you and your values? Why or why not? What could you do differently to improve it? Write down three traits you would like to see your company or your brand represent, and then the steps that you can personally take to bring about such a change.

Nnamdi Asomugha, of the Oakland Raiders, Philadelphia Eagles, and San Francisco 49ers, said he was taught early by his parents, who had fled their native Nigeria, that giving was "what we're supposed to do." Asomugha's off-the-field work encouraged young people to value their education. He told me once in an interview that in order to give back, we needed to make a difference for others by sharing what we have in abundance, whether it's time, wisdom, money, or goods.

We are all role models to somebody. Understanding that others are watching your every step, while at the same time choosing paths of their own, is the Greatest—and most wonderful—burden anyone can carry.

The Great ones understand that what sets them apart is also what makes them role models, and they take that responsibility seriously. They relish the chance to do the right thing.

CHAPTER 16

Records Are Made to Be Broken

They know their legacy isn't what they did on the field. They are well-rounded.

Long before Tom Brady and Peyton Manning, there was an NFL quarterback who could do it all—one Brady and Manning looked up to and idolized as kids. Nicknamed "Captain Comeback," this signal caller could throw, he could run, and, like any Great quarterback, he was more than capable of leading his team to victory when it mattered most in the fourth quarter.

Over the course of his eleven-year career in the NFL, Roger Staubach earned his nickname by leading the Dallas Cowboys to 23 fourth-quarter comebacks, 14 of which came with less than two minutes left in the game. And if the Cowboys were, in fact, America's team, then Roger Staubach was America's quarterback.

Staubach got his start at the Naval Academy, where head coach Wayne Hardin inserted the sophomore into the fourth game of the team's 1962 season against Cornell. Hardin hoped Staubach might kick-start his fledgling offense, and that was exactly what he did. Staubach led Navy to six touchdown drives and a 41–0 victory.

He went on to win the Heisman the following season and was heralded as the best quarterback in Navy's football history. He was drafted in 1964 by the Cowboys, but he didn't join the team until five years later, after honoring his military commitment, which included a voluntary tour of duty in Vietnam.

The 27-year-old rookie didn't win the starting job until his third season in the league, but once the job was his, he wasted little time. Staubach took over the 4–3 Cowboys midseason in 1971 and led them all the way to a Super Bowl title.

Staubach went on to throw 153 touchdown passes, rush for another 20 touchdowns, coin the term "Hail Mary" for his incredible against-all-odds-passes, and win two of four Super Bowl appearances before retiring in 1980.

But despite all his success on the field, Roger Staubach wasn't just a football player. He was one of the first high-profile athletes to understand that his true legacy would be determined away from the gridiron. And off the field he was just as versatile.

"Roger was always one of my football heroes and the older I got, the more I learned about him as a person and not the quarterback," Peyton Manning said. "He's not only a success in business, but he carries himself with dignity and does many positive things in the community."

When he wasn't playing football, Staubach, a devoted husband and father of five, worked in the off-season and went on to found the Staubach Company—his own commercial real estate firm. As CEO, Staubach developed his company into a successful multi-billion-dollar business, with more than a 1,300 employees and working partners positioned all over the world. In 2008, Staubach sold his company to Jones Lang LaSalle for $613 million, which would gross over $100 million in a trust for Staubauch and his children by 2013.

But even more important, Staubach was one of the pioneering few to kick-start the NFL's philanthropic partnership with the United Way. To this day, the NFL's relationship with the United Way is the longest-running and most visible charity of its kind. Staubach was one of the first spokesmen to volunteer on behalf of the United Way, and the ad campaign quickly became one of the most successful in television history.

According to the United Way, when the public-service ads first aired in 1974, the foundation collectively raised $800 million. Today, and more than a thousand commercials later, annual giving to the United Way is more than $5 billion.

Success has always seemed to follow Roger Staubach, no matter where he's been in life, and his story goes to show that a well-rounded and dedicated individual can be a lasting influence on a wide variety of playing fields. He is a father and a husband. He is a Christian, a leader, and an active voice in his community. He is a military man, a businessman, and a football player.

When Staubach retired from football, he had set seven records for the Dallas Cowboys, and he had the second-highest passer rating in NFL history. He was voted into the Pro Football Hall of Fame in 1985.

Now, each one of those records has been surpassed. Staubach is still one of the Greats, but his name at the top has been replaced by another player. The league's partnership with the United Way, however, lives on, and Staubach continues to contribute today as a major spokesperson.

He did something other than just play football—while he was playing football. His NFL legacy is greater than Super Bowls, touchdown passes, or games played. It's about millions of dollars raised and many lives touched.

Too many people become stuck in their own daily routine, or they live in their own little world and fail to see what exists beyond their office walls. Roger Staubach could have made football his entire life, but he knew at the end of the day that touchdowns and a few drops of ink in the record books wouldn't matter all that much.

Because the truly Great, like Roger Staubach, realize that records are made to be broken. They know their legacy isn't what they did on the field. They are well rounded. They use their work on the field to become something special off it. Greatness does not have tunnel vision. It sees beyond the immediate and recognizes that there is a life outside of and after its ambitions.

More from the Truly Great

The Great ones understand that life needs to have another dimension; it needs to not only reach up, but to reach out.

That's the spirit that epitomizes former NBA All-Star Dikembe Mutombo, who has used his success to improve the living conditions in his native Congo. Mutombo's foundation worked toward opening a $29 million hospital in his home country, and he immediately put up $3.5 million of his own money to start the fund-raising effort. When fund-raising stalled, he donated another $15 million to help complete the modern three-hundred-bed facility. When it opened in 2007, it was the first modern hospital built in the area in over forty years.

"This hospital was such a dream and today it is becoming a reality and so important to so many people," Mutombo told the Associated Press. "We think that Congolese people deserve better health care, and we hope that what we are doing here is setting an example so that people can have hope."

Mutombo, who lives in Atlanta with his wife and six children, knew that he could provide people access to medical care they otherwise wouldn't have had. For his efforts, he's been awarded several honors, including the Jackie Robinson Humanitarian Award, *Time*'s European Hero Award, and a mention by name in George W. Bush's State of the Union address in 2007. But what matters to him is that because of his efforts, the Congolese have a better chance at fighting diseases such as malaria, AIDS/HIV, malaria, polio, and other infectious diseases.

Recognizing that he could use his success as a professional athlete to support his native country, Mutombo set out with a plan to improve lives. His long-term vision is focused not on making it to the Hall of Fame, but on being something more than just a basketball player.

Babe Zaharias is routinely ranked as one of the top ten greatest athletes of the 20th century for her unparalleled talent in track and field, golf, and basketball. But it was more than just her performance in competition that makes her truly Great.

In 1932, Zaharias set five world records in one afternoon at the Amateur Athletic Union Track and Field championship. That same year, she also won two Olympic golds and one silver in the 80 m hurdles, javelin throw, and high jump, respectively. Later branching out into gold and becoming a founding member of the LPGA, she won 17 consecutive titles as well as winning every single major golfing championship open to women.

A natural athlete, Zaharias also excelled at basketball, diving, and even billiards, but she was determined to be about more than just sports. She performed on the vaudeville circuit where she proved to be a talented musician both on the harmonic and as a singer; she even recorded several hit records. She enjoyed sewing and made many of her own clothes both for every day wear as well as for golfing. She even took a turn as an actress and appeared in the movie *Pat and Mike* with Katharine Hepburn and Spencer Tracy. After a diagnosis of colon cancer, which would eventually take her life at age 45, Zaharias was an outspoken advocated of cancer research, establishing a fund to help support cancer treatment centers. In short, she was a woman who was always willing to embrace everything life had to offer.

Sporting what is arguably the most remarkable batter's eye in baseball, Ted Williams was a two-time American League MVP, two-time Triple Crown winner—and two-time United States Marine Corps pilot.

On May 22, 1942, Williams was sworn in and served as a flight instructor at the Naval Air Station in Pensacola, Florida, where he trained combat pilots during World War II. After the war ended, he returned to the Boston Red Sox, only to be recalled again during the Korean War. This time, he was deployed overseas and flew a total of thirty-eight combat missions before illness grounded him.

When shrapnel disabled his plane during one mission, he managed to maneuver his aircraft back to a frontline US base for repair before returning to his own unit. When word got out who was there, the troops flocked to see him, and Williams signed autographs and shook hands in a morale boost that was as good as any USO visit.

The five years that his active military service totaled significantly affected his career statistics, and put a number of records out of his reach that he might otherwise have easily broken. That wasn't what mattered to Williams, though. Those closest to him admit that he was disappointed that his name wouldn't be in as many record books, but he never complained about what he felt was his duty. In his mind, something was at stake that was far more important than playing baseball, and he acted upon the call to something beyond his career.

The legacy of Ted Williams can, perhaps, be best summarized by the inscription on his birthday gift from General Douglas MacArthur: "To Ted Williams—not only America's greatest baseball player, but a great American who served his country."

Dick Vitale is the face of college basketball, but most fans don't realize his heart is even bigger than his lungs. One year, a neighbor came by to see Vitale to tell him about a young girl who lived nearby. She recently had been diagnosed with cancer. Vitale's mind immediately went to how he could help the girl's family. He told me,

"My neighbor wasn't asking for money, but I was trying to figure out what I could do."

When Vitale's neighbor came for another visit, she brought the girl, whose name was Payton Wright. "I looked into Payton's eyes and immediately said I'd get involved," he remembered. "I called all those friends and they combined to do something awesome in just a couple of weeks. Together, we created some cushion for the family so that Payton's parents could take time from work to travel for her treatments."

Five years later, the girl died and Vitale took her story public, talking about it on radio shows and even mentioning her during game broadcasts. He made Payton's cause his, pouring his heart and considerable soul into helping the family, and in the process has raised hundreds of thousands of dollars aimed at curing pediatric cancer.

Vitale knows that his real privilege is not sitting in front of a microphone for each game but using the influence and resources that his talents and profession have brought him to impact and enrich the lives of others. He understands that Greatness is not pursuing fame but leaving a legacy. By working with different foundations, Vitale is developing something much more significant than the enthusiastic catch phrases that have made him famous.

"I learned from my mom and dad, who didn't have a formal education, but had doctorates of love," he said. "They told me that if you gave 110 percent all the time, a lot of beautiful things will happen. I may not always be right, but no one can ever accuse me of not having a genuine love and passion for whatever I do."

That's how U2 frontman Bono lives, as well. He got interested in Amnesty International back in 1979; when the Irish band's popularity exploded in 1986, Bono threw himself into charity work and has focused his efforts on fighting poverty.

He understands that his role in the world isn't wrapped up in his job, which is in front of a microphone and onstage. The musician persona is a part of him, but his charity work is bigger to him than his album sales.

Jimmy Carter's legacy didn't even get under way until well after he'd left what many consider a forgettable presidency. Since he left office, though, Carter has stepped in to work for world peace, and in 2002 he was bestowed the Nobel Peace Prize for his efforts.

For many Americans, Carter is the face of Habitat for Humanity, an organization he began to support in 1984 and continues today. Though his age has slowed him down quite a bit in recent years, both he and Rosalyn Carter make it a point to actively volunteer with Habitat at least once a year. He and his wife also contribute to The Carter Center, a foundation that works to advocate for human rights and alleviate human suffering through mediating conflict and promoting peace throughout the world.

It doesn't take much time to contribute to a long-standing goal.

Shaquille O'Neal, one of the most celebrated basketball players the NBA has ever known, is a firm believer in making his life about something more than sports. He has done some work in music and acting, as well as some real estate work with lower-income areas of Orlando. But Shaq made his most unconventional career move when, while still playing for the Lakers, he completed the Los Angeles County Sheriff's Reserve Academy to serve as a reserve officer for the LA Port Authority. Later, when he was playing for the Miami Heat, he became a reserve officer for the Miami Beach Police Department, accepting only one dollar per year in salary.

He completed his BA in 2000 (he left LSU for the NBA draft after just three years), then an online MBA program in 2005. In 2012, he obtained his Ed. D in Human Resource Development from Barry University, and he has plans to attend law school. Shaq gladly takes on such a wide array of pursuits because he wants to be a well-rounded individual and he understands that his life is about more than his time on the court. He seeks out ways to give back to the communities that watch him play, but he also wants to make sure that he is a full person in every way.

None of these figures had to step up. Staubach had no ties to the United Way. Dick Vitale's is one of those rare families where cancer hasn't left a scar. President Carter certainly wasn't hurting for a comfortable home of his own. And Shaq didn't need to pin on a badge to be a valued part of his community. But they all know that life is more about what they do on the field or court, in the broadcast booth, or behind a desk—it's about being and doing more than one thing.

And for the Truly Great in Business

Ray Kroc, founder of McDonald's, had a passion for helping families going through difficult times. As a result, he began the Ronald McDonald House to provide comfortable and convenient temporary housing near hospitals for the families of children undergoing long-term medical care.

Bill Gates, founder of Microsoft, and his wife Melinda have established one of the largest private philanthropic organizations in the world. The Bill and Melinda Gates Foundation, with its endowment topping $42.9 billion, offers grants and other support for a wide variety of projects worldwide. For his genuine interest in bettering life around the globe (and nothing at all to do with computers), Gates and singer Bono shared the title of *Time* magazine's "Person of the Year" for 2005.

One of the three wealthiest people in the world, American industrialist Warren Buffett has pledged to give away 99percent of his roughly $47 billion net worth to charity. The majority of it is partnering with the Gates Foundation for maximum impact, but Buffett has also concerned himself with helping social, environmental, and humanitarian causes close to his heart.

Together with Gates, Buffett announced the Giving Pledge, which urged business magnates to donate half of their wealth to charity either while still living or upon death. The goal, according to the two men, is to help industry leaders look outside their corporate bubble and really see the world around them. By branching out from their pursuit of profit, successful business leaders can give back to help others have a more opportunity to accomplish something in life, as well.

Chris Ortiz, an author and a manufacturing industry consultant, urges his clients to, among other things: "Hire people with passions outside of work...[and] do *not* hire workaholics." The balance of work and life is essential for healthy, stable, and productive employees. The people who only know or only care about their profession are less able to adapt to changing circumstances and have their personal life in order.

A sense of balance, perspective, and gratefulness for one's success is one of the trademarks of a truly Great individual. Professional achievement rings hollow if it is the end to itself. Well-rounded people understand that they are working for something much Greater than just the company's bottom line.

The GREATNESS Challenge

What do you care about? What defines your life beyond the four walls of your office? What causes touch your heart, either for personal reasons or simply because they move you? We all have a passion for something. What have you done lately to cultivate that?

Don't get caught up pursuing honors—trophies and plaques are all just trinkets that will mean nothing in the long run. Instead, pour yourself into something that will have an impact, something that will last. Greatness is not achieved through titles and awards; Greatness is achieved by becoming the most complete person you can be, and then reaching beyond yourself to lift others.

The truth is, when your career is over, it's not about how many awards you have or who you know, but what you did that will last longer than your name.

The truly Great understand that their legacy is much bigger than anything they will ever do in athletics and that their careers are a means of introducing them to new opportunities for growth. That's how it should be for all of us: our careers are the door openers that allow us to do something else.

Most people say they would do more if they had more time, but think of the several extra hours a week that you devote to chasing short-term goals. Now think how much more valuable that time could be for enriching your mind or your talents, or even to someone else for whom a helping hand or an encouraging voice could make all the difference in their future.

Don't get caught up at the office. Remember that there is a world outside your door that is much, much bigger than your own. Every community has multiple opportunities to give back and get involved. All you have to do is look. After all, as Roger Staubach put it so perfectly, "There are no traffic jams along the extra mile."

Some things, like family, faith, and community, are more important than careers and last longer. The best thing about legacies is that everyone can have a positive one. It doesn't take a six-figure income to begin a legacy. It can be something as simple as organizing a book donation to establish a library at a youth center or giving blood. It doesn't have to be earth-shattering to be important. Everyone has the opportunity to be truly Great and to leave behind something bigger than themselves.

Take five minutes and write down the people and things that are most important to you. Then study that list—if you were truly honest with yourself, would you add something to it or take something off? Do you wish you had different responses than were on the list?

Now, consider each person and each goal on the list and think five years down the road, then ten, then twenty. It may remind you how quickly children grow up, how quickly that new car depreciates, or how little time someone with a terminal illness has left. Are you investing your time and energy in the right places? What are you doing to make sure you are well-rounded by looking at what really matters?

Before the 1984 Olympics, a popular commercial ran that featured Bob Beamon, who held the world record for the long jump, offering what seemed to be a boastful challenge to up-and-comer Carl Lewis.

"Back in the Olympic Games of 1968," Beamon said, "I set a world record in the long jump. At the time, some people said no one would ever jump that far again. Well, over the years, I've enjoyed sitting in front of my television set and watching them try. But now there's a new kid, I'm told, who might have a chance of breaking my record. Well, there's just one thing I have to say about that." Here he paused before breaking into a genuine smile. "I hope you make it, kid."

This is the attitude we all should have. If we have a record that holds for a while, then we have every right to be proud. But the record books change. That's what records record, after all—when one person outdoes the accomplishments of the past. That's a sad place to be, if the ever-changing record book is the only place you've left your mark.

What are you doing outside of your career? What are the things that are more important to you than your sales stats or the numbers in your bank account? Are you fostering a real relationship with your family? Are you reaching out in your community? Are you acting upon a calling you know is bigger than yourself?

Personal trainers and dieticians often recommend keeping a food diary for those seeking to lose weight, in which people write down every single thing they eat. Try doing the same thing for a week with your time—carefully track your time and make a note about each activity to which you dedicate yourself. At the end of the week, go back and evaluate your record. Do you notice any patterns or trends that could be turned into something more constructive?

Force yourself to branch out. Set a goal to dedicate a few hours each week to something that has nothing to do with your job or your own goals. How do you feel afterward?

Start small. Your legacy doesn't have to be a large foundation in order to be sustainable or make an impact. Mentor a child, plant trees, train a guide dog, contribute to a larger organization's efforts—these are all small-scale ways to make the future a better place. Take a look at your priority list again. Where can you start? Your contribution—time, money, or goods—can grow over time as you succeed in your business career. The important thing is to get started.

Write down your top five priorities in life. Then, pull out your calendar and take a look at the last two weeks or the last month. Does your calendar reflect your priorities? If not, make some changes to reinforce your priorities. For example, if you listed your No. 1 priority as your children, but you missed two of your daughter's softball games because you worked late, rearrange something. If you do not spend time on your priorities, they're no longer priorities. It's up to you to make changes.

Now, in one sentence, describe what feel you to be your life's calling—the ultimate point of what you want to achieve with the days you're given. Then look over that list one more time and ask yourself, for each person or thing: "If I had to give this up in order to fulfill my calling, would it matter in the long run?" Your answers may surprise you.

Always remember that records are made to be broken. The Great ones do.

AFTERWORD

The GREATNESS Challenge

GREATNESS is a lifestyle, and those who can live it are special people not just because of what they can achieve on the court or at the plate, but because of all that they can do—from the way they treat others, to the way they see themselves, to the way they see their place in society. The truly Great ones have heartfelt pride and special humility. They are fierce competitors and generous givers. They are tremendous individuals, and they are the ultimate team players.

It is important to realize that Greatness cannot be achieved alone. Even athletes in solo sports, such as track and field, tennis, or golf, have a collection of coaches, trainers, and motivators behind them who help craft their sport and their spirit. Greatness is a team effort, even if there is no visible team at competition time. Family and fans, coworkers and encouragers, teachers and mentors—they all contribute to a person's quest for Greatness because they build the individual up and help move him or her forward. Thus, even as we each work toward our own Greatness, we give of ourselves to help others achieve Greatness, as well.

Often, we hear terms like *success, achievement,* and *innovation* or *character, integrity,* and *leadership*—and these are all important concepts. But they address only one part of the whole person. No aspect of Greatness trumps any other part. Each element has an equal share in propelling the individual forward from good to Great. It is the continual honing, adjusting, and improving in every area that makes the difference.

We're all familiar with the old advice: "Do one thing and do it well." This is a good idea in terms of what we produce, but what about who we are? We shouldn't be limited by a few ideals to which we strive. Instead, we should try to encompass as many of these attributes as possible. After all, what is success without integrity? Or leadership without character? All of the catchphrases and buzzwords of motivation are really interconnected ideas that can be fully realized only when they are brought together to complement one another in an individual's thought, preparation, work, and life.

Greatness should be more than just a philosophy or a strategy. It should dictate our choices and impact our actions. It should be both our goal and our constant companion. The desire for Greatness is not the same as ambition, and it's not a hope for fame. It is a personal commitment to espousing the tried-and-true principles that have launched careers, broken records, and helped form heroes on the court, on the field, and in the game of life. Greatness is reaching beyond ourselves to lift others and reaching within ourselves to live with integrity.

It is true that very few of us can ever stand a chance of dominating the court for the NBA, or ruling the links at the Master's, but we can pursue our own personal and professional Greatness with the same attitude and discipline as those who have achieved it in the sporting world.

We each owe it to ourselves to try.

Everyone chooses one of two roads in life—
the old and the young, the rich and the poor, men and women alike.
One is the broad, well-traveled road to mediocrity,
the other the road to greatness and meaning.
The range of possibilities that exists
within each of these two destinations
is as wide as the diversity of gifts
and personalities in the human family.
But the contrast between the two destinations
is as the night is to the day.

— DR. STEPHEN R. COVEY
(American author and motivational speaker)

— APPENDIX 1 —

GREATNESS quotes

Chapter 1: It's Personal

"Winning is not a sometime thing, it's an all time thing. You don't win once in a while, you don't do things right once in a while, you do them right all the time. Winning is habit. Unfortunately, so is losing."

— VINCE LOMBARDI, legendary Green Bay Packers coach

"Never, never, never give up."

— WINSTON CHURCHILL, former British prime minister

"You have to go into the jungle, find the lion, and spit in his face... then shoot him. You guys are not good enough to win on talent alone...you have to want it."

— HERB BROOKS, coach of the 1980 US Olympics Hockey Team

"Most people run a race to see who is fastest. I run a race to see who has the most guts."

— STEVE PREFONTAINE, runner

"You may have to fight a battle more than once to win it."

— MARGARET THATCHER, former British prime minister

"I was made to work. If you are equally industrious, you will be equally successful."

— JOHANN SEBASTIAN BACH, classical composer

Chapter 2: Rubbing Elbows

"The important thought is that the Packers thrived on tough competition. We welcomed it; the team had always welcomed it. The adrenaline flowed a little quicker when we were playing the tougher teams."

— VINCE LOMBARDI, legendary Green Bay Packers coach

"Excellence is a better teacher than mediocrity. The lessons of the ordinary are everywhere. Truly profound and original insights are to be found only in studying the exemplary."

— WARREN G. BENNIS, author of *Becoming a Leader* and founding chairman of the Leadership Institute at the University of Southern California

"Encouragement is oxygen to the soul."

— GEORGE M. ADAMS, American author

"Competition creates better products, alliances create better companies."

— BRIAN GRAHAM, former Cleveland Indians coach and manager

"There are people who when they meet a rival, no matter in what, at once shut their eyes to everything good in him and see only the bad. There are others who on the contrary try to discern in a lucky rival the qualities that have enabled him to succeed."

— LEO TOLSTOY, author of *War and Peace*

"A person is truly great when he is not envious of his rival's success."

— UNKNOWN

"Nothing focuses the mind better than the constant sight of a competitor who wants to wipe you off the map."

— WAYNE CALLOWAY, former Pepsi CEO

"It has meant a lot to me to challenge the best players in the world and to beat them."

— ANDRE AGASSI, tennis player

"Thank God for competition. When our competitors upset our plans or outdo our designs, they open infinite possibilities of our own work to us."

— GIL ATKINSON, historian

Chapter 3: Believe

"Always have faith in yourself. Always have faith in God. Never lose that."

— DREW BREES, New Orleans Saints quarterback

"I believe in God, but I do believe that everybody has something that they worship—sometimes it's materialistic things. Sometimes people worship money. Sometimes they worship power. [Everybody] has something that they are willing to put above everything else. My personal belief is our priorities ought to be our faith, our family, our profession."

— LOU HOLTZ, former Notre Dame and South Carolina football coach

"Great men are they who see that spiritual is stronger than any material force; that thoughts rule the world."

— RALPH WALDO EMERSON (1803–1882), poet, essayist, and philosopher

"To one who has faith, no explanation is necessary. To one without faith, no explanation is possible."

— ST. THOMAS AQUINAS, thirteenth-century priest

"Be faithful in small things because it is in them that your strength lies."

— MOTHER TERESA (1910–1997), Nobel Peace Prize-winning advocate of the poor

"God does not ask your ability or your inability. He asks only your availability."

— MARY KAY ASH (1918–2001), founder of Mary Kay Cosmetics

"The person who has a firm trust in the Supreme Being is powerful in his power, wise by his wisdom, happy by his happiness."

— JOSEPH ADDISON (1672–1719), British essayist and statesman

"A person's proximity to God is measured by his compassion toward his fellow man."

— RABBI SAMUEL BELKIN (1911–1976)

"Live your beliefs and you can turn the world around."

— HENRY DAVID THOREAU (1817–1862), author

"God can only do for you what He can do through you."

— ERIC BUTTERWORTH,
former minister of the Unity City, New York

"There is but one ultimate Power. This Power is to each one what he is to it."

— ERNEST HOLMES (1887–1960), author and spiritual leader

"Life is to live in such a way that we are not afraid to die."

— ST. TERESA OF AVILA (1515–1582)

Chapter 4: Contagious Enthusiasm

"The greatest good you can do for another is not just to show your riches, but to reveal to him his own."

— BENJAMIN DISRAELI (1804–1881),
former British prime minister

"Enthusiasm is everything. It must be as taut and vibrating as a guitar strong."

— PÉLE, international soccer great

"I've never seen a monument erected to a pessimist."

— PAUL HARVEY, syndicated commentator

"A strong, positive mental attitude will create more miracles than any wonder drug."

— PATRICIA NEAL, actress

"A man who is capable of generating enthusiasm can't be whipped."

— EDWARD GEORGE BULWER-LYTTON (1803–1873), poet, novelist, playwright, and politician

"The only disability in life is a bad attitude."

— SCOTT HAMILTON, Olympic gold medalist in skating

"I'm so optimistic I'd go after Moby Dick in a row boat and take the tartar sauce with me."

— ZIG ZIGLAR, motivational author

"Athletics are like everything else. I've never seen a great athlete burn out on their sport, because they truly love what they are doing. People who get burned out on what they're doing are probably doing it for the wrong reasons."

— STEVE HAMILTON, Morehead State University football coach

"Flaming enthusiasm, backed up by horse sense and persistence, is the quality that most frequently makes for success."

— DALE CARNEGIE, American writer and self-development pioneer

"The real secret to success is enthusiasm."

— WALTER CHRYSLER, founder of the Chrysler Corporation

"Every memorable act in the history of the world is a triumph of enthusiasm. Nothing great was ever achieved without it because it gives any challenge or any occupation, no matter how frightening or difficult, a new meaning. Without enthusiasm you are doomed to a life of mediocrity but with it you can accomplish miracles."

— OG MANDINO, author of *The Greatest Salesman in the World*

Chapter 5: Hope for the Best, But . . .

"It's not the will to win that matters—everyone has that. It's the will to prepare to win that matters."

— PAUL "BEAR" BRYANT,
former University of Alabama football coach

"To be prepared is half the victory."

— MIGUEL DE CERVANTES (1547–1616), author, *Don Quixote*

*"If I had eight hours to chop down a tree,
I'd spend six hours sharpening my ax."*

— PRESIDENT ABRAHAM LINCOLN

"Before everything else, getting ready is the secret to success."

— HENRY FORD, innovator and inventor

"Planning is a trap laid down to capture the future."

— HENRY FORD

"Luck is what happens when preparation meets opportunity."

— DARREL ROYAL, former University of Texas football coach

"I will prepare and some day my chance will come."

— PRESIDENT ABRAHAM LINCOLN

"Great things are accomplished only when small things are done."

— JOHN WOODEN, legendary UCLA basketball coach

"Luck favors the mind that is prepared."

— LOUIS PASTEUR, scientist

"I have yet to be in a game where luck was involved. Well-prepared players make plays. I have yet to be in a game where the most prepared team didn't win."

— URBAN MEYER, University of Florida football coach

"Talent alone won't make you a success. Neither will being in the right place at the right time, unless you are ready. The most important question is: 'Are you ready?'"

— JOHNNY CARSON,
comedian and former late-night talk show host

"All things are ready, if our minds be so."

— WILLIAM SHAKESPEARE, playwright

"The difference between someone who is successful and someone who isn't is not about talent. It's about preparation....Adult homework is preparation."

— MIKE SHANAHAN, Washington Redskins coach

Chapter 6: What Off-Season?

"When you're not practicing, remember that someone somewhere is practicing and when you meet him, he will win."

— ED MACAULEY, Basketball Hall of Fame, 1960

"My motto was always to keep swinging. Whether I was in a slump or feeling badly or having trouble off the field, the only thing to do was keep swinging."

— HANK AARON, Major League Baseball Hall of Fame Player and twenty-five-time All-Star

"For me, winning isn't something that happens suddenly on the field when the whistle blows and the crowds roar. Winning is something that builds physically and mentally every day that you train and every night that you dream."

— EMMITT SMITH, NFL's leading rusher and Super Bowl MVP

"I am always doing that which I can not do, in order that I may learn how to do it."

— PABLO PICASSO, artist

"Determine never to be idle...
It is wonderful how much may be done if we are always doing."

— PRESIDENT THOMAS JEFFERSON

"In reading the lives of great men, I found that the first victory they won was over themselves...self-discipline with all of them came first."

— PRESIDENT HARRY S. TRUMAN

*"Even if you're on the right track,
you'll get run over if you just sit there."*

— WILL ROGERS

*"Perfection is not attainable,
but if we chase perfection we can catch excellence."*

— VINCE LOMBARDI, legendary Green Bay Packers coach

*"We are what we repeatedly do.
Excellence then, is not an act, but a habit."*

— ARISTOTLE, philosopher

*"I was made to work. If you are equally industrious,
you will be equally successful."*

— JOHANN SEBASTIAN BACH, classical composer

*"If you're not practicing, somebody else is, somewhere,
and he'll be ready to take your job."*

— BROOKS ROBINSON, two-time World Series champion
and sixteen-time Golden Glove winner

*"Nobody's a natural. You work hard to get good
and then work to get better. It's hard to stay on top."*

— PAUL COFFEY, NHL Hall of Fame defenseman

*"Opportunity is missed by most people
because it is dressed in overalls and looks like work."*

— THOMAS EDISON

"If the people knew how hard I had to work to gain my mastery, it wouldn't seem wonderful at all."

— MICHELANGELO, artist and sculptor

Chapter 7: Visualize Victory

"Don't visualize beating the keeper; visualize destroying the keeper."

— STEVEN GERRARD, international soccer player

"I visualize things in my mind before I have to do them. It's like having a mental workshop."

— JACK YOUNGBLOOD, NFL Hall of Famer

"It's a dream until you write it down, and then it's a goal."

— UNKNOWN

"Plan your work and work your plan. Decide in advance exactly how you are going to get from where you are to where you want to go."

— BRIAN TRACY, motivational speaker

"The trouble with not having a goal is that you can spend your life running up and down the field and never score."

— BILL COPELAND, award-winning author

"Man's greatness lies in his power of thought."

— BLAISE PASCAL (1623–1662),
French mathematician, philosopher, and physicist

"It always seems impossible until it's done."

— NELSON MANDELA, Nobel Peace Prize winner and former president of South Africa

"Visualize this thing that you want, see it, feel it, believe in it. Make your mental blue print, and begin to build."

— ROBERT COLLIER (1885–1950), self-help author

"Goals are the detailed road maps to our dreams."

— MIKE SHANAHAN, Washington Redskins coach

"Dreams are extremely important. You can't do it unless you can imagine it."

— GEORGE LUCAS, cocreator of the *Star Wars* and *Indiana Jones* movies

"Practice does not make perfect, perfect practice makes perfect."

— JOE PATERNO, Penn State football coach

Chapter 8: Inner Fire

"The spirit, the will to win, and the will to excel, are the things that endure. These qualities are so much more important than the events that occur."

— VINCE LOMBARDI, legendary Green Bay Packers coach

"A competitor will find a way to win. Competitors take bad breaks and use them to drive themselves just that much harder. Quitters take bad breaks and use them as reasons to give up. It's all a matter of pride."

— NANCY LOPEZ, golfer

"Success isn't permanent and failure isn't fatal."

— MIKE DITKA, former Chicago Bears coach

"There are no great people in this world, only great challenges which ordinary people rise to meet."

— WILLIAM FREDERICK HALSEY JR.,
World War II US Navy admiral

"It is not the events in our life that define our character, but how we deal with them."

— ERIC HEIDEN, Olympic skater

"It is not the critic who counts; not the man who points out how the strong man stumbles, or where the doer of deeds could have done them better. The credit belongs to the man who is actually in the arena, whose face is marred by dust and sweat and blood, who strives valiantly; who errs and comes short again and again; because there is not effort without error and shortcomings; but who does actually strive to do the deed; who knows the great enthusiasm, the great devotion, who spends himself in a worthy cause, who at the best knows in the end the triumph of high achievement and who at the worst, if he fails, at least he fails while daring greatly. So that his place shall never be with those cold and timid souls who know neither victory nor defeat."

— PRESIDENT THEODORE ROOSEVELT

"The greatness comes not when things go always good for you. But the greatness comes when you're really tested, when you take some knocks, some disappointments, when sadness comes. Because only if you've been in the deepest valley can you ever know how magnificent it is to be on the highest mountain."

— PRESIDENT RICHARD M. NIXON

"Difficulty, my brethren, is the nurse of greatness— a harsh nurse, who roughly rocks her foster-children into strength and athletic proportion."

— PAUL "BEAR" BRYANT,
former University of Alabama football coach

"Never confuse a single defeat with a final defeat."

— F. SCOTT FITZGERALD (1896–1940),
author of *The Great Gatsby*

"Even the knowledge of my own fallibility cannot keep me from making mistakes. Only when I fall do I get up again."

— VINCENT VAN GOGH, artist and painter

"The mark of great sportsmen is not how good they are at their best, but how good they are their worst."

— MARTINA NAVRATILOVA,
winner of 18 Grand Slam tournaments

"Some people think it's a weakness to be behind. Folks, it's not a weakness to be behind—not if you can come back and win it. One of the greatest teaching experiences you will learn in life is to be behind and then come back to win. And until that happens to you, you don't know what kind of a team you've got."

— BOBBY BOWDEN,
former Florida State University football coach

"No man ever achieved worthwhile success who did not, at one time or another, find himself with at least one foot hanging well over the brink of failure."

— NAPOLEON HILL, self-help author

"Sweet are the uses of adversity, which like the toad, ugly and venomous, wears yet a precious jewel in his head."

— WILLIAM SHAKESPEARE

Chapter 9: Ice in Their Veins

"He who is not courageous enough to take risks will accomplish nothing in life."

— MUHAMMAD ALI, former boxing champion

"Pressure is nothing more than the shadow of great opportunity."

— MICHAEL JOHNSON, runner and Olympic gold medalist

"Go out on a limb. That's where the fruit is."

— PRESIDENT JIMMY CARTER

"No one ever achieved greatness by playing it safe."

— HARRY GRAY, president of United Aircraft

"Security is not the meaning of my life.
Great opportunities are worth the risk."

— SHIRLEY HUFSTEDLER, first US secretary of education

"Get action. Seize the moment.
Man was never intended to become an oyster."

— PRESIDENT THEODORE ROOSEVELT

"If you want to succeed, double your failure rate."

— THOMAS WATSON, IBM pioneer

"Limits are self-imposed."

— MIKE SHANAHAN, Washington Redskins coach

"What matters is not necessarily the size of the dog in the fight—
it's the size of the fight in the dog."

— PRESIDENT DWIGHT D. EISENHOWER

"Only those who will risk going too far
can possibly find out how far one can go."

— T. S. ELIOT (1888–1965), author, playwright, poet, and critic

---

"If you're not making mistakes, you're not taking risks, and that means you're not going anywhere. The key is to make errors faster than the competition, so you have more chances to learn and win."

— JOHN W. HOLT JR., coauthor, *Celebrate Your Mistakes*

"He who risks and fails can be forgiven.
He who never risks and never fails is a failure in his whole being."

— PAUL TILLICH, theologian and philosopher

"Everyone has talent. What is rare is the courage
to follow the talent to the dark place where it leads."

— SIR WILLIAM ALTON JONES,
eighteenth-century British philologist and jurist

"What I admire in Columbus is not his having discovered
a new world, but his having gone to search for it
on the faith of his own opinion."

— ANNE-ROBERT-JACQUES TURGOT,
eighteenth-century French economist and statesman

"What would life be if we had no courage to attempt anything?"

— VINCENT VAN GOGH, artist and painter

"There is no passion to be found playing small—in settling
for a life that is less than the one you are capable of living."

— NELSON MANDELA, Nobel Peace Prize winner
and former president of South Africa

Chapter 10: When All Else Fails

"Enjoying success requires the ability to adapt.
Only by being open to change will you have a true opportunity
to get the most from your talent."

— NOLAN RYAN, Hall of Fame pitcher and MLB record holder

"We are not what we know but what we are willing to learn."

— MARY CATHERINE BATESON,
writer and cultural anthropologist

*"There's only one corner of the universe
you can be certain of improving, and that's your own self."*

— ALDOUS HUXLEY, author of *Brave New World*

"The most successful people are those who are good at Plan B."

— JAMES YORKE, mathematician, professor, and researcher,
University of Maryland

*"If you want things to be different,
perhaps the answer is to become different yourself."*

— NORMAN VINCENT PEALE,
preacher and author of *The Power of Positive Thinking*

"We cannot direct the win, but we can adjust the sails."

— DOLLY PARTON, singer and entertainer

*"When it is obvious the goals cannot be reached,
don't adjust the goals, adjust the action steps."*

— CONFUCIUS, Chinese philosopher

*"All of the top achievers I know are life-long learners...
Looking for new skills, insights, and ideas. If they're not learning,
they're not growing...not moving toward excellence."*

— DENIS WAITLEY, motivational speaker and author

Chapter 11: The Ultimate Teammate

"In order to have a winner, the team must have a feeling of unity; every player must put the team first—ahead of personal glory."

— PAUL "BEAR" BRYANT,
former University of Alabama football coach

"All winning teams are goal-oriented. Teams like these win consistently because everyone connected with them concentrates on specific objectives. They go about their business with blinders on; nothing will distract them from achieving their aims."

— LOU HOLTZ, former Notre Dame football coach

"Individual commitment to a group effort—that is what makes a team work, a company work, a society work, a civilization work."

— VINCE LOMBARDI, legendary Green Bay Packers coach

"To become truly great, one has to stand with people, not above them."

— CHARLES DE MONTESQUIEU (1689–1755),
philosopher and social critic

"I long to accomplish a great and noble task, but it is my chief duty to accomplish humble tasks as though they were great and noble."

— HELEN KELLER, deaf-blind author, activist, and lecturer

"A great man is always willing to be little."

— RALPH WALDO EMERSON (1803–1882),
poet essayist, and philosopher

"Few men have the natural strength to honor a friend's success without envy."

— AESCHYLUS, ancient Greek playwright

"Make sure the team members know they're working with you, not for you."

— JOHN WOODEN, legendary UCLA basketball coach

Chapter 12: Not Just About the Benjamins

"To be successful you have to be selfish, or else you never achieve. And once you get to your highest level, then you have to be unselfish. Stay reachable. Stay in touch. Don't isolate."

— MICHAEL JORDAN,
six-time NBA champion and fourteen-time All-Star

"One man can be a crucial ingredient on a team, but one man cannot make a team."

— KAREEM ABDUL-JABBAR, six-time NBA champion and MVP

"You have to be willing to do things the masses would never do; that's how you separate yourself from the masses."

— STEVE BISCIOTTI, NFL owner

"The little money I have—that is my wealth, but the things I have for which I would not take money—that is my treasure."

— ROBERT BRAULT, freelance writer

"Success isn't measured by money or power or social rank. Success is measured by your discipline and inner peace."

— MIKE DITKA, former Chicago Bears coach

"Prospering just doesn't have to do with money."

— JOEL OSTEEN, preacher and author

"The main ingredient of a player's stardom is the rest of the team."

— JOHN WOODEN, legendary UCLA basketball coach

"No one can whistle a symphony. It takes a whole orchestra to play it."

— H. E. LUCCOCK, former Yale Divinity School professor

"A successful team is a group of many hands but of one mind."

— BILL BETHEL, author

"It is not what we take up, but what we give up, that makes us rich."

— HENRY WARD BEECHER (1813–1887),
social reformer, clergyman, and abolitionist

"Focusing your life solely on making a buck shows a certain poverty of ambition. It asks too little of yourself. Because it's only when you hitch your wagon to something larger than yourself that you realize your true potential."

— PRESIDENT BARACK OBAMA

Chapter 13: Do Unto Others

"You don't need to be Bill Gates to be charitable.
You don't even need to give money.
It is the simplest of tasks that can make such a difference."

— WALTER PAYTON, former Chicago Bears great

"We make a living by what we get, but we make a life by what we give."

— WINSTON CHURCHILL, former British Prime Minister

"You do not ever have a thing until you give it away."

— ERNEST HEMINGWAY, author

"Appreciation can make a day, even change a life.
Your willingness to put it into words is all that is necessary."

— MARGARET COUSINS, author and editor

"Everybody can be great...because anybody can serve.
You don't have to have a college degree to serve.
You don't have to make your subject and verb agree to serve.
You only need a heart full of grace, a soul generated by love."

— MARTIN LUTHER KING JR., civil rights activist

"Don't limit investing to the financial world.
Invest something of yourself, and you will be richly rewarded."

— CHARLES SCHWAB, founder of Charles Schwab & Co.

"Give what you have. To someone, it may be better than you dare to think."

— HENRY WADSWORTH LONGFELLOW, poet

"No one will question your integrity if your integrity is not questionable."

— NATHANIEL BRONNER JR.

"Character is destiny."

— HERICLITUS, Greek philosopher

"Life is made up of golden chances, opportunities to do good. One lost is lost forever. If we miss doing a kindness to a friend, we can never do that kindness again. If we might speak a pleasant word, or offer a bit of worthwhile counsel or advice and fail to do so, we can never have that opportunity again. Giving is a way of life."

— A. W. BURTON (1879–1966), businessman and philanthropist

"The best teachers of humanity are the lives of great men."

— CHARLES H. FOWLER (1837–1908), Methodist Episcopal bishop

"Goodness is the only investment that never fails."

— HENRY DAVID THOREAU (1817–1862), author

"You can't live a perfect day without doing something for someone who will never be able to repay you."

— JOHN WOODEN, legendary UCLA basketball coach

A short course in Human Relations

The six most important words: I admit I made a mistake
The five most important words: You did a good job
The four most important words: What is your opinion?
The three most important words: If you please
The two most important words: Thank you
The one most important word: We
The least important word: I

— ANONYMOUS

Chapter 14: When No One Is Watching

"One man practicing sportsmanship is better than a hundred teaching it."

— KNUTE ROCKNE (1888–1931), former Notre Dame football coach

"Success without honor is an unseasoned dish; it will satisfy your hunger, but it won't taste good."

— JOE PATERNO, Penn State University head football coach

"Issue a blanket pardon. Forgive everyone who has ever hurt you in any way. Forgiveness is a perfectly selfish act. It sets you free from the past."

— BRIAN TRACY, motivational speaker

"If you have integrity, nothing else matters. If you don't have integrity, nothing else matters."

— ALAN K. SIMPSON, former Wyoming senator

"You can't go back and make a brand new start, but you can start now and make a brand new end."

— JACK GARMISE

"A person's attitude, effort, and commitment provide the power and passion that makes unique and special things happen."

— JILL STERKLEL, University of Texas women's swimming coach

"Happiness is found along the way, not at the end of the road. People will soon forget the record. What they remember is the way you hustled, the poise you had, the class you showed."

— SHERYL JOHNSON, Stanford University field hockey coach

"What you do speaks so loud I cannot hear what you say."

— RALPH WALDO EMERSON (1803–1882),
poet, essayist, and philosopher

"In looking for people to hire, you look for three qualities: integrity, intelligence, and energy. And if they don't have the first, the other two will kill you."

— WARREN BUFFETT, Berkshire Hathaway CEO

"If we are to be a really great people, we must strive in good faith to play a great part in the world. We cannot avoid meeting great issues. All that we can determine for ourselves is whether we shall meet them well or ill."

— PRESIDENT THEODORE ROOSEVELT

---

*"The quality of a person's life is in direct proportion
to their commitment to excellence,
regardless of their chosen field of endeavor."*

— VINCE LOMBARDI, legendary Green Bay Packers coach

---

*"Example is not the main thing in influencing others.
It is the only thing."*

— ALBERT SCHWEITZER (1875–1965), theologian, musician,
philosopher, physician, and Nobel Peace Prize winner

Chapter 15: When Everyone Is Watching

"A life is not important except in the impact it has on other lives."

— JACKIE ROBINSON, Baseball Hall of Fame

---

*"If you believe in yourself, have dedication and pride
and never quit, you'll be a winner.
The price of victory is high, but so are the rewards."*

— PAUL "BEAR" BRYANT,
former University of Alabama football coach

---

*"We judge ourselves by what we feel capable of doing,
while others judge us by what we have already done."*

— HENRY WADSWORTH LONGFELLOW, poet and author

---

*"Example is not the main thing in influencing others.
It is the only thing."*

— ALBERT SCHWEITZER (1875–1965), theologian, musician,
philosopher, physician, and Nobel Peace Prize winner

"Character is the diamond that scratches every other stone."

— CYRUS AUGUSTUS BARTOL (1813–1900),
Unitarian minister, author

"Have the courage to say no. Have the courage to face the truth. Do the right thing because it is right. These are the magic keys to living your life with integrity."

— CLEMENT STONE (1902–2002),
philosopher and self-help author

"As years passed, it became clear to me that kids see all, not just some of your actions but all. Whether we like or not, we big leaguers are role models. The only question is, will it be positive or will it be negative?"

— CAL RIPKEN JR., Baseball Hall of Fame

"When the first Superman *movie came out I was frequently asked, 'What is a hero?' I remember the glib response I repeated so many times. My answer was that a hero is someone who commits a courageous action without considering the consequences—a soldier who crawls out of a foxhole to drag an injured buddy to safety. And I also meant individuals who are slightly larger than life: Houdini and Lindbergh, John Wayne, JFK, and Joe DiMaggio. Now my definition is completely different. I think a hero is an ordinary individual who finds strength to persevere and endure in spite of overwhelming obstacles."*

— CHRISTOPHER REEVE (1952–2004), *Superman* actor

"Each person must live their life as a model for others."

— ROSA PARKS, activist

"If I am walking with two other people, each of them will serve as my teacher. I will pick out the good points of the one and imitate them, and the bad points of the other and correct them in myself."

— CONFUCIUS, Chinese philosopher

Chapter 16: Records Are Made to Be Broken

"Don't sell yourself short because without that you can't go far in life—because after sports the only thing you know is sports and you can't do anything else with that."

— BO JACKSON, professional football and baseball All-Star

"After the cheers have died down and the stadium is empty, after the headlines have been written and after you are back in the quiet of your room and the championship ring has been placed on the dresser and all the pomp and fanfare has faded, the enduring things that are left are: the dedication to excellence, the dedication to victory, and the dedication to doing with our lives the very best we can to make the world a better place in which to live."

— VINCE LOMBARDI, legendary Green Bay Packers coach

"I am of the opinion that my life belongs to the whole community and as long as I live, it is my privilege to do for it whatever I can. I want to be thoroughly used up when I die, for the harder I work the more I live."

— GEORGE BERNARD SHAW, playwright

"Tomorrow is promised to no one."

— WALTER PAYTON, former Chicago Bears great

"Somebody will always break your records.
It is how you live that counts."

— EARL CAMPBELL, 1977 Heisman Trophy winner
and five-time NFL Pro Bowl player

"We stand our best chance of leaving a legacy to those who want to learn, our children, by standing firm. In matters of style, hey, swing with the stream. But in matters of principle, you need to stand like a rock."

— KEVIN COSTNER, actor

"Do something worth remembering."

— ELVIS PRESLEY, entertainer

"We all leave footprints in the sand, the question is,
will we be a big heel, or a great soul?"

— UNKNOWN

"To laugh often and much; to win the respect of intelligent people and the affection of children...to leave the world a better place... to know even one life has breathed easier because you have lived. This is to have succeeded."

— RALPH WALDO EMERSON (1803–1882),
poet, essayist, and philosopher

"The good that men do lives after them."

— RUTH GORDON (1896–1985), actress

= APPENDIX 2 =

Recommended Reading

Chapter 1: It's Personal

The Mental Athlete, by Kay Porter. Champaign, IL: Human Kinetics, 2003.

Chapter 2: Rubbing Elbows

A Game Plan for Life: The Power of Mentoring, by John Wooden and Don Yaeger. New York: Bloomsbury, 2009.

Chapter 3: Believe

Uncommon: Finding Your Path to Significance, by Tony Dungy and Nathan Whitaker. Carol Stream, IL: Tyndale, 2009.

Chapter 4: Contagious Enthusiasm

The Power of Positive Thinking, by Norman Vincent Peale. New York: Fireside (Simon and Schuster), 2003.

Living the Dream, by Dot Richardson and Don Yaeger. New York: Kensington, 1998.

Ya Gotta Believe: My Roller-Coaster Life as a Screwball Pitcher and Part-Time Father, and My Hope-Filled Fight against Brain Cancer, by Tug McGraw and Don Yaeger. New York: NAL (Penguin), 2004.

Chapter 5: Hope for the Best, But

Turning the Tide: How One Game Changed the South, by Don Yaeger, Sam Cunningham, and John Papadakis. Nashville: Center Street (Hachette), 2006.

Chapter 6: What Off-Season?

Never Give Up on Your Dream, by Warren Moon and Don Yaeger. Philadelphia: DeCapo, 2009.

Reach for the Summit, by Pat Summitt and Sally Jenkins. New York: Bantam Doubleday Dell, 1998.

I Beat the Odds: From Homelessness to The Blind Side and Beyond, by Michael Oher and Don Yaeger. New York: Penguin, 2011.

Chapter 7: Visualize Victory

The Mental Edge: Maximize Your Potential with the Mind-Body Connection, by Kenneth Baum. New York: Perigree, 1999.

Slaying the Dragon: How to Turn Your Small Steps into Great Steps, by Michael Johnson. New York: Regan (Harper Collins), 1996.

Chapter 8: Inner Fire

Running For My Life: My Journey in the Game of Football and Beyond, by Warrick Dunn and Don Yaeger. New York: Harper, 2008.

The Great Eight: How to Be Happy (Even When You Have Every Reason to Be Miserable), by Scott Hamilton and Ken Baker. Nashville: Thomas Nelson, 2009.

Comebacks: Powerful Lessons from Leaders Who Endured Setbacks and Recaptured Success on Their Terms, by Andrea Redmond and Patricia Crisafulli. Hoboken: Wiley, 2010.

Chapter 9: Ice in Their Veins

Celebrating Failure: The Power of Taking Risks, Making Mistakes and Thinking Big, by Ralph Heath. Franklin Lakes, NJ: Career Press, 2009.

Crossing the Line, by Danica Patrick and Laura Morton. New York: Simon & Schuster, 2006.

The Five Dysfunctions of a Team: A Leadership Fable, by Patrick Lencioni. Jossey-Bass, 2002

Chapter 10: When All Else Fails

I've Got Your Back: Coaching Top Performers from Center Court to the Corner Office, by Brad Gilbert. New York: Penguin, 2004.

Chapter 11: The Ultimate Teammate

It's Not about the Truth: the Untold Story of the Duke Lacrosse Case and the Lives It Shattered, by Mike Pressler and Don Yaeger. New York: Threshold Editions (Simon & Schuster), 2007.

The Senior: My Amazing Year as a 59-year-Old College Football Linebacker, by Mike Flynt and Don Yaeger. Nashville: Thomas Nelson, 2008.

Chapter 12: Not Just about the Benjamins

Greatness: The Rise of Tom Brady, The Boston Globe. Chicago: Triumph, 2005.

The Winning Spirit: 16 Timeless Principles That Drive Performance Excellence, Joe Montana and Tom Mitchell. New York: Ballantine Books, 2005.

Chapter 13: Do Unto Others

Never Die Easy, by Walter Peyton and Don Yaeger. New York: Random House, 2000.

Chapter 14: When No One Is Watching

Devoted: The Story of a Father's Love for his Son, by Dick Hoyt and Don Yaeger. Nashua, NH: Eclipse, 2010.

The Winning Spirit: 16 Timeless Principles That Drive Performance Excellence, by Joe Montana and Tom Mitchell. Ballantine Books: New York, 2005.

Chapter 15: When Everyone Is Watching

Lion in a Tiger's Den: Adventures in LSU Basketball, by Dale Brown and Don Yaeger. New York: Hyperion, 1994.

Chapter 16: Records Are Made to Be Broken

100 Heroes: People in Sports Who Make This a Better World, by Robert E. Lapchick. Orlando: NCAS Publishing, 2005.

DonYaeger
AWARD-WINNING KEYNOTE SPEAKER
NEW YORK TIMES BEST-SELLING AUTHOR
FREE
SPEAKING KIT
Visit donyaeger.com for full details!
WHAT MAKES THE
GREAT ONES GREAT
THE HABITS OF HIGH PERFORMING INDIVIDUALS
WHAT THEY'VE SAID
"After hearing Don speak, I immediately decided my team would find significant value by being exposed to his philosophies."
Eric Martorano
Sr. Director, U.S. SMB Channel Group, Microsoft Corporation
"Your presentation was overwhelmingly rated as the best motivational speech my employees had ever heard."
Hector Cavazos
Diversity Coordinator, Chevron
"You possess the unique ability to captivate an audience and take them on an emotional rollercoaster ride!"
Louise Jones
Exec. Dir., Alabama Pharmacy Association
ABOUT THIS PROGRAM
In this program, Don will teach your team the proven and successful habits of the high performing individuals found in this book, and guide your team on a pursuit of greatness.
LIVE KEYNOTE
PRESENTATIONS AVAILABLE
LIVE WEBINAR
PRESENTATIONS AVAILABLE
TO LEARN MORE VISIT
DONYAEGER.COM

Don Yaeger
AWARD-WINNING KEYNOTE SPEAKER
NEW YORK TIMES BEST-SELLING AUTHOR
FREE TRIAL WEBINAR
Take your company training to the next level!
Visit donyaeger.com for full details.
WHAT MAKES THE
GREAT TEAMS GREAT
LESSONS LEARNED FROM CHAMPIONSHIP TEAMS
WHAT THEY'VE SAID
"Don's lessons were a valuable tool for us to all 'speak the same language.' Coaching, culture and teamwork!"
Anthony Robbins
Vice President, BROCADE Federal
"If you want to learn about Great Teams this is where you should go."
Cody Foster
Founder, Advisors Excel
"This program brings coworkers back into the huddle, the dugout, or the court to find that inner-spark, competitive spirit, and desire to become great!"
Jeff Turner
Director Microsoft U.S. SMB Channel Marketing
ABOUT THIS PROGRAM
In his 25+ years of interviewing great team builders, Don has discovered one common denominator: That they are always studying and learning from other great teams.
In this program Don will teach your team exclusive lessons he's learned from some of the greatest leaders of all time.
LIVE WEBINAR
PRESENTATIONS AVAILABLE
LIVE KEYNOTE
PRESENTATIONS AVAILABLE
TO LEARN MORE VISIT
DONYAEGER.COM